Texfake

TEXFAKE

An Account of the Theft and Forgery of Early Texas Printed Documents

by
W. THOMAS TAYLOR

With an Introduction by
LARRY McMURTRY

Austin · W. Thomas Taylor · *1991*

ISBN 0-935072-20-9

For J. J. and Virginia Scheffelin

This book will lose me some friends. But if it lost me all and gained me none, in God's name, as I am a free man, I would publish it.

— Sam Houston

CONTENTS

LIST OF ILLUSTRATIONS

ACKNOWLEDGMENTS

Among the many people who read and scrutinized this manuscript, I would especially thank Paula Tyler and Jill Mason, who rescued the text from serious flaws I was too close to see. And I would like to thank others who, over the long months involved in preparing and publishing this book, were unfailingly supportive in friendship and advice: Bradley Hutchinson, Jennifer Larson, Dorothy Sloan, Decherd Turner, and Ron Tyler.

I would also like to thank Greg Curtis, editor of *Texas Monthly* magazine, who provided me with information from his investigations that proved to be invaluable, particularly the inventory of materials seized by the police in their raid on Dorman David's premises in 1972. The appearance of Curtis' article, and later the well-written piece by Lisa Belkin in the *New York Times Magazine*, was a welcome affirmation of my work. I would also like to acknowledge Monty Jones, who wrote the first article about the forgeries for the *Austin American-Statesman*, and whose computer file name for the story gave me the title for this book.

I owe a particular debt of gratitude to Ralph Elder in the reading room of the Barker Texas History Center at the University of Texas. His cheerful and unfailing help was much appreciated. Indeed, this book could not have been written without the resources available in the Barker Center. There were many helpful people at other institutions as well, including Dora Guerra at the University of Texas at San Antonio; Pat Bozeman at the University of Houston; Kent Keeth at Baylor University; David Farmer at the DeGolyer Library, Southern Methodist University; George Miles at the Beinecke Library, Yale University; Marcus McCorison at the American Antiquarian Society; James Gilreath at the Library of Congress; Houston McGaugh at the Star of the Republic Museum; Gerald Saxon and Marcelle Hull at the University of Texas at Arlington; J. C. Martin at the San Jacinto Monument Museum; Florence Jumonville at the Historic New Orleans Collection; and Chris LaPlante at the Texas State Library.

There are also other individuals who were helpful in various ways, including Kate Adams, Bailey Bishop, Ann Bowden, J. P. Bryan, Jr., Paul Burns, Sara Clark, Fuller French, L. R. French, Jenkins Garrett, Oscar Graham, Jim Grizzard, Michael Heaston, Larry McMurtry, Paul Needham, Steve Saxe, Fred Schreiber, Bill Todd, and John Wheat.

Finally, my entire family—wife Judy, children Kate, Lena, David, and Greg—were always supportive during the last few years, at least when they were not staying prudently out of range of my Irish temper. Indeed, looking back over this entire episode, it is reassuring to see how a certain amount of adversity can serve to strengthen and broaden one's human relationships. It has brought me to the happy conclusion that forgeries just don't matter: friendships and families do.

INTRODUCTION

This is an admirable, necessary piece of work, though I would imagine the author regrets the necessity more than a little. The vast, confused literature of bookselling and book collecting is controlled almost entirely by the myth of the peaceable kingdom—Eden cast rather in the mode of an Edwardian men's club. Pointing out that some of the beasts prowling amid the sofas are actually carnivores is no way to win friends in the book trade.

Any relatively tough-minded book about the book trade is a moral rarity and a very welcome thing. There are so few. The literature of bookselling is mainly advertising; what is being advertised is a peaceable kingdom whose citizens are the honorable, the scholarly, and the mild. One is encouraged to think that a sound system of blackballing will turn back all rogues and scoundrels, should any apply for citizenship.

In demonstrating how a large and not especially expert batch of Texas forgeries rather easily filtered into, and then flooded, the market, Tom Taylor explodes this myth, without once mentioning it. He is concerned to be cool, precise, and fair, and he *is* cool, precise, and fair. While not so constrained as were Carter and Pollard in their famous *Enquiry*, he nonetheless has opted, I think wisely, to write a book that largely restricts itself to laying out the evidence: what was forged, when it appeared, who sold, and who bought.

The result is a convincing and absorbing book, but there are times when one wishes Tom could have let the ghosts come out and dance. His dilemma was that in order to do strict justice to the evidence he has had, for the most part, to omit personality and *mentalité*, by which I mean the attitudes and moral ambiance prevalent in Texas bookselling in the years when the forgeries were made.

The mentality itself is neither rare nor novel, whether one is talking about Texas, American, or international bookselling. What was new was the individual energies, expressed through a kind of post-frontiersmanship, of two unusual dealers, C. Dorman David and John H. Jenkins. Both were mavericks, consciously and proudly so—a two-man herd, conducting a kind of top-speed stampede through the trade, kicking up as much dust as possible as they ran: amid which dust, now that it's settled or settling, we find these forgeries.

I knew both men—not well, but lengthily—and it may be that I can slap on a little of the color that Tom Taylor has had to leave off. I commenced bookselling, under the rubric of Dust Bowl Books, with a leaflet of a catalogue issued from Archer City, Texas, in the summer of 1961. I had no bookshop then, but I was an active scout, and, as such, was an early customer of both Dorman's and Johnny's bookshops.

My first purchase from what was to become the Jenkins Company was made from its then-modest quarters in downtown Austin, and was Johnny's own set of *MAD Comics*, issues no. 1–22. It may, indeed, have been only *one* of Johnny's own sets of these incomparable classics; in any case it escaped Austin but not the pyro-curse which haunted the firm, perishing in a fire in Bethesda, Maryland, some fifteen years later.

My first purchase from The Bookman, Dorman's magisterial establishment on San Felipe Road in Houston, was made not long after he opened (but also, alas, not long before he closed); it was the sumptuous limited edition of Doctor Rosenbach's bibliography of American children's books, and it cost me a mere forty bucks. Two hours later Dorman showed up rather sheepishly at my door, claiming *trahison des clercs* and wanting the book back. I surrendered it reluctantly, but, in negotiating with Dorman, slipped into a series of transactions which provided me, after only a modest additional outlay, with a fine pool table and a Mercedes coupe.

Shortly after that, Dorman's star—so briefly risen—plummeted to earth, flaring brilliantly if catastrophically even as it fell. His undauntable mother, Grace David, took over The Bookman and promptly bought the Yount library from Spindletop country; this was a countryhouse collection which boasted among other treasures, nineteen sets of Maupassant, in various leathers and cloths. Baffled, though not daunted, by all that Maupassant, Grace hired me to manage The Bookman, which I did for about three years, leaving, by happy accident, just about the time a startling pile of documents appeared at the shop one day, left there by Dorman as collateral against monies owed his mother. Whether there were forgeries among them I can't say, but I *can* say that in a less imperfect world the majority of those documents would have been resting quietly in their ancient home: in this case, the Rosenberg Library in Galveston.

I believe I may even, at about this time, have made the acquaintance of that shadowy figure, Bill Gray—he who receives the instructions about what treasures might be found in which courthouse, in the third chapter of *Texfake*. At least I made the acquaintance of *a* Bill Gray, a brilliant antiques picker who once perversely refused to sell me a wonderful hill-country German fly-catching machine (see *Cadillac Jack*, page 12), although he did sell me an equally wonderful roseglow whimsy in the shape of a pig, perhaps turned out by a hill-country German glass blower, from what glass was left in his pipe at the end of the day.

In those days the three collecting Davids, Dorman, Grace, and Diane, were constantly acquiring brilliant *objets* of every conceivable sort; they just as constantly bought, sold, and traded this galaxy of wonders among themselves, with such speed and brio that the only people in Houston who could keep up with which David owned what *objet* at a given moment were the employees of a small moving company who seemed to have decided to devote their lives mainly to moving the Davids, from house to house, marriage to marriage, or wherever.

In the years after losing his shop, Dorman, though addicted and often more or less on the nod, continued to acquire books and objects, if at a somewhat slower pace. Meanwhile, up in Austin, the Jenkins Company was growing, and part of its growth was fallout from the continuous spume of objects Dorman threw off behind him in his descent, more or less like exhaust. There was the Rolls Royce and the railroad car, the cannon collection and the Chinese coins, the Purdey shotguns and the 38,000 lithograph stones (or was it 380,000?). There were boats, wines, and rare tobaccos (these initially had a whole room, with tobacco-compatible shelving, to themselves). There were western landscapes, and, a little later, pre-Columbian artifacts, many of which, alas, turned out to be post-Columbian artifacts, most of them manufactured in the reign of Portillo.

There may even have been a concrete submarine, but I never saw this sub and suspect it was merely part of the vast David apocrypha, a corpus as swollen in its time as the Jenkins apocrypha is today.

Many, many dealers made piranha-like attacks on Dorman's stock, ripping away great hunks of inventory with apparent ease, but—at least until William Simpson came along—Johnny lived the closest and struck the most often.

In the last year of Johnny's life, once the forgeries were exposed and his and Dorman's role in the affair much-debated in the press, one would have thought from reading their published statements about one another that they were as different as the moon and the sun and that they could never have shared an amicable, much less a fraternal, moment. Earlier on, though, each was happy to take credit for the other's achievement. Dorman David told me rather recently that he was the one who taught Johnny (a.k.a. Austin Squatty) to play poker—and I'm sure this assertion would have infuriated Johnny more than any self-exonerating claptrap about the forgeries.

In my view, Dorman and Johnny were the eternal Odd Couple of Texas bookselling: our Mutt and Jeff, Butch and Sundance, Faust and Mephistopheles. Each strove with all his might to become a legend in his own time, and both succeeded; the irony is that through the sad fact of Johnny's death the roots of the two legends are now forever entwined—as in Yeats' poem "The Three Bushes." In this case the forgeries constitute the third bush.

Though they themselves may have liked to think they were mirror opposites, they were, in certain psychological essentials, closer to being identical twins. Both always felt underrated, and both countered with extreme and competitive flamboyance. Both were frontier snake-oil salesmen who *liked*—indeed, gloried in—being frontier snake-oil salesmen. The notion that either of them would have sunk to their knees, rending the air with mea culpas, because they had sold some chump a Texas Declaration of Independence that had just been peeled off the Xerox machine is absurd: their *whole* practice as tradesmen was a hearty "Up yours!" to the genteel canons of the trade, which, after all, are still the canons of a northern European men's club.

Nope: these boys were frontiersmen, and they were sports. Dorman always loved to fool around with old papers and old cuts; he was from the first a better designer than he was a merchant. Making the first few forgeries probably was just horseplay; likewise selling the first few (whoever sold them). It was just boisterous frontier sport, the moral equivalent, in their minds, of sticking a dude on a bronc, or persuading one to rope a bear. A cowboy would call that a legpull, not a crime, even if the bear happened to eat the dude. Frontiersmen turn a traditionally cold eye on inexperience.

Besides that, the frontiersman is apt—if he gets snubbed once too often by the dude—to develop the urge to count coup. The early careers of both Dorman and Johnny involved plenty of snubbing—Tom Taylor's brief account of his attempt to get a little extra discount from H. P. Kraus gives one the tone. In both Dorman's and Johnny's case their very eagerness got them joked about, in various great shops and libraries.

So they counted coup; lots of coup. These forgeries are, in my view, part of that coup. If, in the end, both men proved unclubbable, it wasn't from lack of trying. Dorman gave it up and also gave it the finger, but Johnny tried so hard he became president of the Antiquarian Booksellers Association of America. He was not, as he well knew, presiding over a company of saints. I expect—and, indeed, hope—that he had more fun being Austin Squatty.

But, for all the coup counting, the notion that Dorman and Johnny were the two greatest stagecoach robbers ever to gallop down bookseller's row is absurd, even though it was a notion either man, in certain moods, might have encouraged. If you feel perennially underrated, being overrated for sharp practice is better than never being overrated at all. Johnny, once he became a President, was given to flights of pure-as-the-driven-snowism, but by that time he was only talking to the mirror—or, at least, only the mirror was listening.

But, so far as the trade goes, both men were as lambs compared to several of their tutors. Dorman bought his dazzling opening-day stock at skyscraping prices from the greatest names in the trade; the seasons had scarcely made their turning before the same great names got most of their treasures back at his fire sale—and at fire sale prices. In that company of old grizzlies Dorman was indeed the dude: he threw his rope and they ate him, hide, hair, and toenails.

Now a word about the victims, or, at least, about those who bought. Recent experience has given me some insight about those who buy forgeries, because I have myself now been forged. I don't mean my writing—I mean me.

Shortly after the mini-series of *Lonesome Dove* was aired, to great popularity, forgeries of me—in other words, imposters—began to pop up. Their aims were mainly sexual, though one may have been in it for money. With the help of a detective I now have photographs of four of these imposters. My greatest difficulty so far has been in persuading their "victims" that I am the unique and only-existing first printing of me, and that the men they are being approached by, or are living with, or, in one instance, have become engaged to, are not only forgeries but crude ones at that.

In Tucson, for example, one imposter presents himself to young women at gas stations, claims to be me, claims to be just in the process of casting the sequel to *Lonesome Dove*, claims to have a small part for which the lady in question looks to be perfect. And the man *convinces*, though it seems that his only connection to the film industry (if it's a connection) is that he owns two trained dogs.

In Houston a young woman has been living with, supporting, and planning to marry a man claiming to be me, for about two years. Though she works at McDonald's to support "me," she has apparently never so much as asked to see "my" driver's license; when I reached her mother and informed her that her daughter's fiancé was definitely not myself, the news was neither welcomed nor, so far as I could tell, accepted. The mother did not want to rethink the matter.

The analogy may seem farfetched, and yet precautions just as basic as asking to see a driver's license were omitted in regard to these forgeries time after time. The willingness to believe, contra the dictates of reason, is evidently too human and too powerful to be readily overridden, even in supposedly rationalist professions such as librarianship. It goes with an urge to be larger, to have more, to exceed the ordinary. Dorman and Johnny had this urge to such a degree that at times I think they might even have chosen towering failure over sensible-shoe success.

The urge to collect—or, more basically, to *acquire*—is deeply atavistic and almost always overrides rationality. Few of those afflicted with the need to acquire want to slow things down by asking awkward questions when a chance to get something on the order of a Travis letter comes along. Many of the librarians and dealers and collectors who bought these forgeries would not really have had to reflect very deeply to convince themselves that something was wrong. Items that had been accurately described as "desperately rare" for half a century became, in the space of a decade, rather common. Ross Perot and one or two others who had acquired enough to have brought the fever somewhat under control displayed no willingness to be deceived, and were *not* deceived.

Most of those who *were* deceived have behaved, in my view, almost as disgracefully as the forger and the forgery-merchants. The pettifogging, particularly on the part of libraries, throughout the investigation of these forgeries, has been appalling—though not surprising. Wagon-circling is a frontier tactic still in use in many regions; it seems to be mainly employed now, as it has been in this instance, as a safeguard against embarrassment.

Dorman David, John Jenkins, and William Simpson are not men known for taking the subtle approach to their craft. The two I knew disdained subtlety. Who looks for subtlety on a frontier? Their deals, their trades, their supposed or alleged skullduggery were matters, if not of common knowledge, at least of common gossip: this was true from the moment they went into business. Did they discourage this gossip? Hardly. They didn't work like crazy to become legends in their own time hoping not to be talked about.

For the many citizens of the peaceable kingdom of book collecting who traded with these men regularly now to recoil in horror and attempt to feign shock, bewilderment, and surprise at the contemplation of some pretty slippery dealing is a more than faintly disgusting spectacle. It's a *wholly* disgusting spectacle. The element of crap shoot, pigeon drop, and poker game that went with dealing with Dorman and Johnny was *always* obvious, and, I thought, rather enjoyed by all parties. At least it was enjoyed by me, while it lasted. I don't think it would have surprised me much if the Mercedes coupe I got from Dorman had turned out to be a Studebaker with a brilliant paint job.

Embarrassment can happen whether one knows better or not—certainly there are some faces that ought to be red. But surprise, no. That's hypocrisy. Dorman and Johnny were not merely unsubtle, they were blatant. Dorman even printed his motto, with delicious irony, right there on his business card for all to see. His motto was: "Sell and repent!"

—Larry McMurtry

Part One

Plundering the Past

Chapter One

Texfake

The eastern edge of the University of Texas campus is defined by Sid Richardson Hall, a long, low building with tinted windows deeply recessed in white concrete. Like many other buildings on the campus constructed in the late 1960s, it most resembles a brooding line of defense against invaders. Entering the building does not dispel this impression. The doors leading to the Barker Texas History Center open into a barren lobby, with one small display case, a wall of plaques for large donors, a directory for the building, and an elevator. Although it is a library, there is not a book to be seen. The door on the left leading to the reading room opens to a security desk.

When Dorothy Sloan and William R. Holman approached this desk one morning in late June 1987, they were carrying a document that no doubt became the focus of attention. It was the original broadside printing of the Texas Declaration of Independence, which had been consigned to Sloan, a dealer in rare books, by a collector in Dallas. The collector wanted to sell the document; Sloan very much wanted to buy it. But responding to the sixth sense an experienced dealer develops when holding and examining a document, she was uneasy about it. She wanted to compare the collector's copy with the copy in the Barker Center's Vandale Collection, and she had asked Bill Holman, a retired librarian with thirty years of experience with rare books, to accompany her. Holman is also a distinguished book designer and printer, with a keen eye for typographic nuance.

They carefully compared the two documents, and all seemed fine until Holman laid one copy on top of the other. At that moment he noticed that on the collector's copy the type area was perceptibly smaller—2 to 4 percent, he estimated. Combined with the fact that the printing of the collector's copy was noticeably fuzzy compared with the crisp blackness of the copy in the university's collection, this caused Holman to conclude that the collector's copy was probably a fake. He theorized that it could have been made by photographing a genuine copy and making a zinc printing plate from the negative—fuzzy printing is a common characteristic of printing from zinc plates—and the difference in size was probably the result of the camera being slightly miscalibrated, so that the negative was not a 100 percent image of the original. On July 1 Sloan returned the Declaration of Independence to the collector—along with an equally suspect copy of the Declaration of Causes (Streeter 89)—and there matters might have rested had not Bill Holman and I had one of our occasional lunches at a modest Chinese cafeteria near his son's printing shop. Holman casually related his experience at the library and was surprised when I began asking pointed questions about the documents. The reason for my interest was simple: I had sold three copies of the Texas Declaration of Independence—to the Dallas Public Library, the San Jacinto Monument Museum, and Paul Burns, a private collector in Austin—for a total of nearly $85,000. The possibility that they were fake was not the sort of thing I wanted to hear over a $3 Chinese lunch.

It was especially bothersome because I was not even a dealer in "Texana." My own interests as a dealer were primarily English and American literature, early European printed books, and similar material, all far removed from the lore of the Lone Star state. I had encountered the Texas Declaration of Independence because of my friendship with Ray Walton, another dealer in Austin, who specialized in the history of Texas and the Southwest. Walton had a copy framed on the wall in his office when I dropped in for a visit in 1977. Despite my snobbish disdain for Walton's usual books (a contempt he cheerfully turned back upon my English literature), I could not help being impressed by the broadside hanging on the wall. It is a document that cuts through the mindless chauvinism, the constant polishing of a surface of myth that is crazed with flaws, and brings a person in direct contact with a genuine moment in history. Never mind that, according to reliable reports, the men who signed the document were drunk half the time—they uttered some brave words and backed them up. "Declaration of Independence" is a phrase that resonates for almost any American, and it was printed in large, bold type on the top of the document on Walton's wall.

For a bookseller, if he or she is any good at it, resonance is soon converted into covetousness. I wanted the document, and Walton was only too happy to oblige, after the customary protestations of regret at parting with such a treasure. I left Walton's office full of pride in my new possession, confident that his only misjudgment had to do with price. Eager and green, I was also confident that the world would take notice of a young bookseller with a Texas Declaration of Independence. In the beginning it appeared this would be so, as I sold my copy within a few months for a tidy profit. It seemed such a clever piece of business: My car broke down on the Central Expressway in Dallas, and while waiting for it to be repaired I chanced upon an article in a Dallas newspaper describing the purchase of a copy of the United States Declaration of Independence for the city of Dallas by a group headed by Jack Stroube. While still in the repair shop, I looked up Stroube's number, called him, and suggested that he might like to have a copy of the Texas Declaration of Independence to go along with the Philadelphia document. He agreed entirely and flew to Austin the next week to examine my copy. We made appointments at every library in Austin that held a copy of the document and visited them during that day. The copy at the Texas Memorial Museum was in poor condition, and we did not even bother to compare my copy with it. But we did compare my copy with the copy at the Texas State Library and the three copies at the Barker Texas History Center. It never occurred to us to look at typographic details—all we were concerned about was condition. And much to our satisfaction, the copy that I was offering appeared to be the best of any of them.

After this experience, I was naturally quite pleased to buy another copy from Walton a year or so later, for a slightly advanced price. I distinctly remember noticing and remarking upon the fuzzy quality of the printing of this second copy, but did not find this cause for suspicion. That copy moved quickly, too, and the night of its sale I spent a portion of the profits eating, drinking, and dancing at a Greek restaurant on the Ship Channel in Houston where the waitresses take your shoes and toss them into nets on the ceiling. The hangover from that transaction has lasted over a decade.

Two years later, in 1981, I sold one last copy. I was in the office of Dr. Paul Burns for treatment of an obscure neck ailment. Filling out the customary forms, I noted under "Occupation" that I was a rare book dealer. Burns was pleased—he was a collector of Texana—and asked for a catalogue. I sent him a catalogue that listed my second Declaration of

Independence, and he called to order it. It was sold, but by this time I knew of yet another copy, which had been owned for a number of years by the firm of H. P. Kraus in New York. The price was $30,000—three times what I had paid Walton only four years earlier. I offered it to Burns for that plus a 10 percent commission, and he accepted. I flew to New York to fetch the document.

The firm of H. P. Kraus, in its own building on West 46th Street, was, and may still be, the largest rare book firm in the world. Its proprietor was a legendary if not always beloved figure. A small man, but nonetheless imperious for that, he was well aware of who he was, and well prepared to tell you who you were. We sat down in his outer office and exchanged pleasantries while looking at the document. I was vexed by the realization that my own advancing prices on the Texas Declaration of Independence were working against me—Kraus' catalogue card showed evidence of several price changes, with notes about my price. I thought that Mr. Kraus might bend a bit on his price. The customary 10 percent dealer discount made it $27,000. I offered him a check for $26,000. He gave me a bored look, and replied with his German accent, "Mr. Taylor, business is very, very good right now. I really don't need to sell anything. If you talk to me about spending $3-400,000, perhaps I could do something. But this? This is so little." Some people, it seems, were not much impressed by the young Texas bookseller. The final indignity was that I had no choice but to buy the document at his price. I left feeling rather gloomy, but was brightened by Burns' enthusiasm when I delivered the Declaration to him in Austin.

That was the end of my flirtation with Texana. For various reasons Ray Walton and I did not see so much of each other, and since he had been almost my sole source for such items, I stayed with my usual interests in bookselling. However, over the next five or six years I could not help noticing that copies of the Texas Declaration of Independence seemed to be popping up with remarkable frequency. I visited the Star of the Republic Museum at Washington-on-the-Brazos on the way home from my daughter's summer camp, and there was a copy, proudly displayed in a case of its own. I heard that the University of Houston had received a copy as a gift, and that there was yet another copy, recently acquired, at the DeGolyer Library at Southern Methodist University.

Bill Holman's chance remarks over lunch suddenly provided a clear and unpleasant explanation for the rising count of copies. After brooding over the matter for a few days, I called the three people I had sold copies to and told them that there appeared to be a real possibility that their copies were fake. Though their reactions to the news varied greatly, they had in common a large measure of forbearance, for which I remain grateful. J. C. Martin, director of the San Jacinto Monument Museum, agreed to bring the copy I had sold him to Austin and deposit it at the Barker Texas History Center, so that I could compare it with their Vandale copy, which I considered to be almost certainly genuine since it had been in the library since the 1940s and bore evidence of much earlier ownership. I made careful measurements of the two copies: on the Vandale copy, the length of the headline "Declaration of Independence" was 237 mm; on the San Jacinto copy, 232 mm; the width of a column of type on the Vandale copy was 68 mm; on the San Jacinto copy, 66 mm. And, as was the case with the collector's copy that Holman had examined, the printing of the San Jacinto copy was fuzzy and weak compared to the clear, black printing of the Vandale copy. It appeared that Holman was right—these were forged copies of the Declaration of Independence, printed from photographically produced zinc plates.

However, there were two other pieces of evidence that did not support this conclusion: First, in column 3, paragraph 7, of the San Jacinto copy, the word *denies* was misspelled *donies*. If the San Jacinto copy were made by photographing a genuine copy, where did this error come from? It did not appear on the Vandale copy. Second, while the type area of the San Jacinto copy was narrower than that of the Vandale copy, it was also longer (307 vs. 299 mm); it is possible to enlarge or reduce an image with a camera, but it is *not* possible to reduce it in one dimension while enlarging it in another. More study was needed.

I made sporadic trips around the state (much less heady than the trips of a decade before) to examine other known copies of the Declaration. Every copy I examined fell neatly into one of two groups: of the first, clearly printed and with measurements matching the Vandale copy, all had early provenances, several even directly connected with signers of the document; of the second, poorly printed and with measurements matching the San Jacinto copy, not a single one bore evidence of a provenance earlier than 1970. Unfortunately, nothing helped resolve the problem posed by the two anomalies already mentioned—all of the recent copies had the spelling *donies* and measurements impossible to produce with a camera.

One copy I had not yet examined was Paul Burns'—it was conveniently in a bank in Austin, but I suppose I didn't want to know yet whether it was real. Paul and I went to the bank and pulled the document in its green cloth case from the safe deposit box. Opening it, I was silently jubilant: the printing was black and clear, *denies* was spelled properly. For final confirmation of its authenticity I laid a Schaedler Precision Rule along the headline. My spirits sagged. The measurement matched the suspect copies. After a few moments of reflection, I was puzzled. How could this be? Leaving Paul in a like state of mind, I took his copy to the library to join the other two.

At this point, I asked Jill Mason, a skilled editor and proofreader, to spend as much time as necessary with the three documents, reading each of them letter by letter, word by word, line by line, noting every broken letter, every typo, every repair, every variation of whatever kind. She returned with a long list of notes for each copy, and I returned to the library to see what sense I could make of them.

In the first place it was plain that the Burns copy and the Vandale copy were from the same setting of type. There were twenty-six significantly broken letters that appeared in both documents; except for the discrepancy in measurements, they were a perfect match. The San Jacinto copy, however, contained almost none of these broken letters, and it had one other unique characteristic: in certain places throughout the document, Jill had noticed that letters and even whole words seemed curiously distorted—compressed in one place, expanded in another. Looking at her notes, I noticed that whatever column these distorted letters appeared in, they appeared in the same lines—and looking at the document as a whole, I could see these distortions running along the same lines across all four columns. I glanced at the Burns copy. There, running along exactly the same lines, two vertical and two horizontal, that contained the distorted letters in the San Jacinto copy, were folds and repairs that obscured the text. By chance, I had before me the very copy that could prove that the San Jacinto copy, and every copy like it, was a forgery, because it was the copy that had been used to make them: it had been photographed, enlarged, the letters and words obscured by the folds touched up on the negative (and a number of other things done to it, including the gratuitous misspelling of *denies* and correction of the broken letters), then printed from a zinc plate made from the touched-up negative after it was reduced again to the correct size. I now also knew who the forger might be, because in the meantime I had learned that H. P. Kraus had purchased the Burns copy in 1973 for $5,000 from C. Dorman David of Houston, Texas.

These were useful discoveries, but one critical question remained unanswered. Was the Burns copy genuine? It certainly had every appearance of being genuine, but under the circumstances, this was hardly sufficient. The discrepancy in measurements had to be accounted for. The most likely possibility was that, for some reason, the lock-up of the type on the bed of the press had been altered during printing. When a form of type is placed on the bed of a handpress, wooden pieces called "furniture" are placed around the type to hold it in place, and this arrangement is secured with wedges. A variance in the amount of pressure applied by these wedges—the "squeeze" on the type—could easily account for a 2 mm variation in the length of a line (i.e., 66 mm vs. 68 mm). This was still just a hypothesis—but, as it happens, one that could be substantiated by historical investigation.

Chapter Two

Printing under the Gun

One of the comforting sounds of urban life is the early morning arrival of the newspaper. You hear the lone car moving slowly down the street, the papers landing with a satisfying thump in neighbors' yards. Alert to the sound, you rise from coffee, pad outside, and the worst inconvenience you may suffer in this ritual is when the paper misses its mark, skidding beneath the car, an inch beyond reach. The paper is substantial: four or five sections of a dozen pages each, plus countless inserted advertisements that tend to scatter over the floor as you open the paper to read. A single, medium-circulation daily will consume over a million pounds of paper a week, printing computer-generated text on enormous high-speed presses capable of fifty thousand impressions per hour. It is printed at night, as we sleep, and we expect its arrival in the morning as surely as the rising sun.

One hundred fifty years ago the sun rose many mornings without the appearance of a newspaper anywhere in the fledgling colony of Texas. The first significant newspaper to appear was the *Texas Gazette*, a three-column, four-page weekly edited by Godwin B. Cotten. Published in San Felipe de Austin beginning on September 25, 1829, it appeared irregularly, interrupted by everything from lack of paper and damaged type to the necessity of printing Stephen F. Austin's *Laws, Orders, and Contracts*, the first book printed in Texas. Cotten, who had come to Texas after publishing newspapers in New Orleans and Mobile, described the duties of a country editor in terms that would no doubt horrify a respectable modern editor:

> A Country Editor—Is one who reads newspapers, selects miscellany; writes articles on all subjects; sets types; reads proof; works at press; folds papers; and sometimes carries them; prints jobs; runs on errands; cuts wood; *toats* water; talks to all his patrons who call;

> patiently receives blame for things that never were or can be done; *gets little money*; has scarce time or materials to satisfy his hunger; or to enjoy the quiet of "nature's grand restorer," sleep; and esteems himself peculiarly happy, if he is not assaulted and battered, (or *bulletted and his ears cut off*) by some unprincipled demagogue, who loves puppet shows, and hires the rabble with a treat of corn whiskey, (and that burnt,) to vote him into some petty office.[1]

Though it moved to Brazoria and changed ownership more than once, Cotten's press was the only one in Texas until the fall of 1835, when Gail and Thomas H. Borden, along with Joseph Baker, began publication of the *Telegraph and Texas Register* in San Felipe. Gail Borden is now best remembered for discovering how to condense milk rather than for his newspaper, but in late 1835 and early 1836 his printing office was responsible for recording the history of each passing week, and for printing most of the material required by the provisional government of Texas. The printers took the name "Texas Register" as an indication of their commitment to be an official record of events in the embryo republic, and they did so with an impartiality that was unusual for the time.[2]

Meanwhile, after a lawsuit and two name changes, Cotten's press in Brazoria settled in the hands of Franklin C. Gray, who had previously been foreman of the New Orleans *Commercial Bulletin*.[3] The first issue of his *Texas Republican* appeared in July 1834,[4] and he acknowledged the problem he faced: "We are aware of the many disadvantages under which we labor in an effort to resuscitate and bring into notice and make useful an establishment so effectually dead as this press must be, at present, in the public estimation."[5] Gray did succeed in reviving its reputation, and the paper served as an effective voice for the "war party," led by William H. Wharton, in the months leading up to the Texas Revolution.

The only other press active in Texas at the outbreak of the Revolution was that of D. E. Lawhon in Nacogdoches, which began publication of the *Texean and Emigrant's Guide* on November 28, 1835. Lawhon declared, "Our press and type are new and of an excellent quality and from our experience in the art, we hope for a liberal patronage."[6]

As was true of most pioneer newspaper offices, all three of the presses active in Texas did job printing. In the very first issue of their paper Baker and Bordens ran the following ad:

> BAKER & BORDENS Respectfully inform the citizens of Texas that they have established a Printing Office in the town of San Felipe de Austin, where they are prepared to execute every description of BOOK and JOB PRINTING, at the shortest notice, and upon reasonable terms.
>
> Their extensive stock of materials, being entirely new, and upon the most approved principles, will enable them to do all work entrusted to their charge in the best manner: they therefore confidently solicit a share of public patronage.[7]

Of the jobbing work done by these printers, 95 percent took the form of broadsides, forms, and circulars of four pages or less. They were generally done on short notice, and, while it is clear some proofreading occurred, precision was apparently not expected or delivered.[8]

The most consistent customer for job printing in 1835–1838 was the government of Texas. Reports of important meetings would often be printed up in broadside form, the text in several narrow columns headed by a line or two of larger display type. Since setting type by hand was a time-consuming task, the printers would generally set the columns to the same measure as the columns of their newspapers, allowing them to reprint these reports in the next issue of the paper without resetting the type. Extraordinary events might merit a more dramatic treatment, but even a document as important as the Texas Declaration of Independence, printed by Baker and Bordens, was set up to be reprinted from the same type later.

Understanding the methodology of the Texas printers provided the key to determining the authenticity of the Burns copy of the Declaration of Independence. Looking through the original issues of the *Telegraph and Texas Register* at the Barker Texas History Center, I discovered that the Declaration of Independence was reprinted in the March 12, 1836, issue, a few days after the broadside had been printed. Several corrections had been made—such as adding the names of two signers that had been left off the broadside—but it is over all from the same setting of type—all of the broken letters match. But in this printing the width of a column of type is exactly 66 mm, the same as the Burns copy of the Declaration. This was clear evidence that a separate lock-up in the press, with a different amount of pressure applied by the wedges, had indeed resulted in variant measurements of the width of a column of type in two distinct printings of the Declaration. Thus it was reasonable to conclude that the Burns copy could be genuine; and if it could be genuine, was genuine, since in every respect besides the measurement of the type it was identical to other genuine copies. This was a satisfying discovery (and a great relief—I didn't have another $33,000 to refund!), but it led to another question, which, while not directly relating to forgery, begged to be answered: When and why did the printers stop and unlock the type?

The Texas Declaration of Independence was read and adopted by the convention at Washington-on-the-Brazos on Wednesday, March 2, 1836. Five engrossed holograph copies were prepared, one of which was to be delivered to Baker and Bordens in San Felipe, along with an order for one thousand copies to be printed in handbill form. Owing to various difficulties in preparing the holograph copies, the messenger was not dispatched to San Felipe until the morning of Thursday, March 3.[9] It apparently took about forty-eight hours for express dispatches to get from Washington-on-the-Brazos to San Felipe.[10] The final paragraph from the Declaration of Independence was inserted at the end of the March 5, 1836, issue of the *Telegraph and Texas Register*, suggesting that the type for that issue had already been set when the messenger arrived and the printers were able to get only a bit of it in the paper.

Suddenly, Baker and Bordens found themselves with a lot of printing to do. There were five hundred copies of a four-page newspaper, one thousand copies of the Declaration of Independence, and one thousand copies of Travis' letter from Bexar (Streeter 184—not to be confused with the more famous Victory or Death letter, Streeter 185), which arrived on Tuesday, March 8. Juggling of the newspaper and other printing was not a new situation for the printers. In the *Telegraph and Texas Register* for December 12, 1835, they had noted that "the delay in the publication of this and the previous number of our paper, is owing to a press of public printing."

In the March 12, 1836, issue of the *Telegraph and Texas Register*, Baker and Bordens apologized for their blunder in leaving off the names of two of the signers from the broadside Declaration of Independence—one of them the author of the text, George Childress—explaining that the document was printed "in too much haste, and chiefly in the night." This would probably have been on the night of March 5th, or 6th at the latest, because Asa Brigham, one of the delegates to the convention, had a copy in hand at Washington on the 9th: his copy, in the Streeter Collection at Yale, bears that date. Yet we also know (again, from the March 12 issue) that, "for want of opportunity," all of the copies were not dispatched at the same time. Some had to have left San Felipe by the 7th (to be in Washington by the 9th), but others were not sent, according to the newspaper account, until "late in the week"—probably on Thursday, March 10th, when copies of the Travis letter of March 3rd (Streeter 184) were also dispatched to Washington.[11]

Why were the Declarations sent in two batches? The printers say "for want of opportunity," yet there was a messenger ready to ride for Washington-on-the-Brazos on the 6th or 7th. The messenger, however, was probably a man in a hurry—the delegates at Washington doubtless wanted printed copies of the Declaration as soon as possible. It is useful to remember that, unlike a modern press, which can spit out a thousand sheets of printed paper in a few minutes, this many copies from a hand-press, with a relatively large form of type to be inked by hand and printed on paper that had to be dampened by hand before printing, would require a good many hours of work.[12] Furthermore, one thousand sheets of 13x16-inch paper is a cumbersome load for someone trying to make good time on a horse. Is it possible that the messenger arrived from Washington while the printers were in the midst of working on the newspaper? (It was certainly in type by the time he arrived.) That the printers interrupted work on the paper to take care of the urgent government printing, and after a certain number of copies of the Declaration had been printed, the messenger departed immediately? That having done this, and eager to put the newspaper to bed, the printers removed the type of the Declaration from the press and finished printing the paper, knowing they would then have a few days in which to print the additional copies of the Declaration for delivery to Washington?

This would be idle speculation except that there is contemporary evidence to suggest that this is precisely what happened. At the Barker Texas History Center there is a photostatic copy of the Lamar copy of the Declaration of Independence, located in the State Library. On the reverse is a notation in the hand of E. W. Winkler, the Texas historian (1875–1960):[13]

Another copy in State Library
Public Printing 12 11/16 x 15 7/8

A

Declaration of
Independence
March 5th

1000 copies	
first 100 copies	30.00
900 additional $7.50	67.50
	$97.50

This is a transcription of the printer's endorsement on a copy of the Declaration of Independence that was apparently at one time in the Public Printing Papers at the State Library.[14] The "A" corresponds to the voucher mark recorded on the manuscript bill located in the State Library, presented by Baker and Bordens to the government on July 6, 1836. There are two possible explanations for this endorsement (assuming it accurately reflects the endorsement on a copy that cannot now be identified): either there were two printings of the document, or the printers were simply noting a different billing rate for additional hundreds within a single printing. Normally, the latter would be the more natural assumption. However, I have examined a number of original and transcribed printer's endorsements by Baker and Bordens, and although they almost always bill for printing in multiples of one hundred, not a single one is treated like the Declaration of Independence—that is, with one billing rate for the first one hundred and a second billing rate for additional hundreds. Taken with the previously described historical circumstances, this leads me to believe that there may well have been two distinct printings of the Declaration, separated by two or three days.

If this is the case, the Asa Brigham copy (now at Yale) would have to be from the first printing of one hundred copies, since Brigham had it in hand in Washington on the 9th of March. All the genuine copies that have measurements that match this copy—which is to say all of them I have seen except the Burns copy and a copy at the Alamo—are from this first printing. Which leads to one last question: why, of the twelve surviving copies I have been able to locate, do ten come from the first one hundred, and only two from the second batch of nine hundred? The answer, I think, is this: the first one hundred were delivered immediately to the signers and others present at Washington, all of whom might be expected to care something about the document, preserving it, or sending it back east, as did Brigham. The second, much larger group was for general circulation, a process that never took place because of the chaos that prevailed in Texas between the fall of the Alamo on March 6, 1836, and the victory at San Jacinto on April 21, as much of the population fled eastward in what is known as the Runaway Scrape. Sam Houston's retreating army laid waste to anything that could be of use to the Mexican army; San Felipe itself was put to the torch on April 1, "houses, goods, and all."[15] The building housing the *Telegraph* was the first to be burned,[16] and the printers lost most of the files of their paper in the conflagration.[17] Even far away Nacogdoches had been abandoned by about April 13,[18] and Brazoria was largely abandoned before being burned by Mexicans under General Urrea on April 22.[19] The last issue of Lawhon's *Texean and Emigrant's Guide* appeared in Nacogdoches no later than March 24, 1836; the last surviving copy of the Brazoria *Texas Republican* is dated March 9. The *Telegraph and Texas Register* met a dramatic end: Moved with considerable difficulty to Harrisburg, the press was set up and an issue of the newspaper was being printed on April 14 by "a Frenchman and two North Americans" left behind by their employers, who had fled farther eastward to Columbia, Texas.[20] Santa Anna arrived after only a few copies of the paper had been printed, and he sank the press and equipment into the muddy waters of Buffalo Bayou. One copy of this issue of the paper miraculously survived.[21]

In such circumstances—towns in flames, people fleeing for their lives, much hard work and precious goods left behind—it is not surprising that ephemeral broadsides perished. Even for the printers themselves, carrying out cumbersome quantities of already printed broadsides and newspapers would have been foolish—*un*printed paper would have been much more valuable to them.

The few copies that do remain are mostly in official or personal archives—the Public Printing Papers in the State Archive, the Lamar Papers at the same location, and the Austin Papers at the University of Texas at Austin.[22] An analysis of the entries in the Streeter *Bibliography of Texas, 1795–1845* gives a clear picture of the absolute rarity of Texas imprints dated before May 1836:

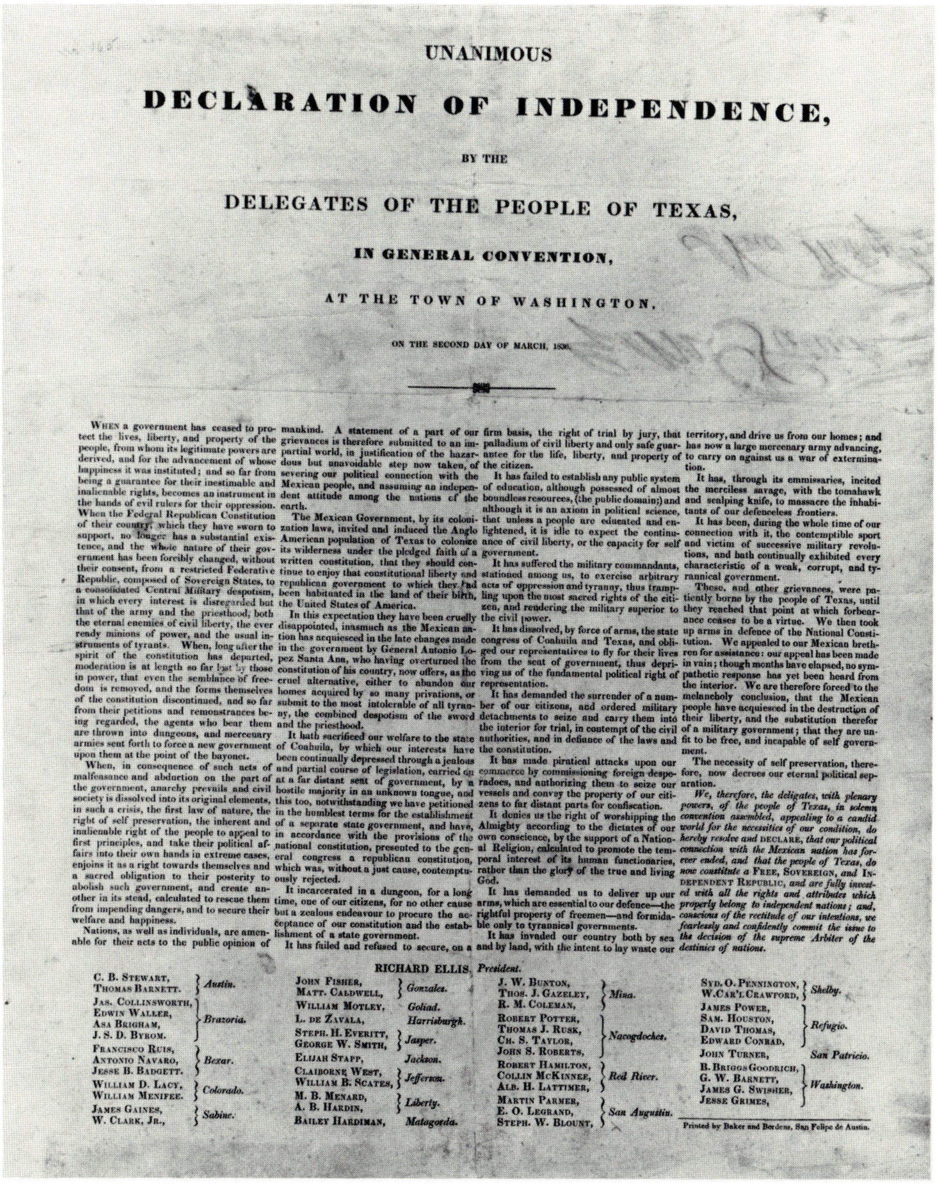

UNANIMOUS

DECLARATION OF INDEPENDENCE,

BY THE

DELEGATES OF THE PEOPLE OF TEXAS,

IN GENERAL CONVENTION,

AT THE TOWN OF WASHINGTON,

ON THE SECOND DAY OF MARCH, 1836.

WHEN a government has ceased to protect the lives, liberty, and property of the people, from whom its legitimate powers are derived, and for the advancement of whose happiness it was instituted; and so far from being a guarantee for their inestimable and inalienable rights, becomes an instrument in the hands of evil rulers for their oppression. When the Federal Republican Constitution of their country, which they have sworn to support, no longer has a substantial existence, and the whole nature of their government has been forcibly changed, without their consent, from a restricted Federative Republic, composed of Sovereign States, to a consolidated Central Military despotism, in which every interest is disregarded but that of the army and the priesthood, both the eternal enemies of civil liberty, the ever ready minions of power, and the usual instruments of tyrants. When, long after the spirit of the constitution has departed, moderation is at length so far lost by those in power, that even the semblance of freedom is removed, and the forms themselves of the constitution discontinued, and so far from their petitions and remonstrances being regarded, the agents who bear them are thrown into dungeons, and mercenary armies sent forth to force a new government upon them at the point of the bayonet.

When, in consequence of such acts of malfeasance and abduction on the part of the government, anarchy prevails and civil society is dissolved into its original elements, in such a crisis, the first law of nature, the right of self preservation, the inherent and inalienable right of the people to appeal to first principles, and take their political affairs into their own hands in extreme cases, enjoins it as a right towards themselves and a sacred obligation to their posterity to abolish such government, and create another in its stead, calculated to rescue them from impending dangers, and to secure their welfare and happiness.

Nations, as well as individuals, are amenable for their acts to the public opinion of mankind. A statement of a part of our grievances is therefore submitted to an impartial world, in justification of the hazardous but unavoidable step now taken, of severing our political connection with the Mexican people, and assuming an independent attitude among the nations of the earth.

The Mexican Government, by its colonization laws, invited and induced the Anglo American population of Texas to colonize its wilderness under the pledged faith of a written constitution, that they should continue to enjoy that constitutional liberty and republican government to which they had been habituated in the land of their birth, the United States of America.

In this expectation they have been cruelly disappointed, inasmuch as the Mexican nation has acquiesced in the late changes made in the government by General Antonio Lopez Santa Ana, who having overturned the constitution of his country, now offers, as the cruel alternative, either to abandon our homes acquired by so many privations, or submit to the most intolerable of all tyranny, the combined despotism of the sword and the priesthood.

It hath sacrificed our welfare to the state of Coahuila, by which our interests have been continually depressed through a jealous and partial course of legislation, carried on at a far distant seat of government, by a hostile majority in an unknown tongue, and this too, notwithstanding we have petitioned in the humblest terms for the establishment of a separate state government, and have, in accordance with the provisions of the national constitution, presented to the general congress a republican constitution, which was, without a just cause, contemptuously rejected.

It incarcerated in a dungeon, for a long time, one of our citizens, for no other cause but a zealous endeavour to procure the acceptance of our constitution and the establishment of a state government.

It has failed and refused to secure, on a firm basis, the right of trial by jury, that palladium of civil liberty and only safe guarantee for the life, liberty, and property of the citizen.

It has failed to establish any public system of education, although possessed of almost boundless resources, (the public domain;) and although it is an axiom in political science, that unless a people are educated and enlightened, it is idle to expect the continuance of civil liberty, or the capacity for self government.

It has suffered the military commandants, stationed among us, to exercise arbitrary acts of oppression and tyranny, thus trampling upon the most sacred rights of the citizen, and rendering the military superior to the civil power.

It has dissolved, by force of arms, the state congress of Coahuila and Texas, and obliged our representatives to fly for their lives from the seat of government, thus depriving us of the fundamental political right of representation.

It has demanded the surrender of a number of our citizens, and ordered military detachments to seize and carry them into the interior for trial, in contempt of the civil authorities, and in defiance of the laws and the constitution.

It has made piratical attacks upon our commerce by commissioning foreign desperadoes, and authorizing them to seize our vessels and convey the property of our citizens to far distant parts for confiscation.

It denies us the right of worshipping the Almighty according to the dictates of our own conscience, by the support of a National Religion, calculated to promote the temporal interest of its human functionaries, rather than the glory of the true and living God.

It has demanded us to deliver up our arms, which are essential to our defence—the rightful property of freemen—and formidable only to tyrannical governments.

It has invaded our country both by sea and by land, with the intent to lay waste our territory, and drive us from our homes; and has now a large mercenary army advancing, to carry on against us a war of extermination.

It has, through its emmissaries, incited the merciless savage, with the tomahawk and scalping knife, to massacre the inhabitants of our defenceless frontiers.

It has been, during the whole time of our connection with it, the contemptible sport and victim of successive military revolutions, and hath continually exhibited every characteristic of a weak, corrupt, and tyrannical government.

These, and other grievances, were patiently borne by the people of Texas, until they reached that point at which forbearance ceases to be a virtue. We then took up arms in defence of the National Constitution. We appealed to our Mexican brethren for assistance: our appeal has been made in vain; though months have elapsed, no sympathetic response has yet been heard from the interior. We are therefore forced to the melancholy conclusion, that the Mexican people have acquiesced in the destruction of their liberty, and the substitution therefor of a military government; that they are unfit to be free, and incapable of self government.

The necessity of self preservation, therefore, now decrees our eternal political separation.

We, therefore, the deligates, with plenary powers, of the people of Texas, in solemn convention assembled, appealing to a candid world for the necessities of our condition, do hereby resolve and DECLARE, *that our political connection with the Mexican nation has forever ended, and that the people of Texas, do now constitute a* FREE, SOVEREIGN, *and* INDEPENDENT REPUBLIC, *and are fully invested with all the rights and attributes which properly belong to independent nations; and, conscious of the rectitude of our intentions, we fearlessly and confidently commit the issue to the decision of the supreme Arbiter of the destinies of nations.*

RICHARD ELLIS, *President.*

C. B. STEWART, THOMAS BARNETT. } *Austin.*
JAS. COLLINSWORTH, EDWIN WALLER, ASA BRIGHAM, J. S. D. BYROM. } *Brazoria.*
FRANCISCO RUIS, ANTONIO NAVARO, JESSE B. BADGETT. } *Bexar.*
WILLIAM D. LACY, WILLIAM MENIFEE. } *Colorado.*
JAMES GAINES, W. CLARK, JR., } *Sabine.*
JOHN FISHER, MATT. CALDWELL, } *Gonzales.*
WILLIAM MOTLEY, *Goliad.*
L. DE ZAVALA, *Harrisburgh.*
STEPH. H. EVERITT, GEORGE W. SMITH, } *Jasper.*
ELIJAH STAPP, *Jackson.*
CLAIBORNE WEST, WILLIAM B. SCATES, } *Jefferson.*
M. B. MENARD, A. B. HARDIN, } *Liberty.*
BAILEY HARDIMAN, *Matagorda.*
J. W. BUNTON, THOS. J. GAZELEY, R. M. COLEMAN, } *Mina.*
ROBERT POTTER, THOMAS J. RUSK, CH. S. TAYLOR, JOHN S. ROBERTS, } *Nacogdoches.*
ROBERT HAMILTON, COLLIN MCKINNEE, ALB. H. LATTIMER, } *Red River.*
MARTIN PARMER, E. O. LEGRAND, STEPH. W. BLOUNT, } *San Augustin.*
SYD. O. PENNINGTON, W. CAR'L CRAWFORD, } *Shelby.*
JAMES POWER, SAM. HOUSTON, DAVID THOMAS, EDWARD CONRAD, } *Refugio.*
JOHN TURNER, *San Patricio.*
B. BRIGGS GOODRICH, G. W. BARNETT, JAMES G. SWISHER, JESSE GRIMES, } *Washington.*

Printed by Baker and Bordens, San Felipe de Austin.

Plate 1. Genuine Texas Declaration of Independence (Streeter 165) (40.5 x 33.2 cm). *DeGolyer Library, Southern Methodist University.*

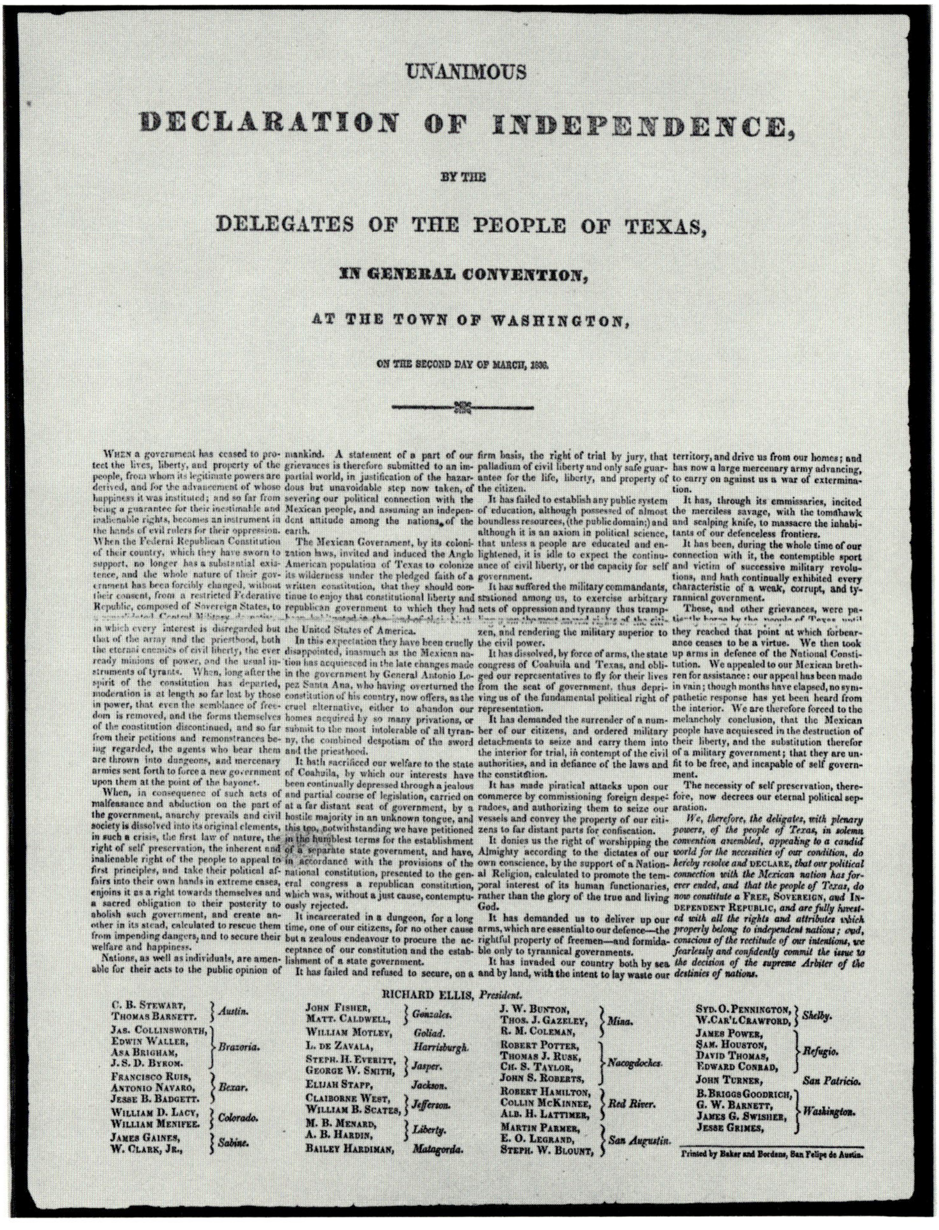

UNANIMOUS

DECLARATION OF INDEPENDENCE,

BY THE

DELEGATES OF THE PEOPLE OF TEXAS,

IN GENERAL CONVENTION,

AT THE TOWN OF WASHINGTON,

ON THE SECOND DAY OF MARCH, 1836.

When a government has ceased to protect the lives, liberty, and property of the people, from whom its legitimate powers are derived, and for the advancement of whose happiness it was instituted; and so far from being a guarantee for their inestimable and inalienable rights, becomes an instrument in the hands of evil rulers for their oppression. When the Federal Republican Constitution of their country, which they have sworn to support, no longer has a substantial existence, and the whole nature of their government has been forcibly changed, without their consent, from a restricted Federative Republic, composed of Sovereign States, to a consolidated Central Military despotism, in which every interest is disregarded but that of the army and the priesthood, both the eternal enemies of civil liberty, the ever ready minions of power, and the usual instruments of tyrants. When, long after the spirit of the constitution has departed, moderation is at length so far lost by those in power, that even the semblance of freedom is removed, and the forms themselves of the constitution discontinued, and so far from their petitions and remonstrances being regarded, the agents who bear them are thrown into dungeons, and mercenary armies sent forth to force a new government upon them at the point of the bayonet.

When, in consequence of such acts of malfeasance and abduction on the part of the government, anarchy prevails and civil society is dissolved into its original elements, in such a crisis, the first law of nature, the right of self preservation, the inherent and inalienable right of the people to appeal to first principles, and take their political affairs into their own hands in extreme cases, enjoins it as a right towards themselves and a sacred obligation to their posterity to abolish such government, and create another in its stead, calculated to rescue them from impending dangers, and to secure their welfare and happiness.

Nations, as well as individuals, are amenable for their acts to the public opinion of mankind. A statement of a part of our grievances is therefore submitted to an impartial world, in justification of the hazardous but unavoidable step now taken, of severing our political connection with the Mexican people, and assuming an independent attitude among the nations of the earth.

The Mexican Government, by its colonization laws, invited and induced the Anglo American population of Texas to colonize its wilderness under the pledged faith of a written constitution, that they should continue to enjoy that constitutional liberty and republican government to which they had been habituated in the land of their birth, the United States of America.

In this expectation they have been cruelly disappointed, inasmuch as the Mexican nation has acquiesced in the late changes made in the government by General Antonio Lopez Santa Ana, who having overturned the constitution of his country, now offers, as the cruel alternative, either to abandon our homes acquired by so many privations, or submit to the most intolerable of all tyranny, the combined despotism of the sword and the priesthood.

It hath sacrificed our welfare to the state of Coahuila, by which our interests have been continually depressed through a jealous and partial course of legislation, carried on at a far distant seat of government, by a hostile majority in an unknown tongue, and this too, notwithstanding we have petitioned in the humblest terms for the establishment of a separate state government, and have, in accordance with the provisions of the national constitution, presented to the general congress a republican constitution, which was, without a just cause, contemptuously rejected.

It incarcerated in a dungeon, for a long time, one of our citizens, for no other cause but a zealous endeavour to procure the acceptance of our constitution and the establishment of a state government.

It has failed and refused to secure, on a firm basis, the right of trial by jury, that palladium of civil liberty and only safe guarantee for the life, liberty, and property of the citizen.

It has failed to establish any public system of education, although possessed of almost boundless resources, (the public domain;) and although it is an axiom in political science, that unless a people are educated and enlightened, it is idle to expect the continuance of civil liberty, or the capacity for self government.

It has suffered the military commandants, stationed among us, to exercise arbitrary acts of oppression and tyranny thus trampling upon the most sacred rights of the citizen, and rendering the military superior to the civil power.

It has dissolved, by force of arms, the state congress of Coahuila and Texas, and obliged our representatives to fly for their lives from the seat of government, thus depriving us of the fundamental political right of representation.

It has demanded the surrender of a number of our citizens, and ordered military detachments to seize and carry them into the interior for trial, in contempt of the civil authorities, and in defiance of the laws and the constitution.

It has made piratical attacks upon our commerce by commissioning foreign desperadoes, and authorizing them to seize our vessels and convey the property of our citizens to far distant parts for confiscation.

It denies us the right of worshipping the Almighty according to the dictates of our own conscience, by the support of a National Religion, calculated to promote the temporal interest of its human functionaries, rather than the glory of the true and living God.

It has demanded us to deliver up our arms, which are essential to our defence—the rightful property of freemen—and formidable only to tyrannical governments.

It has invaded our country both by sea and by land, with the intent to lay waste our territory, and drive us from our homes; and has now a large mercenary army advancing, to carry on against us a war of extermination.

It has, through its emmissaries, incited the merciless savage, with the tomahawk and scalping knife, to massacre the inhabitants of our defenceless frontiers.

It has been, during the whole time of our connection with it, the contemptible sport and victim of successive military revolutions, and hath continually exhibited every characteristic of a weak, corrupt, and tyrannical government.

These, and other grievances, were patiently borne by the people of Texas, until they reached that point at which forbearance ceases to be a virtue. We then took up arms in defence of the National Constitution. We appealed to our Mexican brethren for assistance: our appeal has been made in vain; though months have elapsed, no sympathetic response has yet been heard from the interior. We are therefore forced to the melancholy conclusion, that the Mexican people have acquiesced in the destruction of their liberty, and the substitution therefor of a military government; that they are unfit to be free, and incapable of self government.

The necessity of self preservation, therefore, now decrees our eternal political separation.

We, therefore, the deligates, with plenary powers, of the people of Texas, in solemn convention assembled, appealing to a candid world for the necessities of our condition, do hereby resolve and DECLARE, *that our political connection with the Mexican nation has forever ended, and that the people of Texas, do now constitute a* FREE, SOVEREIGN, *and* INDEPENDENT REPUBLIC, *and are fully invested with all the rights and attributes which properly belong to independent nations; and, conscious of the rectitude of our intentions, we fearlessly and confidently commit the issue to the decision of the supreme Arbiter of the destinies of nations.*

RICHARD ELLIS, *President.*

C. B. STEWART, THOMAS BARNETT. } *Austin.*
JAS. COLLINSWORTH, EDWIN WALLER, ASA BRIGHAM, J. S. D. BYROM. } *Brazoria.*
FRANCISCO RUIS, ANTONIO NAVARO, JESSE B. BADGETT. } *Bexar.*
WILLIAM D. LACY, WILLIAM MENIFEE. } *Colorado.*
JAMES GAINES, W. CLARK, JR., } *Sabine.*
JOHN FISHER, MATT. CALDWELL, } *Gonzales.*
WILLIAM MOTLEY, *Goliad.*
L. DE ZAVALA, *Harrisburgh.*
STEPH. H. EVERITT, GEORGE W. SMITH, } *Jasper.*
ELIJAH STAPP, *Jackson.*
CLAIBORNE WEST, WILLIAM B. SCATES, } *Jefferson.*
M. B. MENARD, A. B. HARDIN, } *Liberty.*
BAILEY HARDIMAN, *Matagorda.*
J. W. BUNTON, THOS. J. GAZELEY, R. M. COLEMAN, } *Mina.*
ROBERT POTTER, THOMAS J. RUSK, CH. S. TAYLOR, JOHN S. ROBERTS, } *Nacogdoches.*
ROBERT HAMILTON, COLLIN MCKINNEE, ALB. H. LATTIMER, } *Red River.*
MARTIN PARMER, E. O. LEGRAND, STEPH. W. BLOUNT, } *San Augustin.*
SYD. O. PENNINGTON, W. CAR'L CRAWFORD, } *Shelby.*
JAMES POWER, SAM. HOUSTON, DAVID THOMAS, EDWARD CONRAD, } *Refugio.*
JOHN TURNER, *San Patricio.*
B. BRIGGS GOODRICH, G. W. BARNETT, JAMES G. SWISHER, JESSE GRIMES, } *Washington.*

Printed by Baker and Bordens, San Felipe de Austin.

Plate 2. Forged Texas Declaration of Independence. *Private Collection.*

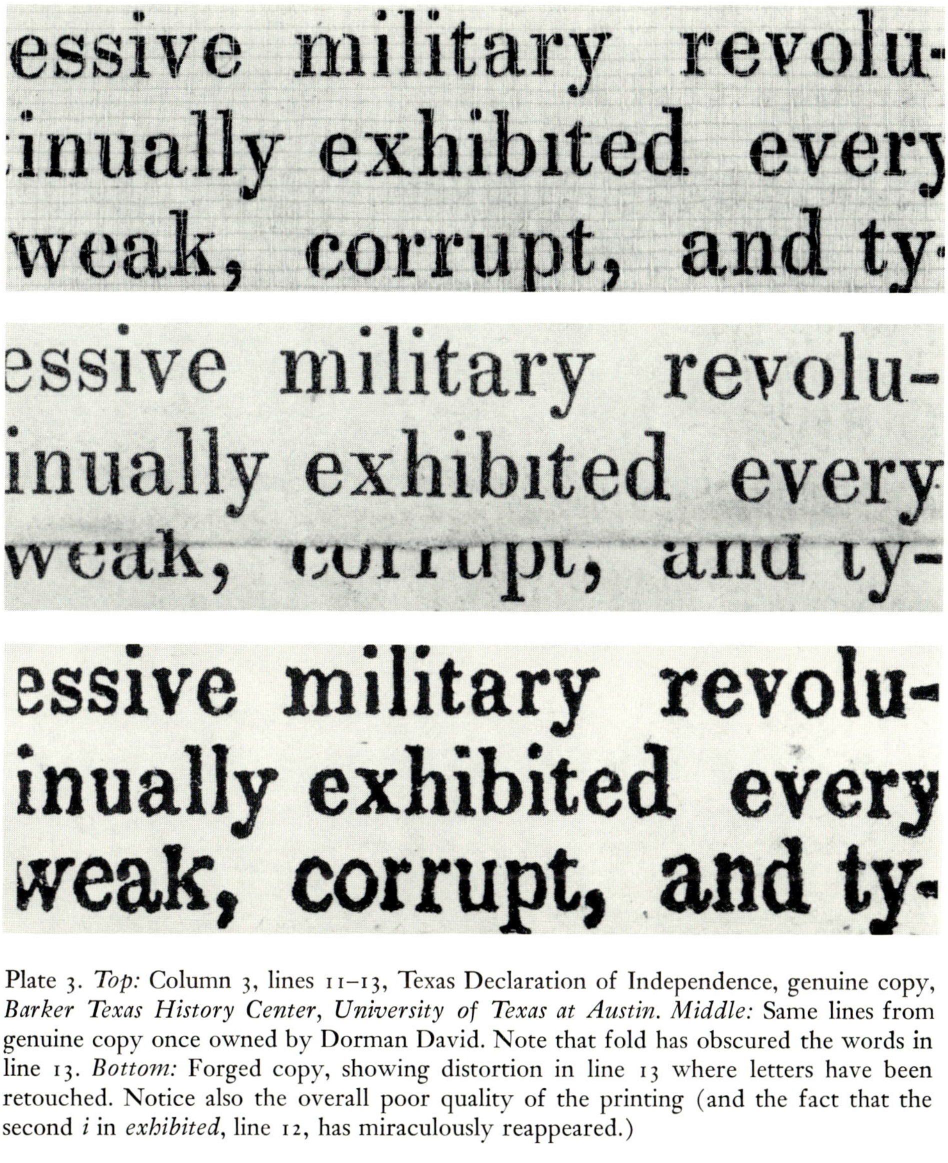
essive military revolu-
inually exhibited every
weak, corrupt, and ty-

essive military revolu-
inually exhibited every
weak, corrupt, and ty-

essive military revolu-
inually exhibited every
weak, corrupt, and ty-

Plate 3. *Top:* Column 3, lines 11–13, Texas Declaration of Independence, genuine copy, *Barker Texas History Center, University of Texas at Austin. Middle:* Same lines from genuine copy once owned by Dorman David. Note that fold has obscured the words in line 13. *Bottom:* Forged copy, showing distortion in line 13 where letters have been retouched. Notice also the overall poor quality of the printing (and the fact that the second *i* in *exhibited*, line 12, has miraculously reappeared.)

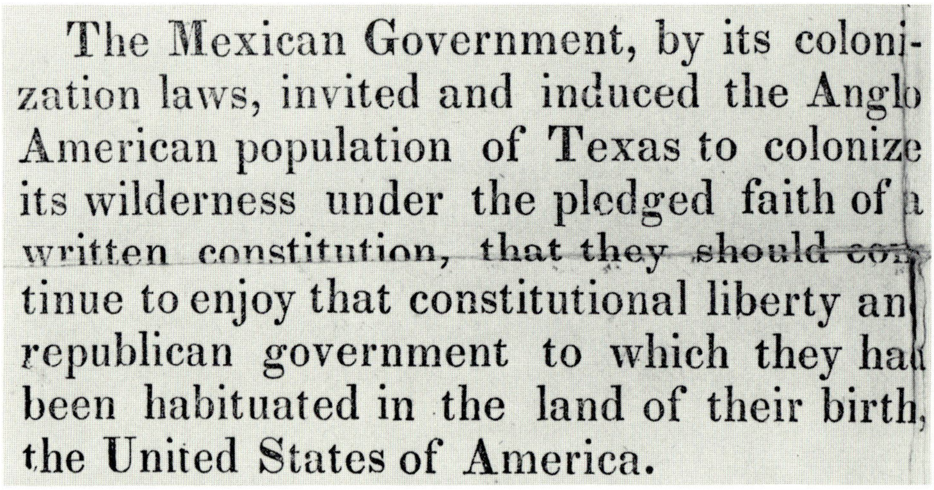

The Mexican Government, by its colonization laws, invited and induced the Anglo
American population of Texas to colonize
its wilderness under the pledged faith of a
written constitution, that they should continue to enjoy that constitutional liberty and
republican government to which they had
been habituated in the land of their birth,
the United States of America.

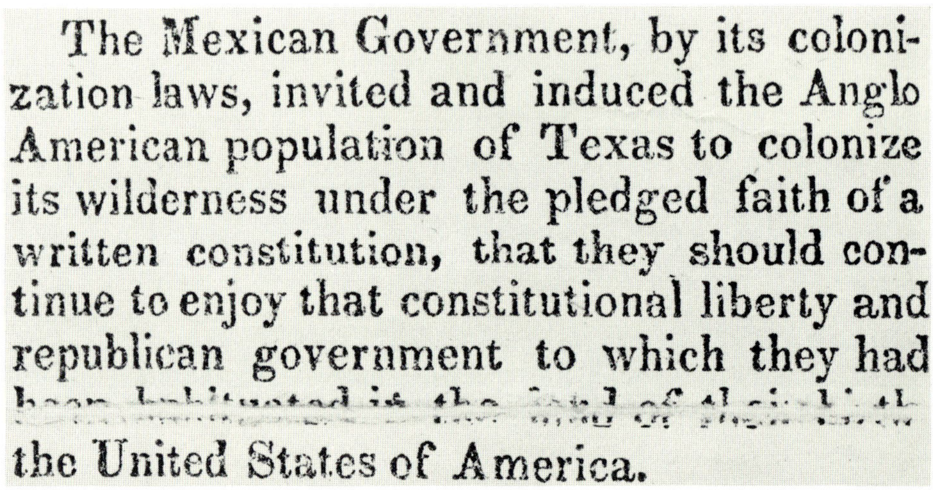

The Mexican Government, by its colonization laws, invited and induced the Anglo
American population of Texas to colonize
its wilderness under the pledged faith of a
written constitution, that they should continue to enjoy that constitutional liberty and
republican government to which they had
[illegible]
the United States of America.

Plate 4. *Top:* Column 2, lines 9–17 of copy used to create forgeries, showing damaged letters along vertical and horizontal folds. *Bottom:* Same lines from forged copy, showing retouched letters, especially in line 13, and along ends of all lines.

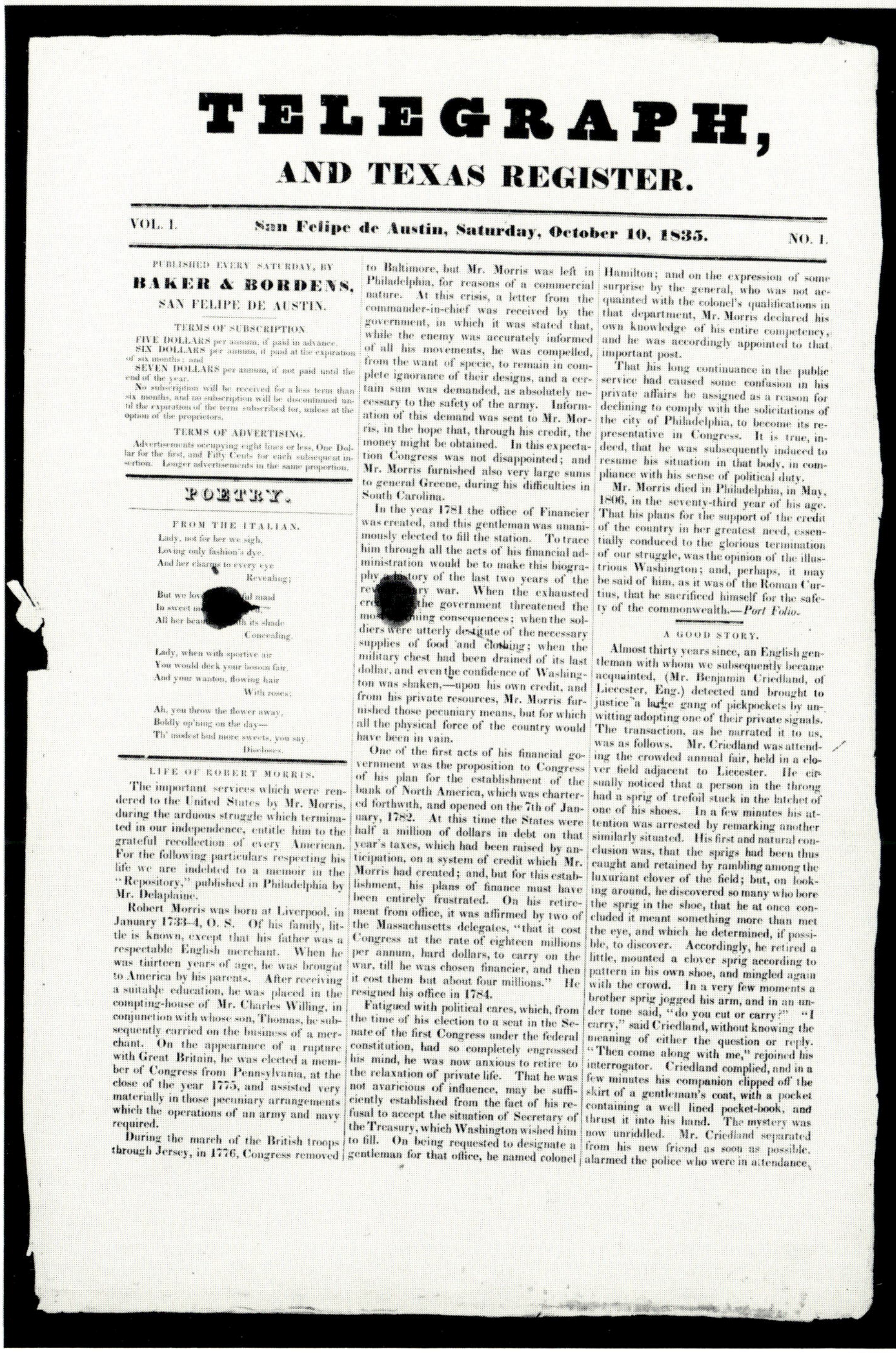

TELEGRAPH,

AND TEXAS REGISTER.

VOL. I. San Felipe de Austin, Saturday, October 10, 1835. NO. 1.

PUBLISHED EVERY SATURDAY, BY

BAKER & BORDENS,

SAN FELIPE DE AUSTIN.

TERMS OF SUBSCRIPTION.

FIVE DOLLARS per annum, if paid in advance.
SIX DOLLARS per annum, if paid at the expiration of six months; and
SEVEN DOLLARS per annum, if not paid until the end of the year.

No subscription will be received for a less term than six months, and no subscription will be discontinued until the expiration of the term subscribed for, unless at the option of the proprietors.

TERMS OF ADVERTISING.

Advertisements occupying eight lines or less, One Dollar for the first, and Fifty Cents for each subsequent insertion. Longer advertisements in the same proportion.

POETRY.

FROM THE ITALIAN.

Lady, not for her we sigh,
Loving only fashion's dye,
And her charms to every eye
Revealing;

But we lov[illegible]ful maid
In sweet m[illegible]d,—
All her bea[illegible]th its shade
Concealing.

Lady, when with sportive air
You would deck your bosom fair,
And your wanton, flowing hair
With roses;

Ah, you throw the flower away,
Boldly op'ning on the day—
Th' modest bud more sweets, you say,
Discloses.

LIFE OF ROBERT MORRIS.

The important services which were rendered to the United States by Mr. Morris, during the arduous struggle which terminated in our independence, entitle him to the grateful recollection of every American. For the following particulars respecting his life we are indebted to a memoir in the "Repository," published in Philadelphia by Mr. Delaplaine.

Robert Morris was born at Liverpool, in January 1733-4, O. S. Of his family, little is known, except that his father was a respectable English merchant. When he was thirteen years of age, he was brougnt to America by his parents. After receiving a suitable education, he was placed in the compting-house of Mr. Charles Willing, in conjunction with whose son, Thomas, he subsequently carried on the business of a merchant. On the appearance of a rupture with Great Britain, he was elected a member of Congress from Pennsylvania, at the close of the year 1775, and assisted very materially in those pecuniary arrangements which the operations of an army and navy required.

During the march of the British troops through Jersey, in 1776, Congress removed to Baltimore, but Mr. Morris was left in Philadelphia, for reasons of a commercial nature. At this crisis, a letter from the commander-in-chief was received by the government, in which it was stated that, while the enemy was accurately informed of all his movements, he was compelled, from the want of specie, to remain in complete ignorance of their designs, and a certain sum was demanded, as absolutely necessary to the safety of the army. Information of this demand was sent to Mr. Morris, in the hope that, through his credit, the money might be obtained. In this expectation Congress was not disappointed; and Mr. Morris furnished also very large sums to general Greene, during his difficulties in South Carolina.

In the year 1781 the office of Financier was created, and this gentleman was unanimously elected to fill the station. To trace him through all the acts of his financial administration would be to make this biography[illegible]tory of the last two years of the rev[illegible]ry war. When the exhausted cre[illegible]the government threatened the mos[illegible]ning consequences; when the soldiers were utterly destitute of the necessary supplies of food and clothing; when the military chest had been drained of its last dollar, and even the confidence of Washington was shaken,—upon his own credit, and from his private resources, Mr. Morris furnished those pecuniary means, but for which all the physical force of the country would have been in vain.

One of the first acts of his financial government was the proposition to Congress of his plan for the establishment of the bank of North America, which was chartered forthwith, and opened on the 7th of January, 1782. At this time the States were half a million of dollars in debt on that year's taxes, which had been raised by anticipation, on a system of credit which Mr. Morris had created; and, but for this establishment, his plans of finance must have been entirely frustrated. On his retirement from office, it was affirmed by two of the Massachusetts delegates, "that it cost Congress at the rate of eighteen millions per annum, hard dollars, to carry on the war, till he was chosen financier, and then it cost them but about four millions." He resigned his office in 1784.

Fatigued with political cares, which, from the time of his election to a seat in the Senate of the first Congress under the federal constitution, had so completely engrossed his mind, he was now anxious to retire to the relaxation of private life. That he was not avaricious of influence, may be sufficiently established from the fact of his refusal to accept the situation of Secretary of the Treasury, which Washington wished him to fill. On being requested to designate a gentleman for that office, he named colonel Hamilton; and on the expression of some surprise by the general, who was not acquainted with the colonel's qualifications in that department, Mr. Morris declared his own knowledge of his entire competency, and he was accordingly appointed to that important post.

That his long continuance in the public service had caused some confusion in his private affairs he assigned as a reason for declining to comply with the solicitations of the city of Philadelphia, to become its representative in Congress. It is true, indeed, that he was subsequently induced to resume his situation in that body, in compliance with his sense of political duty.

Mr. Morris died in Philadelphia, in May, 1806, in the seventy-third year of his age. That his plans for the support of the credit of the country in her greatest need, essentially conduced to the glorious termination of our struggle, was the opinion of the illustrious Washington; and, perhaps, it may be said of him, as it was of the Roman Curtius, that he sacrificed himself for the safety of the commonwealth.—*Port Folio.*

A GOOD STORY.

Almost thirty years since, an English gentleman with whom we subsequently became acquainted, (Mr. Benjamin Criedland, of Liecester, Eng.) detected and brought to justice a large gang of pickpockets by unwitting adopting one of their private signals. The transaction, as he narrated it to us, was as follows. Mr. Criedland was attending the crowded annual fair, held in a clover field adjacent to Liecester. He casually noticed that a person in the throng had a sprig of trefoil stuck in the latchet of one of his shoes. In a few minutes his attention was arrested by remarking another similarly situated. His first and natural conclusion was, that the sprigs had been thus caught and retained by rambling among the luxuriant clover of the field; but, on looking around, he discovered so many who bore the sprig in the shoe, that he at once concluded it meant something more than met the eye, and which he determined, if possible, to discover. Accordingly, he retired a little, mounted a clover sprig according to pattern in his own shoe, and mingled again with the crowd. In a very few moments a brother sprig jogged his arm, and in an under tone said, "do you cut or carry?" "I carry," said Criedland, without knowing the meaning of either the question or reply. "Then come along with me," rejoined his interrogator. Criedland complied, and in a few minutes his companion clipped off the skirt of a gentleman's coat, with a pocket containing a well lined pocket-book, and thrust it into his hand. The mystery was now unriddled. Mr. Criedland separated from his new friend as soon as possible, alarmed the police who were in attendance,

Plate 5. Volume 1, no. 1, of Baker and Bordens' *Telegraph and Texas Register*. *Barker Texas History Center, University of Texas at Austin.*

THE

TEXAS REPUBLICAN.

VOL. I.) BRAZORIA, SATURDAY, JULY 5, 1834. (NUMBER 1.

TERMS:—

THE REPUBLICAN IS PRINTED AND PUBLISHED BY

GRAY & HARRIS,

And will be printed for subscribers every Saturday at $5 per annum, if paid at the end of six months, or $7, if not paid until the expiration of the year.

No discontinuances will be allowed except at the end of the year, and not then until all arrearages are paid.

Advertisements of eight lines or under $1 for the first insertion, and half that price for each continuance—longer ones in proportion—No adveriisement will be withdrawn until paid for, but will be continued at the expense of the advertiser.

ADDRESS

OF THE ALCALDE OF THE MUNICIPALITY OF AUSTIN, TO THE AYUNTAMIENTO, AND THE MEMORIAL OF THAT BODY TO THE GENERAL CONGRESS OF THE UNITED MEXICAN STATES.

TO THE ILLUSTIOUS

AYUNTAMIENTO

OF AUSTIN.

Constitutionally your presiding officer, and convening you a second time, in that character; I feel it my duty to present to to your consideration another subject different from that which impelled me, to call the present meeting.

I allude to the interesting subject of a State Government for Texas.

Situated at that point, where is first received the news from the Interior; and to which point more communications are directed than to any other portion of the province, we have certainly an opportunity of being more correctly informed of the political transactions of the nation, than other portions of the Colony. Our interest however, is not more deep; our feelings not more excited; our anxiety not greater than our other fellow citizens, in every part of Texas, to know what has been done at Mexico, on this all absorbing question—I feel it my duty freely and frankly to communicate to you, all the information I have received on the subject, in hopes, that through you information may go to other portions of the Colony; where otherwise it might not circulate. And not only do I conceive it my duty to communicate to you the information which I may have rec eived; but to express to you with the INDEPENDENCE which should characterize your presiding officer the sentiments I indulge, and the opinions I entertain on the subject. But the sentiments I indulge, and the opinions I entertain, are but those of an individual who, although the humblest among you, feel a gratified delight that not in the darkest period of his life, did he ever shrink from an open and clear expression of his principles. On the present occasion, was he to do so, he would forfeit esteem for himself; he would be wanting in trust and fidelity to his country; he repeats his sentiments are individual, and as an individual he publishes them; he cannot conceive in what manner the office of ALCALDE gives him an exclusive right to advise or admonish the people of Texas, on this all important subject; he was elected for purposes altogether different. The people require of him duties of another sort from those of monitor—nor can he conceive on what principle the Ayuntamiento can base a claim to the right of lecturing the people on the propriety or impropriety of any great political movement? Are we wiser, more informed, more honest or more patriotic than the balance of the community, that we should take upon ourselves the privilege of advising or remonstrating with our fellow citizens on the important point, whether or not the people of Texas should organize themselves into a State. We may depend upon it, the people have too much good sense, too much independence to be influenced by any thing of the sort eminating from us, as a political body; they have been accustomed to think, and to judge for themselves; and they are not to be persuaded that any inward excellence, or extraordinary infalibility, is peculiar to the name of the Ayuntamiento. We cannot induce them to believe that, we as a political body, are more competent to judge of their wants, their rights and necessities, than their whole united talent. But we have, each and every one of us the right of expressing our individual sentiments on this great question; and no source however humble is to be despised, from which light may be derived, to guide us in our onward course.

Such being my sentiments as a member of this body, it will be easily explained to the people of Texas why this Ayuntamiento have never troubled themselves or the people with a manifesto, on the subject of organizing Texas into a state of the Mexican federation. The project of a state government for Texas, did not originate with the Ayuntamientos. It has never been furthered by them; It originated in the good sense of the whole united people of Texas, whose onward course has alone been checked by the interferance and opposition of five of the Ayuntamientos of Texas, if the communications of the people's agent to carry their favorite project into effect are to be relied upon:—For he tells us that the opposition of five Ayuntamientos of Texas, to the state question, weighed more effectually with the Government in hanging it up for the présent, than all other opposition besides. Previous to the adjournment of the people's representatives in convention assembled in April last, a temporary organization throughout Texas took place by means of the appointment of a central committee at this place, and sub-committees in the different precincts, for the avowed purpose of sustaining the people in the fair, just and legal project of a state government. This organization was solemnly deliberated upon by the convention before it took place. It was considered by no means the least important duty that the Representatives owed to the people; they looked upon it as necessary to the consummation of the united purposes of the people. The Ayuntamientos of Texas, were not overlooked in this act of the Convention; but they were excluded from becoming the organ of public opinion at this important crisis, on the grounds that the individual members composing four of the Ayuntamientos of Texas had formally protested against the proceedings of an overwhelming majority of thepeople of their respective municipalities, who were at that period represented in theConvention. These are plain matters of fact, known to three of the members of this Ayuntamiento, two of whom are now present, and who at that time had the honor of being members of the Convention.

The information then, in relation to the state question, is contained in a very narrow compass. Our Constitution has been rejected. Our application refused. We still continue our unnatural connexion with Coahuila. Our fondest hopes, our most cherished anticipations have been blighted. Our earnest entreaties have been disregarded. Our able, our eloquent and PATRIOTIC memorial has scarcely been read, and we have been told, that the grievances of which we complain, find no sympathising friend, in the Government, would receive no redress, from the congress of the nation;—In a word, we have been told that the happiness, prosperity, security and safety of the people of Texas form no part of the policy of the government. They have arrested and now detain our agent Stephen F. Austin on a charge that should lie against the whole people of Texas. They detain him because he has espoused our CAUSE, and *spoke our sentiments*. The project of a state government for Texas was not Austin's; It was the project of the people. Desertion by *us* then, of this *our own cause, would be worse than political apostacy*. It *would be individual persecution; and hypocrisy to the government*. Let us then speak plain to the government on this subject. Let us avow our own acts, by proclaiming *the truth*, that the people of Texas *once harmonized in the great end of a state government*. A respectful memorial on the subject from this Ayuntamiento, and from the different Ayuntamentos of Texas, to the government might be attended with great good to the citizens and the country. As citizens of Texas, and members of this body, *let us try it*.

R. M. WILLIAMSON.

TO THE GENERAL CONGRESS

OF THE UNITED MEXICAN STATES.

The Ayuntamiento of Ausin would respectfully approach the Congress of the nation on the subject of the imprisonment of STEPHEN F. AUSTIN the delegate of Texas, to the National Congress asking for the erection of that province into a separate state of the Republic. The right of approaching the National Congress and asking for a redress of grievances, they have ever been taught to consider as one of the most invaluable guarantees of the Constitution and any invasion of that right should be regarded by all the true friends of freedom, with feelings of just alarm, and as giving cause for just complaint. Was the imprisonment and trial of Stephen F. Austin, a matter only of individual consideration, this Ayuntamiento would be the last to interfere between him and the law. Was he arrested for an offence chargeable only on him, it would be considered by this body an act of arrogant indelicacy to raise the voice of complaint. But such is understood not to be the fact. The accusation against him, if we are correctly informed, is based on his letter to the Ayuntamiento of Bexar, & bearing date the 2d day of October, 1833—and that accusation we understand to be *Treason*. Your memorialists have too high an opinion of the intelligence of the Mexican Judiciary, to believe that any expression contained in that letter can be tortured into any thing like treason. They apprehend no danger to Colonel Austin; entertaining, as they do, no idea that any wrong has been done by him. But your Memorialists feel persuaded that the secret and unprincipled efforts of their enemies have succeeded in infusing into the councils of the nation the opinion that the people of this province were [illegible] and refractory, and ready for revolt; and that the letter of Col. Austin, alluded to, was not only intended for, but would bring about that result. They are persuaded that this suspicion of the fidelity of the people of this province, has been the cause of the arrest of their delegate; and this Ayuntamiento, acting under the responsibility of their office, and the sacred and solemn obligations into which they have entered, gladly avail themselves of this opportunity of giving a public and unqualified denial to all such charges—and for themselves and the people of the jurisdiction tendering to the government, "their lives, their fortunes and their sacred honor" in sustaining the constitution and laws of their adopted country. Your Memorialists are not unaware, that many circumstances have occurred in this province to induce the impression abroad, that we were a contentious and disorganised people, and that we were contemplating opposition to the government. But they are also aware that an examination into the causes which led to these occurrences, will satisfy the government that they were not the work of design, or caused by any feeling inimical to the integrity of the Mexican Republic. They not only do not fear—but they invite a minute and rigid inquiry into the causes of the disturbances of Texas; and if the whole history of the Americans, from the first settling of this colony up to the present period, is laid open to inspection, it will be found that forbearance and circumspection of conduct and an earnest desire to conciliate the Mexican authorities, and prove themselves worthy and useful citizens of the country has been their ruling principle.

Invited by the liberality of the Mexican Nation, the citizens of this province left their own dear and native Republic, and settled a wilderness—where the savage, the beasts and the storms alike contended for empire. They conquered the savage, and gave him the mountains for his bounds; they subdued the wilderness to the purposes of agriculture, and now present to the Mexican Nation, a country on the whole face of which one universal assurance of its future greatness and prosperity is inscribed. But they brought along with them their own native notions of freedom and independence—Their republican notions of the liberty of speech and action; and surely it cannot be a matter of astonishment, if, after enduring every privation, and overcoming every obstacle, they beheld with republican indignation the constituted civil authorities of the country controlled by military usurpation. A civil war raged throughout Mexico, and its blighting effects extended to this province—the military usurped the civil authorities; our citizens were incarcerated against law and without trial—the state authorities proved incompetent to our protection, and rallying with one accord under the banner of Santa Anna, we vindicated our own wrongs, & restored the civil authorities of thecountry. The occurrences at Velasco, Anahuac & Nacogdoches were bro't about by the arbitrary and unconstitutional acts of the Military. They were not the work of intrigue on our part, nor brought about by design. Necessity alone was their mother, and a restoration of law & order their good effects. The necessity, however, that drove the people of this province to the expulsion of the troops from thiscountry had also placed them in a situation of fearful responsibility. The cause of Santa Anna was not only uncertain, but the great probability was, that he could not sustain himself. The situation of the Mexican confederacy was such as to make every patriot weep. The fondest hopes of liberty appeared to have been blighted; and surveying the condition of the Republic naught presented itself to view but one wide extended ocean of blood. The constitution had been torn in a thousand fragments, & scattered to all the winds of the heavens; the sun of freedom appeared to have dawned for the last time upon unfortunate Mexico; for her confederacy broken and destroyed had gone down bathed in the blood of many of the best citizens of the country. The fearful question was put and left unanswered—What will be the result? What should Texas do? It was not uncertain, but highly improbable that the government would ever again be united upon the Republican Federative principle. It was more probable that a Royal government would be the issue—and necessity required that the people of this province should take some precautionary steps for such an emergency. The most misrepresented and exagerated accounts of the disposition of the inhabitants of Texas towards the Mexican government, had been carried to Mexico. We were denounced in the public prints as rebels, and it was said an armed soldiery was contemplated to be sent against us. Under these circumstances all eyes were directed to a convention of the people, and with an almost unanimous voice, that convention was called which deputised Stephen F. Austin, and sent him to Mexico, as the bearer of the Memorial asking that Texas be admitted as a state of the Mexican Nation. That convention was composed of individuals elected by the people from every part of Texas; and we can safely affirm that Stephen F. Austin was commissioned as the bearer of the Memorial by nine-tenths of the people of Texas.

This Ayuntamiento is not disposed to be the eulogist of Colonel Austin. He opposed the people in their call of the convention—He opposed them in asking for a state government; and he was beaten for President of the convention purely on account of his known hostility to these measures—He has ever recommended that all our memorials should be through the medium of the Ayuntamientos.—He was the most uncompromising opponent Texas had to encounter in the call of a convention; and had his recommendations been pursued, the military would yet have been in Texas. Law and order would now have been subservient to military rule; and the history of our grievances would never have reached the cabinet of Mexico; but the people were not to be controlled, and he was forced to follow in the wake. The Ayunta-

[*Concluded on fourth page.*]

Plate 6. Volume 1, no. 1, of the Brazoria *Texas Republican. Barker Texas History Center, University of Texas at Austin.*

rant's Guide.

.Y BY D. E. LAWHON,

SATURDAY, JANUARY 2, 1836. No. 6.

Texean and Emi...

BY D. E. LAWHON,

ADVERTISEMENTS

Constitution of the MEXICAN UNITED STATES.

MISCELLANEOUS.

KOSCIUSKO IN LOVE.

CATHEDRAL AT MEXICO.

(Niles' Weekly Register.)

KATHLEEN MAVOURNEEN.

THE RESURRECTION.

Plate 7. Volume 1, no. 6, of D. E. Lawhon's *Texean and Emigrant's Guide. Barker Texas History Center, University of Texas at Austin.*

BAKER & BORDENS

Respectfully inform the citizens of Texas that they have established a ***Printing Office*** in the town of

SAN FELIPE DE AUSTIN,

where they are prepared to execute every description of **BOOK** and

JOB PRINTING,

at the shortest notice, and upon reasonable terms.

Their extensive stock of materials, being entirely new, and upon the most approved principles, will enable them to do all work entrusted to their charge in the best manner: they therefore confidently solicit a share of public patronage.

San Felipe de Austin, October 10, 1835.

Plate 8. Ad in the first issue of the *Telegraph and Texas Register* (enlarged). *Barker Texas History Center, University of Texas at Austin.*

No. of copies located	No. of entries
0*	24
1	76
2	31
3	16
4	10
5 or more	6

*i.e., a document that is known to have existed, but of which no copy survives.

Although the Streeter *Bibliography* was published in 1955, my examination of numerous institutional and private collections in recent years has uncovered very few additional *genuine* copies of these documents. Nor have they been common in the trade, even in the stocks of great Americana dealers. Edward Eberstadt and Sons' famous catalogue 162 on Texas, issued in 1963, contained 336 Streeter items (only three institutions hold more), but of these only three were Texas imprints dated before May 1836.

This is not to suggest that materials printed after May 1836—broadsides especially—become dramatically more common. They don't. What this does demonstrate, beyond question, is that the printed history of this particular period hangs on the slenderest thread. It also brings into focus the glaring problem faced by dealers, collectors, and librarians touched by the desire to possess the icons of this history—there was simply no available supply. The bibliographic entrepreneurs of Texas were to solve this problem by two simple expedients—theft and forgery.

Notes

1. *Texas Gazette*, May 15, 1830.
2. For the founding and editorial policy of the paper, see Joe B. Frantz, *Gail Borden, Dairyman to a Nation*, 82–110.
3. McMurtrie, "Pioneer Printing in Texas," *Southwest Historical Quarterly*, 183n.
4. In partnership with A. J. Harris, who retired after only seventeen issues.
5. *Texas Republican*, July 25, 1834.
6. *Texean and Emigrant's Guide*, November 28, 1835.
7. *Telegraph and Texas Register*, October 10, 1835.
8. D. E. Lawhon noted in the first issue of his paper that "some typographical errors appear on the first side of this week's paper, caused chiefly by our hurry of business,

but we hope to improve in the next . . ." (*Texean and Emigrant's Guide*, November 28, 1835).

9. Gray, *From Virginia to Texas*, 124.

10. *Telegraph and Texas Register*, Saturday, March 12, 1836, reported that on Sunday, March 6, the Travis letter to the president of the convention (Streeter 184) had been ordered to be printed, but was not received by Baker and Bordens until eleven o'clock Tuesday morning, indicating that it took forty-eight hours to get the text from Washington-on-the-Brazos to the printers in San Felipe.

11. See Streeter's note to no. 184 (*Bibliography*, Part I, 1:171).

12. That Baker and Bordens dampened their paper before printing (which was the general practice of the time) is confirmed in the issue of December 17, 1836, in which they complain with some bemusement, "What will the public think of the devils of the press, when the very paper wetted down for publication, has been frozen?"

13. There are a number of other photostats with similar notes on the reverse in Winkler's hand in the Barker Center's collections.

14. The State Library has no record of this copy; it was apparently not in the library when Thomas Streeter compiled his bibliography in the early 1950s. It may well have been exchanged or sold as a duplicate before that time.

15. Gray, *From Virginia to Texas*, 150.

16. Frantz, *Gail Borden*, 107n.

17. *Telegraph and Texas Register*, September 27, 1836.

18. Webb, *Handbook of Texas*, 2:515.

19. Webb, *Handbook of Texas*, 1:207. Although this was a day after the Battle of San Jacinto, the news would not have reached Urrea. In any case, Gray's equipment must not have been badly damaged because he was printing again by the middle of May (see Streeter 126, dated May 12).

20. Santa Anna, "Manifesto," 74.

21. At the Houston Public Library. (See Streeter, *Bibliography*, Part I, 2:525.) At least one of the printers survived as well, rescued by Texan forces near San Jacinto (Tolbert, *The Day of San Jacinto*, 119).

22. Thomas Streeter's great collection of Texana, which formed the basis for his *Bibliography of Texas, 1795–1845*, benefited from exchange of duplicates from these collections. For instance, he acquired his copies of Streeter 145 and 185 from the Texas State Library, and Streeter 130 from the Benjamin C. Franklin Papers at the University of Texas at Austin.

CHAPTER THREE

Looting Texas Libraries

On August 2, 1971, Austin police arrested a suspect in the theft of an 1840 map of Texas from the downtown public library. Searching his car, they found instructions from an accomplice:

1. Get as much as you can!
2. Get maps in these county clerk's offices.
3. Get all the old books you can.
4. Keep different counties separated.

With these general instructions was a roadmap of Texas with thirteen county seats marked, and a sheet of more detailed suggestions:

Fort Bend—C[ounty]/Seat—Richmond
Here the D[istrict]/Clerk's office hasn't anything but a few documents. You can still get some stuff from it (plenty in the 1850's). Easy to get stuff out of here. In the C/Clerk's office you can get a briefcase full but it'll take a couple of hours. I have gotten a lot of early items out. You still ought to be able to get a briefcase full. Everything is in one room. Library here in Richmond, 52,000 Volumes.

Houston—C/Seat—Crockett
Never been here. Just get a lot of shit, books, maps also. Library here in Crockett has 20,000 Volumes.

Brazoria—C/Seat—Angleton
District Court here is the only thing I haven't tried. In County Court there is *S.F. Austin's Probate*—It is filed under No. 1 of probate records. Bill, I'll give you $30.00 for this probate alone. It is in a manilla folder (Legal Size). Bill, there is a pretty good library here in Angleton (111,000 Volumes) if you want to check it out.

Fayette—C/Seat—LaGrange

Bill, I have explained the situation on the County Court. In the District Court there is a suit filed under *No. 19*, (The suit over Galveston). I want it and will give considerable allowance.

Montgomery—C/Seat—Conroe

Bill, you know the deal on this place. Get all the stuff you can get in District clerk's and County Clerk's office. Volume is the key here. Get as much as you can and go back 2 or 3 times if it is as easy as you say. Bill, I will make allowance for the items you get after the Republic of Texas.

Travis—C/Seat—Austin

Bill, unlike these other counties this one was created 4 years after the others (1840). I am completely unknowing of this county—get what you can. Remember to check for maps and books.

Robertson—C/Seat—Franklin

Don't know much about this one either. Get what you can.[1]

The suspect also had in his possession five maps from the University of Texas library, and Texas Ranger George Brakefield characterized the thieves as part of a "highly organized group" with a "very sophisticated operation."[2] Four days later a Waco dealer was discovered trying to sell three documents stolen from the State Archive, and it soon became clear that the Austin and Waco incidents were linked to an attempt by a man identifying himself as "Mr. Smith" to sell a number of important prints and documents to the Amon Carter Museum in Fort Worth. Unfortunately for Mr. Smith, Margaret McLean, microfilm archivist at the Carter Museum at the time, had been Thomas Streeter's chief researcher in Texas for his *Bibliography of Texas*, and she immediately recognized several of the documents "Smith" was selling as being from the collections of the State Archive and the Barker Texas History Center at the University of Texas.[3]

Only six weeks before these events, an auction had been held in the Fontaine Ballroom of the posh Warwick Hotel in Houston, featuring seventy-seven glittering pieces of historical Texana "From the Collection of C. Dorman David." An introduction to the catalogue proclaimed that "[David] has one of the largest collections of Texana in the world," which he was able to form because he "collected Texas manuscripts when they were rarely sold to the public." This was true: they were rarely sold to the public because the public owned them in the first place. Lot 5, a splendid Stephen F. Austin letter written while he was imprisoned in Mexico City in October 1835, is published on page 8 of volume 3 of *The Austin Papers* (Barker). It belongs to the University of Texas. Lot 10, a dramatic letter from Peter Dimitt from Goliad written October 21, 1835, begins, "The hour has come when your country requires the services of every man in it," and ends with the question, "Shall we sleep or shall we awake and act like men?" The stuff of chauvinists' dreams, it is published on page 11, volume 1, of Binkley's *Official Correspondence of the Texan Revolution*, with the location given as Domestic Correspondence, Texas State Library. Likewise lot 15, Ben Milam's and Edward Burleson's report to Stephen F. Austin from Bexar on December 7, 1835, is published as belonging to the University of Texas;[4] lot 23, a James Bowie letter from the Alamo, is published as belonging to the Texas State Library;[5] lot 26, a letter from James Morgan describing in detail the Battle of the Alamo (noted by David in the catalogue as "the most exciting yet seen"), is published as belonging to the Rosenberg Library in Galveston;[6] lot 30, an army order signed by Sam Houston on the San Jacinto battlefield, is published as belonging to the Texas State Library.[7] In all, seventeen of the seventy-seven lots in the sale appear to belong to public collections, a determination made by research no more sophisticated than consulting three of the books conveniently listed by David among "Reference Books Used" on page 3 of his catalogue: *The Writings of Sam Houston*, *The Austin Papers*, and *Official Correspondence of the Texan Revolution*. These seventeen lots represent the cream of the material—roughly 40 percent of the total value of the lots sold—and more detailed research would probably prove more of the materials to have a clouded provenance.

Two days after the auction, the sale was touted in Marge Crumbaker's society column in the *Houston Post* under the headline "Texana Sale Nets $23,000."[8] The largest purchasers at the sale were mentioned by name, and Ms. Crumbaker closed her account by remarking that "the sale drew dealers and collectors from across the country." Despite all this publicity, the existence of a published catalogue, the ease of identifying the apparently missing material, the ready availability of the names of the buyers at the sale, the arrests being made in Austin and Waco, nothing happened for almost a year.

The audacity of the David sale, and the improbable lack of response to it, may seem amazing today. But David was merely working well-plowed ground: by 1971 the wholesale disappearance of documents from state institutions, and their dispersal at public auction with little adverse consequence, was a common occurrence. On November 21, 1967, Parke-Bernet Galleries (at the time, the largest auction house in the United States) held an auction entitled "TEXAS: Autograph Letters and Manuscripts by Stephen F. Austin, James Fannin, Sam Houston, and others. Including Many from the Year 1836. Rare Books from the Collection of Robert E. Davis, Waco, Texas." Lots 3, 4, 5, 6, 7, and 8 were all Stephen F. Austin letters that are published as belonging to either the University of Texas or the Texas State Library.[9] Lot 17 is a fine letter, dated March 8, 1836, from William Bryan, general agent for Texas in New Orleans, regarding raising of money for the week-old republic. It is published in *Official Correspondence of the Texan Revolution* as belonging to the Texas State Library.[10] Letters from David G. Burnet, James W. Fannin, and six out of ten Sam Houston letters appear to belong to the Texas State Library.[11] In all, at least forty-two of the 125 lots in the sale appear to belong to the Texas State Library, the University of Texas, or the Rosenberg Library in Galveston, according to the standard published sources.[12] They fetched a total of $10,415, roughly 50 percent of the sum realized by Davis from the entire sale. There is nothing to suggest that Robert Davis, proprietor of the Texian Press in Waco, was himself responsible for removing anything from a state institution.[13] This is simply to note that the largest auction house in America held a well-publicized sale which should have been of interest to certain Texas librarians, had they known of it.

And they did know of it. In the weeks between the arrival of the auction catalogue in Austin and the date of the sale, in an atmosphere that one former employee of the Barker Texas History Center described as "frantic hush-hush," arrangements were made for the Eberstadts to represent the University of Texas at the Davis sale and to buy back many items that officials of the Texas State Library believed to be state property. The Eberstadts dominated the sale, purchasing sixty-eight of the 125 lots, accounting for nearly 70 percent of the value of the sale, including thirty-six lots on behalf of the University of Texas for $6,525.[14] Why neither the University nor the State Library repurchased all of the material that appears to be theirs is a mystery. Nor is it clear why the Texas State Library used the University of Texas to repurchase its materials. The documents purchased were held at the University of Texas from November 1967 to November 21, 1968. At that time a letter from Frances H. Hudspeth, Executive Assistant to Harry Ransom, Chancellor of the University of Texas, to Fred Folmer, University Librarian, noted that twenty-five of the thirty-six lots purchased had been transferred to the Texas State Library and the remainder added to the university's collections. The inventory attached to this letter leaves no doubt that the officials involved in this transaction—including Chester Kielman, then director of the Barker Texas History Center, and Dorman Winfrey, then director of the Texas State Library, both of whom received carbon copies—believed that most of the documents purchased by the university already belonged to the state: those transmitted to the State Library are described as "State Property," with detailed provenances added.[15] And a former employee of the State Library distinctly recalls being handed the stack of documents by Winfrey, being told that they had been "recovered" in New York and that he was to return them to the collection and never mention it to anyone.

Although this transaction is clearly etched in the memories of their subordinates, both Kielman and Winfrey today say they have no recollection of it.[16] Robert Davis, whose friendship with Winfrey dates from the early 1960s, when his Texian Press published Winfrey's first two books,[17] naturally remembers the sale, but says "there was never any problem with it." No one from the state ever approached him about the documents. Such documents were circulating freely at the time, according to Davis, who says he acquired most of his from Dorman David and Austin dealer John Jenkins. It never occurred to anyone to question where they came from: "That's just the way it was. I didn't have any problem with it then, and I don't have any problem with it now."[18]

Apparently no one had a problem with it. On July 26, 1968, eight months after the sale of his documents, Davis was appointed to the Library and Historical Commission, the board charged with overseeing the State Library. He became chairman of this board in 1972 and served in this capacity until his term expired in 1979.[19]

With the precedent set by the Davis sale, it is not surprising that the Dorman David auction in 1971 proceeded unmolested by the authorities. The only consistent course for Winfrey and the State Library to pursue would have been to buy back their documents at the sale. Finally, on June 14, 1972, a year after Dorman David's auction, police raided his shop in Houston. The operation did not go smoothly. David was not at his shop, so he had to be brought from his nearby home. He refused to open the shop, so police kicked the door in. Although enough books and documents were confiscated to fill a fifty-four-page inventory, and some proved to be stolen, it was immediately clear that they had missed the mother lode: none of the precious documents they believed David possessed was in his shop.[20] And since they had not secured a search warrant for his house, the police were stymied.

In the end, it didn't matter—although there were documents from the State Library among those seized, the state declined to prosecute. Various counties in Texas were contacted regarding documents of theirs in the haul, but none pursued the matter—Washington County even denied it was missing anything, though the quantity of republic-period Washington County documents that have freely circulated since then would suggest otherwise.[21] Only Lamar Tech University pressed charges, and these, too, were eventually dropped.

Why did the State Library (and others) behave this way? There was, of course, the problem of the Davis sale—if it were uncovered, officials would have had a hard time reconciling it with a prosecution of David. Why shouldn't David profit as handsomely as Davis had from his "State Property"? But beneath that lie the motivations that led to the unfortunate response to the Davis sale in the first place—fear and embarrassment. One employee of the State Library described it as "a rape victim mentality," and it was in keeping with the prevalent attitude at most libraries in the 1960s. If there was a theft, you kept it quiet, at all costs. Nowhere would this fear be more compelling than at the Texas State Library, with a commission containing a powerful ex-governor (Price Daniel); a meddlesome legislature; and a local press always in search of a story. Dorman Winfrey's chief concern, according to several people who worked for him, was to keep the boat unrocked. An employee intent on pursuing the apparently massive thefts from the library was told he was making things difficult and criticized for lack of judgment.

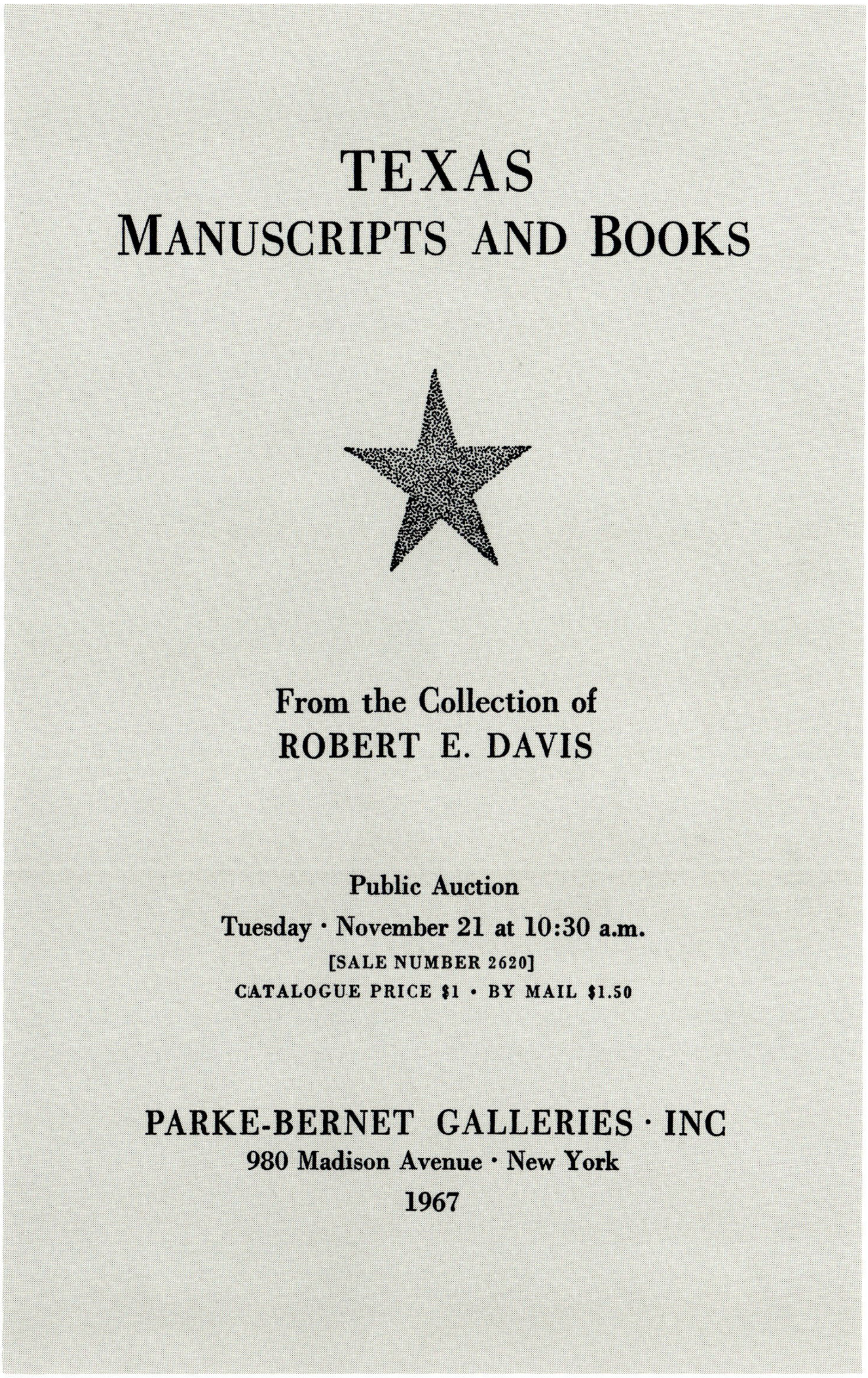

TEXAS
MANUSCRIPTS AND BOOKS

From the Collection of
ROBERT E. DAVIS

Public Auction
Tuesday · November 21 at 10:30 a.m.
[SALE NUMBER 2620]
CATALOGUE PRICE $1 · BY MAIL $1.50

PARKE-BERNET GALLERIES · INC
980 Madison Avenue · New York
1967

Plate 9. Cover of the Robert E. Davis sale catalogue, November 21, 1967 (23.3 x 15.3 cm). *DeGolyer Library, Southern Methodist University.*

SALE OF

RARE TEXAS HISTORICAL

MANUSCRIPTS AND AUTOGRAPH MATERIALS;

BEING LETTERS, DOCUMENTS, AND BROADSIDES

FROM THE COLLECTION OF

C. DORMAN DAVID

TO BE SOLD

TO THE HIGHEST BIDDER AT THE

WARWICK HOTEL HOUSTON

FONTAINE BALLROOM

JUNE 22, 1971

AT EXACTLY 8:10 P.M.

AUCTIONEER: TOM CLOUD

Plate 10. Cover of the sale of Dorman David's "collection," June 22, 1971. *DeGolyer Library, Southern Methodist University.*

For those of you who are unfamiliar with Dorman David, he has been a dealer in rare books and Texana for 11 years. He opened the Bookman in Houston in 1961 and left the store in the care of Grace David in 1965. Since that time he has been selling privately to universities and individuals. Mr. David collected Texas manuscripts at a time when they were rarely sold to the public. He started with a Stephen F. Austin letter and continued buying in Louisiana and Texas until today he has one of the largest collections of Texana in the world. The material for sale is what he accumulated relating to Texas heroes and other miscellaneous subjects that found no place in any of his personal collections. Much of this material is beyond price estimation but a guideline price is offered for the buyer's orientation. These price estimations are moderate. Mr. David will be at the Bookman on the designated days and can show anyone interested catalogues from the past 20 years with prices on items related to the ones for sale.

Many schools and universities would like to have the materials from this sale. However, they do not have budgets that allow expenditures in this direction. Anything purchased from this sale can be given to a school and used as a tax exemption; one-third of your income can be given to this end. Anything purchased will be appraised at its full value, so as not to be an expense to you as a donation. The University of Houston for instance, has a nice start in collecting this type of material and would welcome any addition to their collection.

Plate 11. Page 5 from the David catalogue, with a biographical statement that gives a good sense of the flavor of the period.

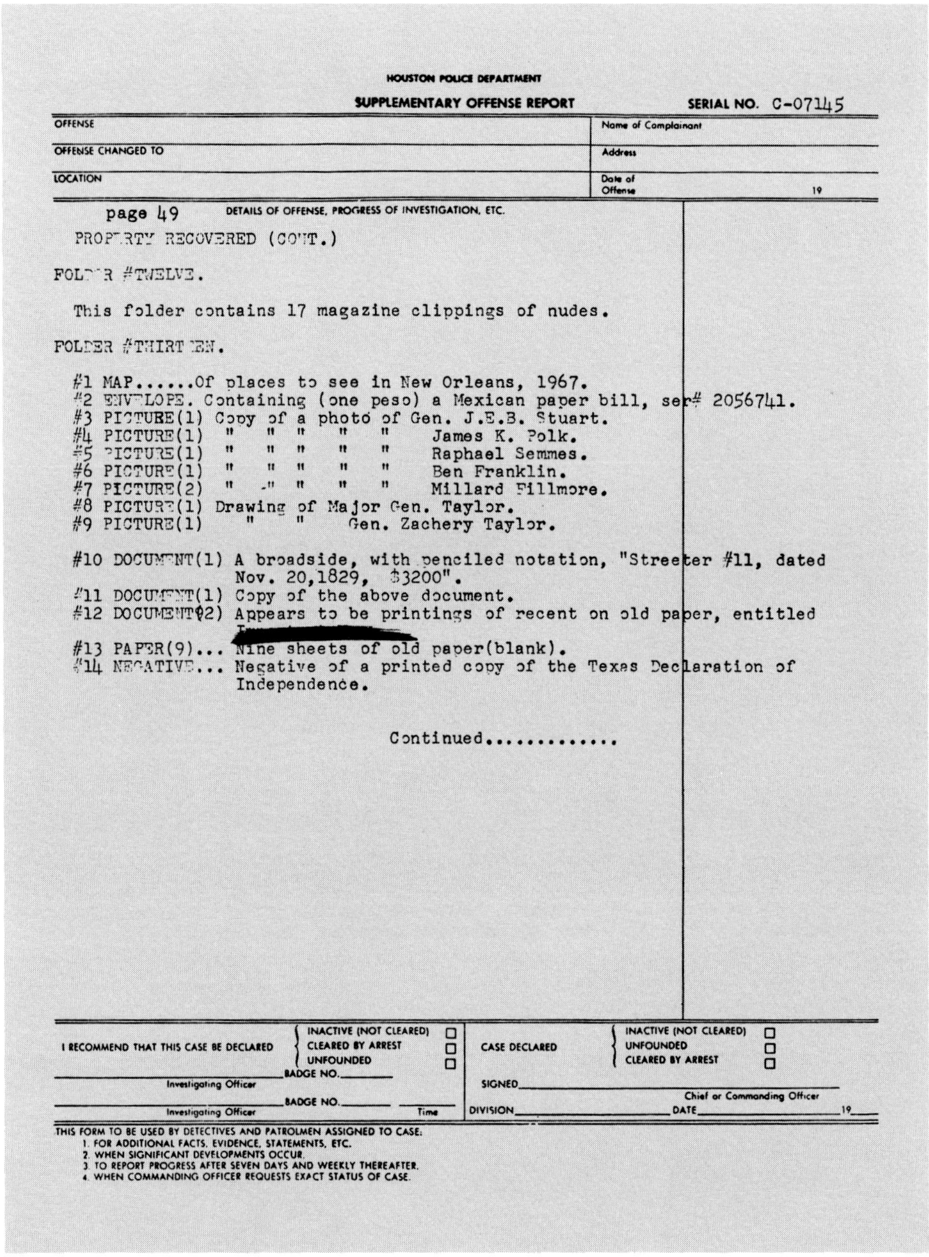

HOUSTON POLICE DEPARTMENT

SUPPLEMENTARY OFFENSE REPORT

SERIAL NO. C-07145

OFFENSE	Name of Complainant
OFFENSE CHANGED TO	Address
LOCATION	Date of Offense 19

page 49 DETAILS OF OFFENSE, PROGRESS OF INVESTIGATION, ETC.

PROPERTY RECOVERED (CONT.)

FOLDER #TWELVE.

This folder contains 17 magazine clippings of nudes.

FOLDER #THIRTEEN.

#1 MAP......Of places to see in New Orleans, 1967.
#2 ENVELOPE. Containing (one peso) a Mexican paper bill, ser# 2056741.
#3 PICTURE(1) Copy of a photo of Gen. J.E.B. Stuart.
#4 PICTURE(1) " " " " " James K. Polk.
#5 PICTURE(1) " " " " " Raphael Semmes.
#6 PICTURE(1) " " " " " Ben Franklin.
#7 PICTURE(2) " " " " " Millard Fillmore.
#8 PICTURE(1) Drawing of Major Gen. Taylor.
#9 PICTURE(1) " " Gen. Zachery Taylor.

#10 DOCUMENT(1) A broadside, with penciled notation, "Streeter #11, dated Nov. 20,1829, $3200".
#11 DOCUMENT(1) Copy of the above document.
#12 DOCUMENT(2) Appears to be printings of recent on old paper, entitled [redacted]
#13 PAPER(9)... Nine sheets of old paper(blank).
#14 NEGATIVE... Negative of a printed copy of the Texas Declaration of Independence.

Continued............

I RECOMMEND THAT THIS CASE BE DECLARED: INACTIVE (NOT CLEARED) ☐ CLEARED BY ARREST ☐ UNFOUNDED ☐

CASE DECLARED: INACTIVE (NOT CLEARED) ☐ UNFOUNDED ☐ CLEARED BY ARREST ☐

Investigating Officer ______ BADGE NO. ______

SIGNED ______ Chief or Commanding Officer

Investigating Officer ______ BADGE NO. ______ Time

DIVISION ______ DATE ______ 19__

THIS FORM TO BE USED BY DETECTIVES AND PATROLMEN ASSIGNED TO CASE:
1. FOR ADDITIONAL FACTS, EVIDENCE, STATEMENTS, ETC.
2. WHEN SIGNIFICANT DEVELOPMENTS OCCUR.
3. TO REPORT PROGRESS AFTER SEVEN DAYS AND WEEKLY THEREAFTER.
4. WHEN COMMANDING OFFICER REQUESTS EXACT STATUS OF CASE.

Plate 12. Page 49 from the police inventory of materials seized during the raid on Dorman David's premises. Items 10–14 relate to the forgeries. *DeGolyer Library, Southern Methodist University.*

It is unclear whether even the Library and Historical Commission was aware of the extent of the thefts and the manner in which they were handled. In the face of what had actually transpired, it is otherwise hard to understand how Frank P. Horlock, chairman of the commission at the time of the David sale, and the raid on his shop, could make the following statement to the *Houston Post* in September 1972:

It's my position as chairman we'll use every legal means to recover any document or any other historical item that has been the property of the people of Texas and has been at any time placed in the permanent archives of the state. . . . If they [historical items] ever belonged or were catalogued into the archives they had to be removed illegally. The state does not buy and sell documents.[22]

Horlock was appointed to the board in 1970. Perhaps he had not been told about the Davis sale; James M. Moudy, the only commission member from 1970 whom I have been able to locate (aside from Davis) does not recall thefts ever being discussed at commission meetings. A desire to keep the board in placid ignorance might also explain why University of Texas funds were apparently used to purchase items at the Davis sale (though this does not explain what was in it for the university). In any case, Horlock was soon replaced as board chairman by Davis, and until recently there have been only sporadic recoveries of documents stolen from the state.

During the intervening years, documents with apparently clouded provenance have circulated among dealers, collectors, and librarians with relative ease. When someone is found in possession of a document that has been published as belonging in an institution (particularly the State Library), the person generally offers one of two explanations. These explanations have gained credence through endless repetition, but they are nevertheless spurious and need to be laid to rest:

1. *The State Library traded or simply gave away documents, and with poor record-keeping there is no way to know what documents left its custody in this manner.*

This is an insidious half truth. In early times there is no doubt that documents were handled casually. For instance, there is a broadside General Council Circular of November 14, 1835 (Streeter 93), at the Alamo Museum Library that was obviously once in the Public Printing Papers at the State Archive—originally presented to the government for billing purposes, it bears Baker and Bordens' price notations on the reverse. The document was given to Moses Austin Bryan in the 1890s and bears a note in his hand, "This paper was given to me by Mr. McCall during the month of July that I spent at the capital making out a list of the surviving veteran soldiers of the Republic of Texas."[23] However, most of the documents in current question were still located in the state institutions where they had been originally deposited when they were recorded in published correspondence or bibliographies of printed documents, some as late as 1955. The contention is that feckless librarians traded or simply gave away to casual autograph seekers many of the documents now in circulation.

It is true that trades were made—the broadside version of Travis' Victory or Death letter (Streeter 185) was traded to Thomas Streeter in 1953—but at the time, it was a duplicate.[24] Virtually all research libraries routinely trade or sell duplicates in their collections to obtain other needed materials, and both sides benefit from these exchanges. The University of Texas also made at least one exchange of a duplicate with Thomas Streeter.[25] If a person owns a document which can be demonstrated to have been a duplicate in a public collection, it is as reasonable to suppose that it was exchanged as that it was stolen. But there is no documentary evidence that any state institution traded away the literally scores of unique and invaluable manuscripts by Travis, Bowie, Houston, Burnet, and others that have appeared on the market since 1965, nor over half the printed history of the Texas Revolution, most of it unique, which is now missing from the State Library. This rumor of wholesale trading of unique material has gained currency from its usefulness, not its truthfulness, and in the absence of any hard evidence to support it should be dismissed.

2. *The manuscript documents in circulation in private hands are contemporary copies of the documents reported in institutional collections.*

Here again a thread of truth has been stretched to make a garment of falsehood. There were often multiple copies made of important government documents—the Texas Declaration of Independence, of which five manuscript copies were made (only one survived), is an excellent example. It is reasonable to suppose that multiple copies were sometimes made of other official government documents.

However, much of the material on the market is not of an official nature. Moreover, an examination of the standard published volumes of Texas documents shows that relatively few contemporary copies are cited as manuscript sources for the printed transcriptions—which would not be the case if multiple copies had been routinely made and "originals" perished with normal frequency (suggested by the one-in-five survival ratio for the Declaration of Independence). More damning to this argument, however, is that when a collector or dealer claims that a manuscript document in his hands is a "copy," the institutional "original" from which he claims it derives is generally missing. Of course, this should not be the case. The complaint of the dealer returning a document to a library that has forcibly claimed it that, "When you find your original, I want my copy back," is transparently implausible and self-serving, yet continues to find sympathy in Texas.

There is one other piece of evidence damning to both the "trade" and "copy" theories. Namely, if these were true, there should have been a more or less consistent—or even declining—supply of these documents in commercial circulation throughout the period from roughly 1900 to the present. Instead, there was a remarkable increase in the number of these documents after 1965, when the first major thefts occurred. I have yet to be shown a significant Texas document once in a state collection that has a provable provenance outside of state custody between the time it was published as belonging to the state and 1965. To be brief and blunt: the documents in circulation that appear to be unique originals stolen from state institutions are almost certainly just that.

However, there is also a rationalization for owning these documents that is not so easily dismissed: *If the State Library and other institutions deliberately and persistently concealed the extent of the thefts from their libraries, and even bought back material they fully believed to have been stolen from the library, why should a person who bought a document in good faith, with no way to know that it was stolen, be forced to surrender it at great loss?*

This argument will strike a responsive chord in anyone with a sense of justice, and it is difficult to judge where equity lies. The documents clearly belonged to the state and were removed illegally—should the present administrators of the State Library, trying to do a responsible job to reclaim these documents for future students and historians, be hamstrung by the actions of their predecessors? [26] On the other hand, should honest collectors and dealers be harassed by the state because of owning documents they had no way of knowing were stolen, by virtue of the concealment by those same past administrators? The common denominator of complaint, and rightly so, is with the administration of the State Library in the 1960s and 1970s, which did not deal forthrightly with the thefts that afflicted the library. The present confusion and animosity is a sad legacy to this generation of bibliophiles.

Beyond that, however, is the enormous destruction to the historical record of this state that they witnessed and scarcely blinked at. The public auctions described previously are only the tip of the iceberg—many more such documents may have circulated privately and quietly, and with each passing year the deliberate concealment of their theft has made the chances of recovery more remote.

The potential problems lurking below the public surface are exemplified by the broadsides printed in Texas before 1837 that were once in the Texas State Library. Several of these appeared in the Robert E. Davis sale in 1967. For instance, lot 74 is a copy of "Meeting of the Citizens of San Felipe" (Streeter 132A), a dramatic broadside that includes the first printing of William Barret Travis' Victory or Death letter from the Alamo. Streeter recorded a copy of it at the Texas State Library in 1955, but it is now missing. However, E. W. Winkler made photostats of a great many of the broadsides in the Texas State Library besides the Texas Declaration of Independence mentioned in the preceding chapter. A number of these copies are now at the Barker Texas History Center at the University of Texas at Austin. By comparing the photostat of the missing State Library copy of "Meeting of the Citizens of San Felipe" with the illustration of the broadside on page [17] of the auction catalogue, it is demonstrable that they are the same copy. All of the paper creases and small repairs are identical, with one significant exception: there is a large area of the top of the broadside in the auction catalogue that has a repair that does not appear on the photostat. This "repair" was made to deliberately obscure evidence that the broadside belonged in the Public Printing Papers in the State Library—Winkler records on the photostat that the original document was docketed on the back with Baker and Bordens' charges for printing it.

The Public Printing Papers would be a rich source for an archival thief: Baker and Bordens apparently presented to the government a copy of every piece they printed, docketed with billing notations on the reverse. Aside from these dockets, which could be erased or obscured, there was no way to identify the broadsides as belonging to the library, since the collection was not catalogued by item. The thieves took advantage of this, but apparently it was not always deemed necessary to obliterate the dockets: in the Davis sale, lot 75 ("Friends and Citizens of Texas," Streeter 133), lot 94 (broadside proofs of the first land law, Streeter 168 or 207), and lot 101 (law certificate, not in Streeter) are all catalogued as being docketed on the verso. There are at least seven broadsides with descriptions that suggest they were once the property of the state of Texas.[27]

This is bad enough, but it only hints at the plundering of the historical record that took place at the Texas State Library. In 1955 Thomas Streeter recorded in the holdings of the library fifty-four broadsides printed in Texas before 1837.[28] As of August 1990, thirty of these were missing.[29] Of the thirty missing broadsides, fifteen were the only known copies.[30] Thanks to E. W. Winkler's photostats, there is at least some record of thirteen of these. But for two broadsides—one dated November 1836 by Thomas Borden, brother of Gail, proposing Fort Bend as the seat of government (Streeter 116), and another of the same date, describing a proposal for statehood in the Union that Streeter (no. 158) describes as "an important factor in the history of the annexation of Texas"—there now exists no record at all. The texts are not printed elsewhere.

As regards manuscripts, there is at present no good record of what is missing, so an accurate estimate is difficult to make. Unfortunately, given what is known from the public sales of such materials, the laconic assessment of one Texas collector may not be off the mark. When it was suggested to him that there might be forgeries of manuscripts as well as printed broadsides, he remarked, "Why would anyone bother to forge a manuscript, when they were so easy to steal?"

Notes

1. Notes obtained in the arrest of Bill Gray, August 2, 1971. Photocopy of typescript, 4 pages. DeGolyer Library, Southern Methodist University, Dallas, Texas.

2. "Documents Recovered in Waco," *Austin American-Statesman*, August 7, 1971.

3. "Couple Helps Crack 'Hot Document' Ring," *Fort Worth Star Telegram*, August 10, 1971.

4. Barker, *Austin Papers*, 2:280.

5. Barker, *Austin Papers*, 3:290.

6. Jenkins, *Papers of the Texas Revolution*, 4:296, no. 2540.

7. Williams and Barker, *Writings of Sam Houston*, 1:425.

8. *Houston Post*, June 24, 1971. David may not have been pleased with the results of the sale—his pre-sale estimates printed in the catalogue total over $39,000.

9. Lot 3, Austin to Fisher, Barker, *Austin Papers*, 2:1036–1037 (Texas State Library); lot 4, Austin to Smith, Jenkins, *Papers of the Texas Revolution*, 4:110, no. 1833 (Texas State Library); lot 5, Austin to Smith, Barker, *Austin Papers*, 2:312 (University of Texas); lot 6, Austin to Burnet, Jenkins, *Papers of the Texas Revolution*, 8:241, no. 9005 (Texas State Library); lot 7, Austin to Wharton, Barker, *Austin Papers*, 3:476 (University of Texas); lot 8, Austin to Catlett, Barker, *Austin Papers*, 3:476 (University of Texas).

10. Binkley, *Official Correspondence*, 1:487.

11. Lot 18, Burnet to Hardeman, Binkley, *Official Correspondence*, 2:836 (Texas State Library); lot 26, Fannin to Belton, Jenkins, *Papers of the Texas Revolution*, 1:370, no. 554 (Texas State Library); lot 36, Houston to Congress, Williams and Barker, *Writings of Sam Houston*, 1:497 (Texas State Library); lot 37, Houston to Pollitt, Williams and Barker, *Writings of Sam Houston*, 2:33 (Texas State Library); lot 41, Houston to Seguin, Williams and Barker, *Writings of Sam Houston*, 2:57 (Texas State Library); lot 44, Houston to government, Williams and Barker, *Writings of Sam Houston*, 2:256 (Texas State Library); lot 45, Houston to Birdsall, Williams and Barker, *Writings of Sam Houston*, 2:268–69 (Texas State Library); lot 46, Houston to Pollitt, Jenkins, *Papers of the Texas Revolution*, 8:202, no. 3951 (Texas State Library).

12. Lots 1, 3, 4, 5, 6, 7, 8, 16, 17, 18, 20, 23, 26, 34, 36, 37, 39, 40, 41, 44, 45, 46, 49, 50, 52, 57, 58, 60, 63, 67, 74, 75, 76, 84, 85, 86, 87, 94, 101, 118, 123, 124. This list is compiled using published sources: the 1968 inventory of lots purchased by the University of Texas on behalf of the State Library; and in some cases internal evidence provided by the auctioneer's description (such as Baker and Bordens' dockets on the verso of broadsides).

13. Nor was Davis alone in selling documents of dubious origin at auction. In 1965 Hamilton Galleries in New York sold a fine Sam Houston letter that is published as belonging to the University of Texas (*American Book-Prices Current*, 1965, p. 934. The catalogue mis-dated the letter c. 1845—it is actually dated February 16, 1837. Williams and Barker, *Writings of Sam Houston*, 2:56).

In 1967 the same auctioneer sold a three-page manuscript by Sam Houston, "To Head Chiefs of the Witchetaws, Ionies, Wacos . . . and Other Tribes," that is published as belonging to the Texas State Library (*American Book-Prices Current*, 1968, p. 1148. Williams and Barker, *Writings of Sam Houston*, 4:334). In 1968 Hamilton sold a two-page proclamation signed by Houston and Anson Jones convening Congress in 1844, that apparently belongs in the Texas State Library (*American Book-Prices Current*, 1969, p. 1454. Williams and Barker, *Writings of Sam Houston*, 4:385). In 1969 they sold an agreement, dated May 24, 1836, between Thomas Tobey and the Republic of Texas that also appears to belong in the Texas State Library (Jenkins, *Papers of the Texas Revolution*, 6:365, no. 3146). In 1970 they sold a Stephen F. Austin letter to David G. Burnet that appears to belong to the Texas State Library (*American Book-Prices Current*, 1970, p. 1273. Jenkins, *Papers of the Texas Revolution*, 8:241, no. 4005). That same year Roger N. Conger, another resident of Waco, who later became president of the Texas State Historical Association, consigned to Parke-Bernet a group of Texas-related books and manuscripts that began with a superb letter from Stephen F. Austin to R. R. Royall, written the day before Austin left for the United States to raise money. It is published in the *Austin Papers* (Parke-Bernet Sale 3019, April 7, 1970, lot 108; Barker, *Austin Papers*, 3:202), as belonging to the University of Texas. Lot 156 is a letter from David G. Burnet that is published as belonging in the Comptroller's Papers at the Texas State Library (Jenkins, *Papers of the Texas Revolution*, 6:340, no. 3112).

14. This information was compiled from a copy of the Davis sale catalogue marked with buyers' names by a person present in the room.

15. A photocopy of this letter is available at the DeGolyer Library, Southern Methodist University, Dallas, Texas.

16. Author's notes from telephone conversations with Dorman Winfrey and Chester Kielman, October 1990.

17. *History of Rusk County* (Waco: Texian Press, 1961); *Julian Sidney Devereaux and His Monte Verdi Plantation* (Waco: Texian Press, 1962). Davis also published Winfrey's *Indian Tribes of Texas* in 1971.

18. Author's notes from telephone conversation with Robert E. Davis, October 5, 1990.

19. *Biennial Reports of the Texas Library and Historical Commission*, 1968–80.

20. After the raid, in late 1972, David sold a superb series of letters by Travis, Austin, and Houston to a private collector, and in October 1973 sold his genuine Declaration of Independence to H. P. Kraus.

21. There are, for instance, a large number of official Washington County documents in the University of Houston library, received as gifts from Houston area collectors; some have also appeared in William Simpson auction catalogues.

22. "State Begins Crackdown," *Houston Post*, September 17, 1972.

23. Presumably John Dodd McCall, who was comptroller of public accounts in Austin from 1887 to 1895 (Webb, *Handbook of Texas*, 2:101).

24. See pages 109–110 for details of this transaction.

25. R. R. Royall, "To the Citizens of Texas," Streeter 130, according to a note in E. W. Winkler's hand laid in an empty file in the B. C. Franklin Papers at the University of Texas at Austin.

26. The present state archivist, Chris LaPlante, has taken an admirably aggressive stand on the recovery of stolen state documents, and is apparently receiving support for his efforts—in November 1990 the Texas attorney general filed suit against one estate to reclaim documents that show evidence of once belonging in the State Archive. Even more recently, Jim Grizzard, one of Dorman David's chief customers/victims, voluntarily returned to the state over $50,000 worth of unique manuscripts he believes were stolen from the State Library, accompanied by a $30,000 check to help catalogue what

is missing from the library, and a challenge to other collectors and dealers to follow his example.

27. Lots 74, 75, 76, 90, 94, 99, and 101.

28. Defined as a single sheet printed on one or both sides. The Streeter numbers are: 9, 22, 26, 48, 49, 58, 61, 71, 74, 77, 78, 81, 82, 84, 86, 88, 90, 92, 92A, 96, 97, 101, 102, 103, 105, 106, 111, 112, 114, 116, 118, 131, 132, 132A, 133, 134, 137, 142, 143, 145, 146, 148, 149, 151, 153, 158, 159, 165, 170, 172, 173, 174, 180, 185.

29. Streeter numbers: 9, 22, 58, 74, 77, 81, 84, 86, 92, 101, 102, 105, 106, 111, 112, 116, 131, 132A, 133, 134, 137, 143, 145, 151, 153, 158, 170, 172, 174, 185.

30. Streeter numbers: 81, 84, 101, 102, 105, 106, 112, 116, 131, 133, 134, 143, 151, 158, 170.

Chapter Four

Who Printed What

The identity of the person or persons responsible for actually removing the documents from the State Library has never been established, and at this point probably never will be. But for the other means of enlarging the supply of Republic-period Texas documents—forgery—a substantial body of evidence does exist. The trail begins in 1973, when a copy of the printed broadside version of William Barret Travis' Victory or Death letter from the Alamo appeared as lot 67 in a sale at Parke-Bernet Galleries scheduled for October 30.[1] It caught the attention of Ray Walton, who got in contact with John Peace, then chairman of the University of Texas Board of Regents and an avid collector of Texana. Peace desired the document and commissioned Walton to bid for it. I accompanied Walton on the trip. Neither of us had attended a New York auction before, so we were anxious as lots 1 through 66 were sold. When the Travis letter came up, Walton did not indicate his bids by a discreet nod or a flick of a finger or pencil; he stuck his hand high in the air, index finger raised, and held it there until the hammer fell at $5,000. The prize was his.

Walton later remarked that this sale "caused quite a stir; nobody had paid that much for a copy of it before."[2] That is an understatement—before this copy appeared, no copy had been publicly offered for sale at any price.[3] But between 1973 and 1986 at least ten more copies of this prize broadside appeared and were sold. Something was obviously wrong. Here was an important document, no copy of which had been sold, anywhere, before 1973. Now a copy was appearing about every sixteen months. But because almost all of these sales were private, and only one copy went on public display,[4] an individual purchasing the document, or an institution acquiring it as a gift, might well have been unaware of the other transactions and not question its authenticity or provenance.

One person who did ask questions was the well-known Texas billionaire H. Ross Perot. He was offered a copy of the Travis broadside in late 1985 by Gary Hendershott, an Arkansas dealer. Perot, not noted for being easily fooled, did not take its authenticity for granted. Instead, he asked Don Etherington, then head of conservation at the Harry Ransom Humanities Research Center at the University of Texas at Austin, to examine the document. Etherington first attempted to compare it to the copy recorded by Streeter at the Texas State Library, but finding that copy missing, he flew to New Haven with Perot's copy to compare it with the Streeter copy at Yale.[5] On January 13, 1986, Etherington and George Miles, curator of Western Americana at Yale, compared the two documents carefully. They concluded that the Perot copy was a forgery because of a lower-case *a* in the word *flag* at the end of line 6, which was deformed in a way that could not occur with metal type (see illustration, page 135). Perot returned the document to Hendershott, who returned it to the dealer from whom he had acquired it, John Jenkins in Austin. I learned of this incident while I was working on the Declaration of Independence. It now appeared that there were two forged documents. This raised a troublesome question: how many more might there be?

Answering this question was not nearly as difficult as one might think. The Declaration of Independence proved to be a kind of Rosetta Stone, the patterns it exposed being common to many of the other forged documents. Eventually, I simply looked for rare early Texas broadsides that had suddenly become less rare; that displayed anomalies in the type matter explainable only by touching-up of a photographic negative; and that had as their earliest traceable owner one of three dealers whose names turned up consistently as the earliest source of the forged Declarations: Dorman David, John Jenkins, and Houston auctioneer William Simpson. My search was also made easier by the fact that several people were already suspicious of one or more documents. One person called and said, "You might want to look at Streeter 89." A dealer brought several documents he was leery of to my house; three proved to be forgeries. Jennifer Larson, a bookseller in San Francisco, was asked by an insurance company in January 1988 to appraise books and documents claimed by Jenkins as damaged in a September 1987 fire. With a sharp and objective eye, she was suspicious of several documents. When later she got in touch with me, I was able to confirm for her that two of the documents she questioned were indeed fakes; and she was able to lead me to another forged document.

Another lead came when I was at a bookfair in Dallas. Displayed in a dealer's booth was a little handbill entitled "Columbia Jockey Club," announcing a horse race to take place on May 4, 1835. The first copy known had appeared in 1974 and was described in the revised edition of Streeter, published in 1983, as no. 64.1. Michael Heaston, an Americana dealer in Austin, indicated to me that he had doubts about the document; he also was willing to have the document sent to him on approval. When it arrived in Austin, I examined it carefully. The printing was not good, and looked suspiciously like the mottled printing of the forged Declarations. But there was none of the telltale tampering with the type itself, and I did not know the document's provenance. So I took the handbill to the Barker Texas History Center to compare it with an F. C. Gray imprint, Gray being the only printer in the region at the time. The type did not match the first F. C. Gray imprint I looked at. However, since Gray's typographic material had passed through several hands before he acquired it (it originally belonged to Godwin B. Cotten), it was possible that there had been a number of typefaces in his shop. I compared the text type in the Jockey Club handbill to fifteen additional F. C. Gray imprints, as well as to his newspaper (which might be expected to utilize most if not all of his available types). Nowhere did the type on the Jockey Club handbill appear. This engaging piece of Texana had not been printed by F. C. Gray; and if not by F. C. Gray, then not in Texas in April 1835.

It was a member of my staff who provided the essential clue to determining the nature of the document. I returned to my shop with the handbill and related my experience at the library. Bradley Hutchinson, a knowledgeable pressman, looked at the type and said, "That looks like Century to me." We consulted the standard reference book on the subject of modern typefaces, Jaspert, Berry, and Johnson's *Encyclopedia of Type Faces*. As he suspected, the typeface was indeed Century, which did not exist until 1896, when it was commissioned as a new face for *Century* magazine. Furthermore, the type on the handbill appeared to be the Linotype version of the face, which did not appear until even later. For certain confirmation, I took the text to G&S Typesetters, the only remaining Linotype shop in Austin, and had them set the text in Linotype Century; it was an exact match. The Jockey Club handbill was not a forgery; it was a complete fabrication. The text and even the adorning woodcut were authentic,[6] but they had not been used in concert to make a piece of printing in 1835. This knowledge led to the discovery of two more fabrications: "The Town of Houston" (Revised Streeter 112.1) and "Glorious News" (not in Streeter), the former printed from Linotype Bodoni, the latter once again from Century.

By the summer of 1988, I had accounted for fifty-four copies of thirteen bogus documents—ten of them forgeries, three of them fabrications. Although numerous copies remained to be discovered, there was at this point sufficient evidence to pursue the next logical question: Who made them? In two instances Dorman David had owned the original used to make forgeries.[7] I had been told by an acquaintance of his that in the mid-1960s she had watched him staining and baking paper to make it appear old. Then Dorothy Sloan brought word that, confronted about the forgeries by J. P. Bryan, Jr., a Houston collector, David had admitted to making the Declaration of Independence. Sloan had David's address; she suggested we pay him a visit at his home in Pass Christian, Mississippi.

To my surprise, David agreed to see us, so on September 1, 1988, Dorothy Sloan, her daughter Jasmine, and I flew to New Orleans and drove from there to Pass Christian. Our conversation with David was casual and relaxed; he readily conceded making the Declaration of Independence but maintained that he had not meant to deceive anyone. He had intended the documents to be part of a portfolio of facsimiles of early Texas documents relating to immigration, and he had never made a secret of his project. Lots of people had known of it. He described in some detail how he photographed the original documents, blew up the negatives, sometimes as much as ten times the original size, touched them up as necessity or whim moved him, reduced them, had an unmounted zinc cut made from the reduced negative, and printed from that.

David was similarly casual in his later conversations with Gregory Curtis for an article in *Texas Monthly* magazine.[8] He provided a rather romantic account of making "old" ink by collecting carbon from candle smoke in a bag, and applying the ink to the plate with leather ink-balls of the kind used in the early nineteenth century, which he made himself. "He put a piece of paper on top of the inked plate, and with a small wooden mallet he tapped each letter one by one," Curtis wrote. "He lifted the sheet after each tap to check the result."[9] David's description of the process he used is obviously fanciful, because following it would inevitably produce printing that looked like smeared lipstick. It is probable that David knows more than he admits about printing with equipment more sophisticated than "a small wooden mallet": in his second catalogue, issued in December 1963, he wrote in a foreword, "This is our second catalogue, our second venture in printing on our own press. Please bear with us in our attempt to learn the trade."

But by 1988 David was ambiguous about how well he had learned his trade. To Gregory Curtis he said, "I was never satisfied with anything I did,"[10] and he expanded on this to David Hewett for an article in *Maine Antique Digest*: "I was still experimenting, but I didn't have a good finished product. . . . I did make some sheets, but they were very crude and may have passed [as authentic] to somebody, but I don't know who."[11] However, David's modesty sometimes deserted him. In an interview with Lisa Belkin, reporter for the *New York Times*, David stated, "I'm an artist. I believe in my heart that if I wanted to I could make something no one could detect."[12] And despite his protestations to the contrary, he did allow himself the satisfaction of deceiving at least one collector with four of his creations in the early 1970s; the collector has receipts, signed by David, to prove it.[13]

About the extent of his trade—how many documents he made—David was equally contradictory. To Hewett he said he made "about five of them."[14] *Which* five was another question. The Declaration of Independence he consistently claimed as his work. Beyond that, little was clear. He told Hewett that he made the Declaration of Causes (Streeter 89).[15] When asked about the same document by Lisa Belkin, he said, "I don't know about that."[16] Likewise, when I asked David about the "Town of Houston" fabrication (Revised Streeter 112.1), he professed no knowledge of the document at all. Asked by Lisa Belkin if he made it, he said, "That sounds right."[17]

As Belkin aptly noted in her article, David had lived a life that would put a strain on anyone's memory; he was addicted to heroin during the period that many of these documents were produced. Gregory Curtis reported that, "Old friends who might stop by would see him in the bathroom with a needle in his arm. Others would come in to find him sitting loopy-eyed in front of the television; he had twisted the dials to make the colors bizarre."[18] Given these circumstances, it is possible that

David really has no clear recollection of what he did during those years. Or it may be that, as another person put it, "Dorman has a problem with reality."

Whatever the reason, David is obviously an unreliable witness. For a more reliable estimate of which documents he made, it is necessary to return to the documents themselves, to discern what the patterns of manufacture, provenance, and other physical evidence can reveal about their origins. There are at present (November 1990) fifteen documents known to have been forged or fabricated. The evidence regarding each (exclusive of David's own testimony) can be summarized as follows: [19]

AUSTIN'S NOTICE TO COLONISTS (Streeter 11): David reproduced the top half of this document in his catalogue 14 in 1966; there were two copies in the police inventory of material seized during the 1972 raid. David sold the earliest located copy of this forgery to a collector in April 1973. It was made from a reproduction in a book, and is incorrectly sized—the same technique produced the same results in two other instances (Streeter 150 and 1246—see below). The forgeries also show evidence of retouching in the negative, the telltale sign of David's handiwork.

COLUMBIA JOCKEY CLUB (Revised Streeter 64.1): Although there is nothing to directly link this fabrication to David, the technique of using a genuine contemporary text to create a fabricated document from modern Linotype is common to two other documents ("The Town of Houston" and "Glorious News") that can be linked to him.

DECLARATION OF CAUSES, Spanish edition (Streeter 88): The only known forgery of this document is at Baylor University. It is a photocopy on old paper of the copy now in the Peace Collection at the University of Texas at San Antonio. It had to have been made before 1974, when the Peace Collection was received as a gift. However, all of the forged documents that definitely originated with Dorman David were printed letterpress from plates (with the possible exception of "A Public Meeting"—see below); there is no evidence to link him to this forgery.

DECLARATION OF CAUSES, English edition (Streeter 89): The entire document has been extensively retouched while in negative form, and it was probably made from a reproduction. In addition, the earliest recorded sale of a copy of this forgery was made by David in April 1973.

THE TOWN OF HOUSTON (Revised Streeter 112.1): This fabrication was made by taking a genuine text from the columns of the *Telegraph and Texas Register* for August 30, 1836, and creating a broadside from it. In the inventory of the police search of David's shop in 1972, there is on page 47 the following entry, "No. 4 Document (1) Clipping entitled 'The Town of Houston' dated Aug. 30, 1836."

PAGÉS WANTED POSTER (Revised Streeter 119.1): Dorman David acquired the only known genuine copy of this from Morris Cook in 1964; the forgery is incorrectly sized and is missing two rules, flaws of the kind found in other forgeries that can be definitely linked to David.

IMPORTANT NEWS (Streeter 136): There were two copies of this item listed on page 49 of the police inventory of David's property, with the notation, "Appears to be printings of recent [date] on old paper." The forgery shows evidence of extensive retouching to the negative.

ARMY ORDERS (Streeter 150): This was made from a reproduction in a book, and the size is incorrect, as in two other instances (Streeter 11 and 1246); the earliest recorded sale was made by Dorman David in October 1971.

DECLARATION OF INDEPENDENCE (Streeter 165): Dorman David owned the genuine original from which the forgeries were made; the negative is listed on page 49 of the police inventory of his shop; the document displays evidences of retouching to the negative; David sold a forged copy in October 1971 to a collector.

TRAVIS' VICTORY OR DEATH LETTER FROM THE ALAMO (Streeter 185): Has evidence of retouching in the negative; the earliest known sale of a forged copy was made by David to a Houston collector in the early 1970s (probably before the Peace copy was sold at Parke-Bernet in 1973).

AUSTIN'S GRANT APPLICATION (Streeter 1082): Now at the University of Houston, the copy used to make the forgeries was once owned by Dorman David; the forgeries show evidence of retouching in the negative.

NEW ORLEANS RECRUITING POSTER (Streeter 1246): This was made from a reproduction in Walter Lord's *A Time to Stand*, as was Streeter 150, and like both of the other documents made from illustrations in books (the other is Streeter 11), it is the wrong size.

GLORIOUS NEWS: This is a fabrication utilizing Linotype Century type, as in Revised Streeter 64.1; the earliest recorded sale was made by Dorman David to a collector in the early 1970s.

A PUBLIC MEETING: This is a unique hybrid of a genuine source and original type, made by photocopying a slightly modified newspaper article onto old paper. The newspaper used to create this forgery was in the inventory of material seized from Dorman David's property in the 1972 police raid.

SAM HOUSTON PROCLAMATION (Winkler/Friend 202): This is the only forgery I have encountered that is not from the period covered by Streeter (1795–1845). The original used to make the forgeries is at the University of Houston, unfortunately with no indication of provenance; the forgeries do, however, show evidence of retouching to the negative.

Given that David made his acknowledged forgeries using retouched negatives, the presence of retouching—often unnecessary, sometimes whimsical—would in itself be strong evidence that David made a document. Combined with the earliest known sale or possession of a forgery by David, and/or his possession of an original document (or other material, such as the newspaper clipping for Revised Streeter 112.1) that can be demonstrated to have been used to make the forgeries, this evidence is compelling. Such evidence exists for seven of the fifteen documents listed above: Austin's Notice to Colonists (Streeter 11), the English Declaration of Causes (Streeter 89), Pagés Wanted Poster (Revised Streeter 119.1), Important News (Streeter 136), The Declaration of Independence (Streeter 165), Travis' Victory or Death Letter (Streeter 185), and

Austin's Grant Application (Streeter 1082). For Army Orders (Streeter 150) and the New Orleans Recruiting Poster (Streeter 1246), the evidence is different but still fits the pattern: Both were made from reproductions of copies in the University of Texas library that appear in Walter Lord's *A Time to Stand*, a book David admired—he called it the "Best History of the Alamo" in his list of "Reference Books Used" on page 3 of the catalogue of the Warwick Hotel auction in 1971. Neither is the exact size of the original. This use of a reproduction and the subsequent incorrect sizing are identical to the technique and flaw in Streeter 11. In addition, the earliest recorded sale of Streeter 150 was made by David, and, taken with the other evidence, this suggests that David was also the creator of the forgeries of both these documents.

The three fabrications, "Columbia Jockey Club" (Revised Streeter 64.1), "The Town of Houston" (Revised Streeter 112.1), and "Glorious News," follow identical patterns of text selection and manufacture, and for "The Town of Houston" there is the additional fact that the newspaper clipping that was the source for this document was found in David's possession during the police search of his premises. This same evidence—the presence of the newspaper source for a forgery in the 1972 raid—exists for "A Public Meeting."

Overall, the web of evidence—the way one document relates to another, the way the provenances relate to the document, the way all of this relates to Dorman David's own (albeit contradictory) descriptions of his activities—combined with the important negative evidence that nothing has surfaced to suggest that these documents were created by anyone else—indicates that Dorman David was the probable creator of most of the fifteen forged or fabricated documents thus far discovered.

Whatever documents Dorman David may or may not have made, however, it is apparent that he was not the chief marketer of his creations. Of the nearly sixty specimens of the fifteen bogus documents now known, only five can be traced directly to him. And the last confirmed date of a sale of one of the documents by David was April 10, 1973. Where did the rest come from, and who brought them onto the market? Did they know, or should they have known, what it was they were selling?

Notes

1. Streeter 185 (*Bibliography*, Part I, 1:172).
2. Hewett, *Maine Antique Digest*, 29-A.
3. Streeter acquired his by exchange from the Texas State Library—see page 109.
4. One was displayed at the San Jacinto Museum.
5. The Yale copy is certainly genuine—it is still attached to Streeter 145, with which it was originally printed in 1836.
6. See the individual entry for this item, page 76, for more details.
7. The Declaration of Independence (see page 102) and Streeter 1082 (see page 111).
8. Curtis, *Texas Monthly*, 184.
9. Ibid.
10. Ibid.
11. Hewett, *Maine Antique Digest*, 30-A.
12. Belkin, *New York Times Magazine*, 74.
13. The documents were Streeter 89, 150, 165, and 185.
14. Hewett, *Maine Antique Digest*, 30-A.
15. Ibid.
16. Belkin, *New York Times Magazine*, 74.
17. Ibid.
18. Curtis, *Texas Monthly*, 183.
19. For details regarding this evidence, see the individual entries for the documents.

Chapter Five

Who Sold What

After the raid on his premises, Dorman David's career collapsed. He was indicted for possession of stolen property and for possession of narcotics. He jumped bail and lived as a fugitive for seven years.[1] Shortly after his arrest he made a few more significant sales—a group of superb (mostly stolen) letters and assorted forgeries to a Houston collector, and the genuine Texas Declaration of Independence to H. P. Kraus in October 1973. At roughly the same time he also sold all of his remaining stock—eight to ten large boxes holding approximately five thousand documents[2] —to William Simpson: "I had to sell everything I owned then. It was tough. Auctioneer Bill Simpson helped me unload the material I had when I went out of business."[3]

Simpson, a "theatrical, good-humored man with a white goatee," who "was once the acolyte of Ezra Pound," opened his auction gallery in Houston in 1964.[4] He has acknowledged buying the material and claims that he then traded most of the printed material to John Jenkins.[5] I can recall seeing boxes of documents bearing Dorman David's distinctive cost code at the Jenkins Company premises shortly after I began in business in 1972. For his part, Jenkins, who was found dead of a gunshot wound in April 1989 (whether by homicide or suicide is still a debated issue), stated, "I bought many things from [David]. But Simpson got the bulk of his stock. Simpson got boxes, thousands of pieces."[6] Jenkins also shifted blame to Simpson for one of Dorman David's contentions—that he sold Jenkins the plates used to make the forgeries. David claims that in late 1970 or early 1971 (he must have the dates wrong, because the raid wasn't until 1972)—"I got down to the last three boxes I had, and John Jenkins bought them for around $300. He said 'Well it's the last things I'm going to buy from you,' and I said, 'Yes, they're the last things I have.' I can't remember all that was there, but the printing plates were."[7]

Not surprisingly, Jenkins denied this: "I've never seen any such plates.

I think he may have confused me with someone else. He may have in fact sold these plates to the Simpson Galleries in Houston because that is the source for most of these things."[8]

The plates, of course, are something of a red herring; the real question is, What became of the inventory of forgeries? There was more than one copy of some of the forgeries found during the police raid, and it seems probable that more than one had been made of the others as well. Again, Jenkins put the blame squarely on Simpson: "They [Simpson's] have acknowledged selling the bad pieces to me. Over the last twenty years, I bought maybe twelve [bad] pieces from the Simpson Galleries. . . ."[9] Jenkins provided the *Maine Antique Digest* with receipts from Simpson for a copy of "Dec. of Causes" (Streeter 88 or 89), dated April 16, 1974, and for a Declaration of Independence sold to an investor group formed by Jenkins called "India Inc.," dated October 21, 1971.[10]

However, Simpson Galleries also denies having had the plates,[11] and furthermore takes issue with Jenkins over the number of bogus documents they sold to him. Shortly after the article in the *Maine Antique Digest* appeared, I telephoned William Simpson and asked him directly if he had sold Jenkins twelve of the documents. He emphatically denied it. He said he had sold Jenkins only three or four, and in addition said that he had acquired a number of *his* forgeries from Jenkins. He reasserted this to Calvin Trillin for a profile on John Jenkins in *The New Yorker*, and Trillin neatly summed up the dispute by saying that their mutual accusations had "a certain symmetry."[12]

Besides Jenkins, Simpson has also claimed "fine old Houston families" as a source for some of the forgeries that he has sold, auctioned, and appraised.[13] Besides Simpson, Jenkins added the Eberstadt Collection ("three or four"), Dorman David ("two or three"), and other people in the trade ("maybe one or two").[14] There is a certain vagueness here, and the one specific new source mentioned—the Eberstadt Collection—will not stand close scrutiny.[15] Jenkins stated that the Eberstadts made large purchases from David;[16] but the Eberstadts had retired by the late 1960s, well before David is known to have sold a fake. Two of the three documents known to have been in the Eberstadt Collection of which forgeries do exist—Streeter 88, 89, and 165—can be accounted for and are genuine (the present location of Streeter 88 is unknown).[17]

In the end, only one thing is clear: the two invoices from Simpson to

Jenkins aside, neither David nor Jenkins nor Simpson ever produced a shred of documentary evidence to account for their ownership of any of these forgeries.[18] Thus we are left with the curious spectacle of the three principals in this affair standing in a circle, pointing accusing fingers at one another. What is significant is that no one has pointed a finger at anyone else. And if they could not agree among themselves as to who was the source of the forgeries, this should not obscure the fact that there are a number of things they have agreed on:

1. Dorman David made many of the forgeries.
2. When Dorman David went out of business around 1973, he sold most if not all of his remaining stock, some five thousand items, to William Simpson.
3. William Simpson sold or traded some portion of David's stock to John Jenkins.
4. Since that time (1973), of the fifty-seven forgeries that have been discovered (not including unlocated copies) by November 1990, twenty-three can be traced to John Jenkins and seventeen to William Simpson. (The remaining seventeen copies are in the possession of owners—five dealers, three institutions, and one collector —who cannot determine the ultimate origin of their documents.)

As far as I am aware, none of these statements is in dispute. Indeed, when the entire affair is distilled to its essence, only one question of any importance remains: Did Jenkins and Simpson know that the documents they were selling were forgeries? Or, if that question cannot be answered (as indeed may be the case), *should* they have known they were forgeries?

The involvement of William Simpson is difficult to assess because there is a paucity of evidence. He sold very few of the forgeries to their present owners: most were sold to collectors who subsequently donated the materials to libraries, and in a number of cases the donor is deceased. In cases in which the donor is still alive, there is still little incentive on the part of either donor or donee to pry into the matter, and none has.

According to newspaper accounts, William Simpson has been generally unavailable for comment regarding the forgeries he sold. His son, Ray, who now manages Simpson Galleries, said to a Houston reporter in December 1988 that, "Sometime many years ago, when there was a tremendous amount of documents which we don't see any more, a few slipped through my daddy's fingers." He added that since restitution had been made, the matter should be laid to rest.[19]

However, at the time he said this, officials at the Star of the Republic Museum and the University of Houston, which between them own nearly a dozen forgeries that originated with William Simpson, had not heard anything from either of the Simpsons. This was seven months after the forgeries were exposed. Elizabeth Wachendorfer, University of Houston library development officer, said, "I'm not very happy about it. I guess I expected a call."[20] In the end, it didn't matter if he called, because the University of Houston, having acquired many of their forgeries as gifts from collectors who acquired them from William Simpson, was not in a position to demand restitution—and Simpson didn't offer. Those who eventually demanded it—including the Star of the Republic Museum—did get their money back, but of the seventeen forgeries handled by Simpson, I know of only three for which he has been required to refund the purchase price. As Gregory Curtis noted in *Texas Monthly*, selling forgeries can be a "highly profitable, successful, even gentlemanly business."[21]

On the one occasion I managed to reach William Simpson by telephone, shortly after the article appeared in the *Maine Antique Digest*, he volunteered a story about the broadside "The Town of Houston," which had been mentioned in the press as one of the fabrications I had discovered. He related to me that this document had been printed by a gentleman in Houston, a collector of Texana and a printer, for the Texas Centennial celebrations in 1936. He told me a name that I did not recognize and have since forgotten. I asked if I could talk with the gentleman. No, Simpson said, he passed away about ten years ago. A pity, he said—you would have enjoyed knowing him, both of you being printers.

Nearly a year after hearing this from Simpson, I was visiting the Star of the Republic Museum to examine its Streeter-period broadsides. Among them was a copy of the "Town of Houston" broadside, and a check of the museum's accession records revealed that they had purchased it from Simpson in 1978 for $350. That is not a trivial sum, and the curator was certainly under the impression that the document was printed in 1836, not 1936. Putting together Simpson's story and his sale, one could only conclude that he sold to the museum for $350 a piece of paper he knew to have been a mere souvenir printed in 1936. This would be unseemly enough; but the alternative is even less attractive. Ray Simpson denies they knew anything about forgeries: "Dealers like ourselves, we were just innocent, we were caught up in a web." [22]

At the time of his death, John Jenkins was under investigation by the Travis County District Attorney for his role in selling forgeries and for his possible involvement in the fire at his premises in September 1987.[23] With his death, those investigations ceased, and any chance of being able to say with certainty whether he knew at the time he sold them that the documents in question were forgeries was lost. One could speculate endlessly, but it would seem much more useful to devote attention to a few questions that remain approachable: Regardless of whether he knew, in the first instance, that the documents coming from Houston were forgeries, *should* he have known, at some point, that they were? What was that point? And what did he do at that point? These questions also have the advantage of rendering irrelevant the finger-pointing over who was the ultimate source of the forgeries. If Jenkins found himself buying the same supposedly rare documents over and over again from one source, that in itself is problematic.

Unlike Simpson, who shies from publicity, Jenkins thirsted for it, and he had an uncommon knack for telling good stories. Jenkins found that reporters would print whatever he told them and that his friends would be amused by his tales, not inclined to hold him to the facts. Calvin Trillin, in his *New Yorker* profile on Jenkins, tells of him spinning tales at poker games: "If someone said that the story being told didn't sound like the precise truth, Jenkins might say, 'O.K. Let's see hands. How many want a good story and how many want the truth?'" [24]

Jenkins told his story of the forgeries twice, in writing and in some detail. The first time was in a long letter to the insurance investigator looking into his claim for the September 1987 fire. Publicly, Jenkins downplayed this fire. To a *Houston Post* reporter he said, "It was a very minor fire. It didn't affect much of the books. It was in the mailroom and office. It was more of an inconvenience." He described his losses as "some computers and typewriters and things." [25] By this time, however, reporters were becoming more skeptical of Jenkins' stories, and upon calling the state fire marshal's office the *Post* discovered that Jenkins had filed a claim of between $250,000 and $500,000, and that the claim included a number of documents, such as the Texas Declaration of Independence and the Travis letter, which were subsequently revealed to be forgeries.

Employed by the insurance firm to verify the value of the documents in Jenkins' fire claim, San Francisco bookseller Jennifer Larson came to Austin on January 21, 1988, not expecting to find anything amiss—she respected Jenkins and his reputation. What she discovered changed her opinion quickly: among many other problems, she was quite suspicious of the authenticity of several Texas Revolution broadsides in the claim, and she expressed her doubts to the insurance adjustor. Jenkins' letter of March 7, 1988, was in response to these suspicions. Jenkins showed me this letter during a visit to my office the week following the first newspaper story of the discovery of the forgeries, which appeared in the April 8, 1988, edition of the *Austin American-Statesman*.[26]

Jenkins' second account of the forgeries is in a report dated November 2, 1988, and distributed to the Board of Governors of the Antiquarian Booksellers Association of America (ABAA), a trade organization.[27] It is obvious that he never expected this report to be compared to his earlier letter to the insurance investigator, because the two accounts, written eight months apart, give entirely contradictory versions of the history of the forgeries, particularly as regards his own and other people's beliefs about the nature of the documents in the decade preceding their public exposure. In his November report to the ABAA, Jenkins stated unequivocally that it had never occurred to him to doubt the authenticity of the now questioned broadsides. He said that everyone—dealers, collectors, librarians, and scholars—had accepted them as unquestionably genuine. He further stated that during the Texas Sesquicentennial in 1986 much new material appeared on the market, and for the first time he and others got an inkling of how many more copies there were of some broadsides than the number found by Streeter in 1955. Of course, Jenkins had more than an inkling of this—he had sold at least fourteen of these documents before 1986—but he asserted that even after the Sesquicentennial it never occurred to him to question them.

In the March 1988 letter to the insurance investigator, he had offered a different version of events.[28] He said that in the past it had been impossible to make certain judgments about these broadsides; that various dealers often disagreed about the authenticity of a piece; that fifteen or twenty years ago some broadsides were released under doubtful circumstances; and that everyone had debated for years regarding the genuineness of these and other earlier facsimiles. He said that he had more knowledge in the field of the Texas Revolution than anyone else, yet he had never felt secure about the absolute genuineness of broadsides of the period. Nevertheless, the prudent procedure seemed to be to continue selling the documents in the absence of absolute authentication, always with an unconditional right of return. Indeed, Jenkins continued, any piece that could be authenticated beyond doubt would bring a much higher price than what he asked for them, just as any document that could be proved a forgery would be worthless. He cited the Declaration of Independence in the insurance claim: if it could be proved genuine, it would be worth twice what he was claiming; if it proved fake, it was worthless. He sought a fair compromise, thereby establishing an entirely new concept in the staid world of bibliography: the $20,000 semi-real document.

One additional remark made by Jenkins in his report to the ABAA is revealing. In a paragraph discussing (but not naming) Dorman David, Jenkins stated that he had not seen David for fifteen years, but that David had often talked to him of making a portfolio of facsimiles of rare Texas broadsides. This is an unintended confirmation of Dorman David's account, first published two months later, which might otherwise be dismissed as unreliable:

> I had considered offering a portfolio of facsimile printed Texana items to my customers and had printing plates made. There were about five of them. They included the Texas Declaration of Independence, the Declaration of Causes, and some others.
>
> I was still experimenting, but I didn't have a good finished product. I was buying blank paper from John Jenkins, and I was going to print some. He was aware of what I was doing, but so was anyone else who came into my store.[29]

If we accept that Jenkins had not seen David for fifteen years, then, by his own account, Jenkins knew from the very beginning—before 1973—that Dorman David might be making facsimiles of important Texas documents. Contrary to what he wrote to the ABAA in November 1988, there was considerable reason for Jenkins to doubt the authenticity of *any* Texas broadsides from the Revolution, a fact he acknowledged in his letter to the insurance investigator. By his own account, the following was true:

1. Jenkins knew as early as 1973 that Dorman David might be making a portfolio of facsimiles.
2. Jenkins knew that broadsides had been released under suspicious circumstances around the same time.
3. For years Jenkins had debated the authenticity of these documents with other dealers.
4. Jenkins was not confident to authenticate any of these documents.

In his report to the ABAA Jenkins fell back on what Calvin Trillin called his "abiding interest in quantity." He said that the Jenkins Company was, by far, the largest dealer in Texana, with a larger stock than all other dealers combined and sales amounting to 80 percent of all Texana sold during the past two decades. He referred to multiple copies of rare Texas broadsides overflowing from the huge Eberstadt stock, much of which he said was still in inventory. He concluded by saying that the sales of twenty forgeries during these twenty years was thus a trivial part of his sales of similar items of Texana.

Putting aside the bombast, the credibility of his statements hinges on the premise that the broadsides of the Texas Revolution can be lumped together with similar items of Texana. They cannot. In terms of both their rarity and their textual interest they hold a unique place in Texas history—which is why they are desirable, expensive, and worth forging. Jenkins said in his report that he sold thousands of Texas imprints of every kind, but the ambiguity of that phrase obscures the possibility that he sold very few imprints of a particular kind: genuine Texas broadsides from the Revolution. The same holds true for the huge Eberstadt stock (of which, in fact, little remained by 1988). While it may have overflowed with multiple copies of many things, Revolution-period broadsides were not among them: there were only single copies of a thimbleful. Finally, the equation of twenty pieces in twenty years with his entire sales for the period contains an obvious fallacy: while twenty pieces do represent a tiny fraction of *total* sales for the period, in any given month when one is in need of cash, $5,000 or $10,000 can be a useful sum of money. And as anyone who knew John Jenkins will testify, he was often in need of cash.

All of this said, it remains true that the Jenkins Company was then a large rare book firm, with an effective staff and substantial sales. If the Jenkins Company had handled single examples of twenty different broadsides scattered over a twenty-year period, the firm would not need to have been one of the largest in the world, as Jenkins often claimed, to have sold them without suspecting a problem. However, his sales of forged documents presents a somewhat different pattern: no copies of some, one copy of others, two copies of still others, but six forged copies of the Texas Declaration of Independence and at least seven forged copies of the Travis Victory or Death letter.

The first copy of the Texas Declaration of Independence that can be associated with John Jenkins is the one for which he provided a receipt to the *Maine Antique Digest* to prove that it was purchased from William Simpson. The purchase occurred in October 1971, and it is unclear to me whether this copy represents one that cannot now be located or is, in fact, one of the copies sold by Jenkins later in the 1970s. There is another untraced copy, which appeared as item 34 in Jenkins' catalogue 85, issued in late 1974 or early 1975. Again, there is no way of knowing whether this represents a distinct but now unlocated copy or is one of the identified copies.

The first copy of the Texas Declaration of Independence that can be traced from its present owner to Jenkins with some certainty is by coincidence the only genuine copy I know of that he sold. This is the genuine copy (see census, page 104, no. 4) that appears to have been in the Eberstadt Collection when it was purchased by Jenkins in 1975. It had been at Yale before that institution acquired Thomas Streeter's collection, and was probably exchanged as a duplicate to the Eberstadts subsequent to that time. It was purchased from the Eberstadt Collection shortly after it arrived in Texas by Ray Walton, who sold it to a private collector in Texas whose identity remains unknown to me. I have not been able to examine this copy, but Walton assures me that he has, and, on the basis of information that I provided him, he further assures me that it is genuine. However, when the University of Texas purchased the Eberstadt Collection from Jenkins later in 1975, there was *another* Texas Declaration of

Independence in it—a forgery. Jenkins closed out the decade by selling a copy to Ray Walton in late 1976 or early 1977, a copy to Fred White, Jr., in 1978, and another to Ray Walton in 1979. The next time that John Jenkins sold a copy of the Texas Declaration of Independence, it was to a Dallas collector in 1986. This was the copy that was sent to Dorothy Sloan as a possible consignment and that Bill Holman condemned as a forgery. It was returned to the collector, and a few weeks later, the collector allowed me to examine the document in Dallas. I took careful measurements of it and confirmed to him that its measurements did not conform to a genuine copy, and that, in my opinion, it was probably fake. The collector returned the document to Jenkins because of doubts as to its authenticity. This is the same copy that appeared in the Jenkins Company fire insurance claim in September 1987—this can be proved from the existence of a unique paper flaw, a stitch mark running across the document where a repair was made in the mold used to form the sheet of paper, present when I examined the document in the collector's office and when Jennifer Larson later examined the document for the insurance company. In defense of the price he claimed for the Declaration in the fire loss, Jenkins stated that he had sold it for the price listed in the claim ($20,000), and then later traded an equal amount of material to get it back from the purchaser. He did not mention the fact that he had to give the collector the material to make restitution because the collector believed the Declaration to be fake.

If Jenkins had wanted to know the reasons the document was returned as a forgery, it would have required no great effort. The collector could have (and may have) told him of his experience with Dorothy Sloan, Sloan could have told him about Bill Holman's observations, and Holman himself could have told Jenkins of the evidence that the Declaration of Independence was a forgery. If he was at all concerned about whether any of the copies he had sold were genuine, it would have required little effort for him to arrive at the certainty he claims was so elusive. He appears to have made no attempt to do so.

Jenkins' transactions involving copies of the Travis letter (Streeter 185) show a similar pattern. He sold one or two copies at dates I have not been able to determine, one in 1976, and then copies in 1983, 1984, 1985, 1986, and 1987. In his report to the ABAA, Jenkins lumped this broadside with other material, saying that he almost always had one or more Travis broadsides in stock, but that he also had multiple copies of many other rarities from the Eberstadt and his own inventory. He cited the presence of eight or ten copies of many Mexican imprints listed by Streeter as unique or near unique. Of course, Travis' letter is not a Mexican imprint, and it stands apart from virtually any other rarity—it is one of the most important documents in Texas history. It is striking that Jenkins unblinkingly claimed to have always had in stock at least one copy of a broadside that no one else had owned a single copy of for one hundred thirty years.

Jenkins also listed the Travis letter in his 1987 insurance claim. He did not claim the Hendershott/Perot copy that had been examined at Yale and returned as a forgery in January 1986; in his letter to the insurance examiner he stated that he took that one home for his own collection, believing it fully authentic. In the letter, Jenkins casually dismissed Don Etherington's and George Miles' conclusions, asserting that he personally knew, based on his unique expertise, that almost all the known copies of that broadside were variant one from another. He volunteered that paper was scarce in Texas and that Baker and Bordens would print on anything that was available, and that the quality of printing suffered from the adverse circumstances under which they were operating.

Jenkins was indeed uniquely qualified to know, by virtue of having handled hundreds of Texas broadsides in the process of compiling his *Papers of the Texas Revolution*, published in 1973, that this is untrue. Baker and Bordens did indeed have to print on anything that was available, but all that was available was a single stock of unwatermarked wove paper: every single Baker and Bordens imprint I have examined (at least eighty) was printed on this paper. Also, there is remarkably little variance in the quality of printing in Baker and Bordens' imprints. With the exception of the newspaper, all of the printing from their presses that I have examined is black, clear, and well executed.

In any case, the basis upon which Etherington and Miles—and later I—determined that the Travis broadsides are fake is quite simple, and has nothing to do with "variants" and paper stocks. Jenkins lamented in his letter to the insurance adjustor that there had not been dependable ways of judging the authenticity of these Texas Revolution broadsides, but in fact no high science or extraordinary expertise was needed to assess the Travis broadside. The evidence is simple and conclusive (see page 109) and was available to Jenkins by January 1986. Yet there is no indication that Jenkins attempted to determine the authenticity of any of the copies he had sold. Indeed, he maintained in his report to the ABAA that at the beginning of 1987—the end of the Sesquicentennial and a year after the Hendershott copy was returned—it did not occur to him to question the authenticity of the Travis broadside, or any other document.

Notes

1. Curtis, *Texas Monthly*, 184.
2. Ibid., 185.
3. Hewett, *Maine Antique Digest*, 30-A.
4. Lewis, "Rare Papers . . . ," *Houston Post*, A-10.
5. Curtis, *Texas Monthly*, 185.
6. Lewis, "Rare Papers . . . ," *Houston Post*, A-10.
7. Hewett, *Maine Antique Digest*, 30-A.
8. Ibid.
9. Ibid.
10. Ibid. However, I cannot correlate either of the documents noted on these receipts to any copy of the documents I have been able to locate: the only copies of Streeter 88 or 89 sold by Jenkins after 1973 that I can locate were Streeter's and were from the Eberstadt Collection. The earliest Declaration of Independence I can locate that was sold by Jenkins was in 1975 (two copies, one to Ray Walton and one to the University of Texas at Austin). This is rather a long time to make investors wait.
11. Ibid.
12. Trillin, *The New Yorker*, 91.
13. Author's telephone conversation with William Simpson, January 1989.
14. Hewett, *Maine Antique Digest*, 30-A.
15. The Eberstadt Collection, the fabled stock of the booksellers Edward Eberstadt and Sons, was purchased by Jenkins in 1974. Containing approximately 40,000 items, by most reliable accounts it was acquired for approximately $2.5 million.
16. Report from John Jenkins to the Board of Governors of the ABAA, November 2, 1988, p. [2]. Because this report might be construed as being protected by copyright, I have paraphrased its contents. A photocopy of the original is available at the DeGolyer Library, Southern Methodist University, Dallas, Texas.
17. I have checked the list of forgeries against a copy of Streeter that has each item that was in the Eberstadt's collection marked as such. These are the only three marked to indicate their presence in the Eberstadt Collection. Yet there were at least three forgeries in the "Eberstadt Texas Collection" when it was purchased by the University of Texas in 1975–Streeter 165 (Declaration of Independence), Streeter 1246 (New Orleans Recruiting Poster), and Streeter 150 (Army Orders). I believe the copy of Streeter 165 that was originally part of the collection was genuine copy no. 4 (see census, page 104, sold–along with a considerable amount of other important Texas material–to Ray Walton before officials of the University of Texas viewed the collection.
18. It has been suggested that there is also no documentary evidence–no "paper trail"

—for many of the transactions included in the census of documents in this book (see Part II). However, there is a fundamental difference: none of the parties to any of the transactions—including Jenkins, Simpson, and David—has disputed the accuracy of these entries, and all have been given the opportunity to do so. The only disagreement is over the ultimate source of a document when it involves Jenkins and Simpson.

19. Lewis, "Rare Papers . . . ," *Houston Post*, A-10.

20. Ibid.

21. Curtis, *Texas Monthly*, 107.

22. Belkin, *New York Times Magazine*, 76.

23. Jenkins' business was struck by fire three times: in 1969, when he was located in downtown Austin; on Christmas Eve 1985, when his entire plant burned; and again in September 1987. The last fire was ruled arson.

24. Trillin, *The New Yorker*, 82.

25. Lewis, "Inquiry Ongoing . . . ," *Houston Post*, A-10.

26. Jenkins had called me one morning out of the blue, beginning the conversation with "Tom, I've been a fool." He brought several documents for me to examine, showed me the letter to the insurance investigator, and was at some pains to thank me for finally clearing up the mystery surrounding the Texas Revolution broadsides. After this date Jenkins always had praise for what I was doing—a stark contrast to his attitude only days before the article appeared, when he was assuring a dealer who bought a Texas Declaration of Independence from him that I was an idiot who knew nothing about Texana and was only out to make trouble. In fairness, it should also be said that before and after the forgeries were publicly exposed Jenkins was always willing to refund the purchase price to anyone who returned a document because of doubts as to its authenticity.

27. Since the forgeries were first publicly exposed in April 1988, efforts had been made to get the Board of Governors of the ABAA to confront the issues raised by the sale of these forgeries by members of the association. There was a notable reluctance to do so. Dorothy Sloan tried to bring the matter to the Board's attention, but was rebuffed, and resigned in protest. Likewise, in September 1988, I wrote a letter to the chairman of the ABAA's ethics committee, with a copy to the president, outlining the problems and urging that the Board of Governors authorize the association's attorney to investigate the matter. This letter was never shown to the Board, and long afterward officers of the association were still retailing the pleasant fiction that no complaints had been received. I also resigned from the association. However, I have since come to the realization that the ABAA's conduct, however misguided, was typical of the response to be expected from any trade organization to allegations of wrongdoing on the part of members—especially members who are former presidents of the organization (Jenkins was president from 1980 to 1982). Also, it should be noted that the ABAA has since compiled a registry of questioned imprints that should be very helpful in preventing the unwitting sale of known forged documents in the future.

28. Letter from John Jenkins to William Buck, Maxson Young Associates, March 7, 1988. Because of copyright, the contents of this letter have been paraphrased. A photocopy of the original is available at the DeGolyer Library, Southern Methodist University, Dallas, Texas.

29. Hewett, *Maine Antique Digest*, 30-A.

Chapter Six

A Sad Legacy

The beginning of miseries for the world of historical Texana might well be marked by the appearance of Dorman David's catalogue 6, a tempting array of 130 items ranging from Revolution-period broadsides to famous books of the Civil War to Ike Whitley's "comically illustrated" *Rural Life in Texas*. Issued in 1964, the catalogue contained an engaging introduction by Houston writer George Fuermann, in which he states:

> Dorman David possesses, or is possessed by, a natural hedonism that is more commonly the fortune of emperors, film stars and other lesser gods. He is hard put to see why anyone would trouble to sell, or another to buy, a commonplace book or document when Thomas W. Streeter has shown the way to 1,661 treasures. It is that aspect of Mr. David's imagination that will, soon after this catalogue is mailed, create among collectors an agitation that will bear some resemblance to a snuttering of monkeys. This catalogue, this extravagant wish book, will create a dreadful yearning in the specialist.

A passionate desire to possess important historical material was nothing new—Thomas Streeter was certainly infected by it, as had been countless collectors before him. But theirs had been a largely quiet passion, and the end toward which the efforts aimed had a bent toward scholarship—Streeter's *Bibliography of Texas*, both monumental and meticulous, stands as example. What took hold in Texas with the arrival of Dorman David was something quite different—public, flamboyant, it was a frenzied acquisitiveness that fed on the almost visceral reaction of many Texas men to the genuinely stirring events of the state's past. David, and Jenkins and Simpson after him, offered collectors a chance to participate vicariously in this history by owning manuscripts and printed documents that were central to its creation. With the demand side of the economic equation so well primed, it should not be surprising that dishonest individuals attempted by theft and forgery to remedy the lack of supply.

What *is* surprising, and ultimately tragic, is that the very libraries that were being plundered by thieves and defrauded by forgers were so pitifully acquiescent in the destruction and pollution of the heritage it was their duty to protect. Ranging from deliberate concealment of theft, to looking the other way when gifts of dubious provenance or authenticity were received, to simple unwillingness to pursue matters that might prove difficult when problems were exposed, Texas libraries set an example of avoidance that has had, and will continue to have, destructive consequences both tangible and intangible. Discretion was not only the better part of valor—it replaced it altogether.

Dealers and collectors were only too willing to cooperate. In the case of both the thefts and the forgeries, there existed a powerful need not to know what had happened, to avoid asking where all the documents were coming from. Like rotten eggs that no one wants to break, they passed from dealer to collector, in careful hands, all the while touted as the golden eggs of our history. I am convinced that the Texas forgeries—some quite skillful, others equally amateurish—were able to circulate largely undetected for twenty years in part because of the pervasive need not to look closely at a document, because one did not want to face the possibility that it had been stolen. For instance, in the case of the printed broadside version of William Barrett Travis' Victory or Death letter from the Alamo, it is clear that the forged copies derive from a genuine original once in the State Library, but now missing. If it had been widely known that this broadside had been stolen from the State Library, it seems improbable, even given the lax standards of the time, that thirteen copies of the document could have changed hands, sometimes several times each, without someone checking a copy to see if it was stolen, and discovering instead that it was forged.

The dealers and collectors who were in one way or another involved in the marketing of stolen and forged documents did not and probably will not suffer adverse consequences as a result of these actions. In Texas we have an unfortunate habit of romanticizing our villains, and the names linked to this affair may well become part of a lore sanitized of greed and fraud. After all, the highwayman is always more interesting than his victims, especially victims so willing, scoundrels so charming.

Nor will the situation improve until the attitudes underlying these actions change. Many collectors of Texana, both avocational and professional (the distinction is often blurred), have been gripped by simple covetousness, the idea that the possession of a given document is more important than tedious notions of ethics, integrity, or even common sense. It is an attitude exemplified by a librarian who, when asked why he continued to do business with a bookseller whose honesty he doubted, replied that he would do business with the devil if he had materials students and scholars needed. The devil, of course, is always keen to do business, but has his price.

For me, there has been one overwhelmingly positive outcome of my involvement with this affair—a rediscovery of the richness of Texas history, and a fascination with the printing of the genuine broadsides of the Texas Revolution. Thus I have tried to give the reader a taste of something besides rotten eggs—something of the flavor of the period, of the adversity and adventure that is a true part of our history, however overworked it may sometimes seem. In the individual descriptions of the documents that follow, the story surrounding each text is told, in a way that I hope will tempt the reader toward something beyond curiosity about the machinations of thieves and forgers, to investigations into the enduring historical legacy that is deservedly cherished by Texans.

Part Two

The Forged Documents

A Note on the Description of Documents

On the following pages each of the Texas broadsides of which forged or fabricated copies exist is described in detail, along with the historical circumstances surrounding the original printing of the item (or, in the case of fabrications, the historical circumstances that would have surrounded the item if it were authentic). In some cases the material presented is new: the account of Pagés' activities in Texas explores events that have not been described before, and the account of the printing of the Travis letter clears up some recent confusion regarding its original production.

The census for each document has been compiled with great care, and copies have been sent to every person or firm involved for review and correction. Certain of these documents are in private collections, and I have not been able to examine them; both their nature as forgeries and their provenance are dependent on information given to me over the telephone. However, none of the entries in the census has been disputed. It should be noted that as far as I am aware, none of the dealers involved in selling the forged documents has been unwilling to make restitution to purchasers when it was demanded (in many cases, it was not). Moreover, there is no evidence whatever to suggest that most of the people involved in transactions with these documents had any knowledge of the nature of the documents in which they were dealing.

As a matter of courtesy the names of all private collectors and donors have been eliminated except in the instances where those collectors have publicly acknowledged ownership of one or more of the documents. Of course, many dealers are in some sense collectors, and many collectors deal in books to a certain extent as well. When a question arose as to whether a person was a dealer or a collector, I made a judgment based on the dominant aspect of that person's activities with books and manuscripts. The location listed for a document is where it was first discovered; many of the forgeries are now elsewhere, after being returned for restitution.

Despite the care taken in the compilation of this census, a few documents may have been double counted, and, in a few cases, documents may have been undercounted. It is sometimes impossible to know whether a document listed in a dealer's catalogue is the same document that appeared five years later in another location. Moreover, I strongly suspect that in the months following the exposure of these documents as forgeries, copies were returned about which I have no knowledge. And it would not surprise me if there are more copies in public and private collections yet to be discovered.

Austin's Notice to Colonists

(Streeter 11)

In September 1829, Godwin B. Cotten established a press in San Felipe from which he issued the most important newspaper in Texas before the Revolution, the *Texas Gazette*, nicknamed the "Cotton Plant." Noah Smithwick, the most engaging chronicler of life in early Texas, described Cotten as "a genial old bachelor of fifty or thereabouts, his aldermanic proportions making him a conspicuous figure. His signature, G. B. Cotten, prompted an inquiring individual to ask the significance of the initials. 'Why d__n it, can't you see? Great Big Cotten, of course. . . .' "[1] He was also the host of convivial parties for the local bachelors: "Collecting a jovial set of fellows, he served them up a sumptuous supper in his bachelor apartments at which every guest was expected to contribute to the general enjoyment according to his ability."[2]

Stephen F. Austin "never participated in any of these jamborees,"[3] but he did use Cotten's paper to publish translations of Mexican laws and decrees regarding the colony, and to serve as a voice for his policies. Indeed, the greater part of most issues was devoted to such matters.[4] Publication of the newspaper was temporarily suspended after the issue of November 7, 1829, to allow the press to print Austin's *Translation of the Laws, Orders, and Contracts on Colonization*, which has the distinction of being the first book printed in Texas. Although Cotten promised to restore publication of the *Gazette* by the first Saturday in December, printing the book apparently took longer than anticipated, and the newspaper did not resume publication until January 23, 1830. During the interruption Cotten also printed a variety of forms and notices for Austin related to the business of colonization, including twenty-five copies of the present broadside, which outlines the steps necessary for an immigrant to establish himself in Austin's colony. These were printed on November 20, and more were printed on December 1 at an additional cost to Austin of $4.[5]

Only one genuine copy of this document is known today, and it is located in the General Land Office in Austin. The three copies that have surfaced since 1970 are forgeries and derive from the General Land Office copy—letters and words damaged in the original have been obviously retouched on the forged copies.

It is clear that the forgeries were not reproduced *directly* from the Land Office copy, because the size of the type area in the forgeries is 14 percent larger than that of the genuine copy. Since the forger did not have access to the original, he apparently photographed the reproduction in Streeter (Part I, vol. 1, plate 4, facing page 16). Not knowing the correct amount to reduce this illustration (which is considerably enlarged, with measurements given for only the overall size of the document), he created a forgery with an obvious flaw. The same technique—copying from a reproduction in a book—produced the same defect in the forgeries of Sam Houston's Army Orders (Streeter 150) and the New Orleans Recruiting Poster (Streeter 1246). In each case, the document is known by only one genuine copy, so that unless a potential buyer had access to the original, and a reason to measure it, this error could remain undetected.

Census

Genuine copies:

1. Texas General Land Office, Austin.

Forgeries:

1. Private Collection, Houston. Acquired from William Simpson.
2. John Jenkins, Austin. Listed in fire claim, September 1987.
3. Private Collection, Houston. Purchased from Dorman David on April 10, 1973, according to a bill of sale signed by David.

Notes

1. Smithwick, *The Evolution of a State*, 61.
2. Ibid., 71.
3. Ibid., 72.
4. Cotten had purchased two lots for $45, and being unable to pay for them offered to print all of the official publications of the *ayuntamiento*, beginning in January 1830.

(Charles A. Bacarisse, "The Texas Gazette, 1829–1831," *Southwestern Historical Quarterly*, 56:240.)

5. "Austin in Account with G. B. Cotten," Barker, *Austin Papers*, 2:562–563.

Columbia Jockey Club

(Revised Streeter 64.1)

The Brazoria *Texas Republican* for April 11, 1835, contains an advertisement announcing a horse race to be held "over the Columbia Turf" by the Columbia Jockey Club on Monday, May 4. A subsequent ad in the issue of May 2 announced the entrance of several notable horses, including "John Chaffin's sorrel horse *Gambler*, P. R. Splane's brown horse *Rocket*, [and] D. Random's Kentucky bay horse *Pedlar*."

These were not casual races; early Texans were passionate about the Turf and wagered large sums on their horses. *Rocket* and *Gambler* engaged in a match race on October 1, 1835, for $1,000, which was presumably won by *Rocket*, since his owner was offering to race him against all comers for up to $10,000 in November.[1] It cost between $100 and $150 just to enter a horse in the Columbia Jockey Club's May race.

For little more than that ($375) Yale University acquired in 1975 a previously unrecorded broadside announcing the race, which was duly entered in the 1983 revised edition of Streeter's *Bibliography of Texas* as number 64.1. Unfortunately, the broadside is a complete fabrication. The text was taken verbatim from the April 11, 1835, ad in the *Texas Republican*. However, the illustration in the newspaper ad was different from the illustration used on this broadside, and I have not found any instance of the use of this cut by F. C. Gray, the printer of the *Texas Republican* and the only printer in Texas who could have printed the broadside. The first use of this cut that I was able to locate was in the *Texas National Register* (Washington-on-the-Brazos) for July 3, 1845. I also examined the type in fifteen different F. C. Gray imprints, in addition to the newspaper, and did not find a type matching that used in the broadside. The type turned out to be 12-point Linotype Century for the text and 12-point Linotype Century Bold for the headline, type designs that did not exist until 1896.[2]

Given the time required to check all this, it would be encouraging to think that the creator of this document had gone to at least as much trouble to discover his text and illustration in their original sources. However, his predilection for using reproductions of original sources in modern books (see also Streeter 11, 89, 150, 1246) suggests a more convenient source, which I only discovered much later—Malcolm D. McLean's *Fine Texas Horses: Their Pedigrees and Performance, 1835–1845* (Fort Worth: Texas Christian University Press, 1966). The ad from the *Texas Republican* is reproduced on page xvi, the illustration from the *Texas National Register* on page xix.

Census

Fabrications:

1. Yale University, Beinecke Library. Purchased from Glen Dawson, a Los Angeles dealer, in 1975. Mr. Dawson cannot recall from whom he acquired the item.
2. Baylor University, Texas Collection. Received as part of a gift of 167 items from Dallas dealer John N. Rowe on December 21, 1987.
3. Gary Hendershott. Hendershott is a dealer in Little Rock, Arkansas; he listed and illustrated a copy of this document as item 21 in an undated catalogue (c. 1986). He says he acquired it from a private collector who got it from "a dealer in Texas."

Notes

1. Hogan, *Texas Republic*, 130. If *Gambler* did lose the race, his owner Chaffin got at least a measure of revenge: in a later issue of the *Texas Republican* he posted notice that as deputy sheriff he was levying a lien against Splane for three Negroes, in satisfaction of an unpaid claim. Splane's fortunes apparently continued to deteriorate, as he withdrew his nomination for senator from Brazoria in August 1836, citing his "pecuniary situation" (*Telegraph and Texas Register*, August 30, 1836). Perhaps *Rocket* had lost a few expensive races in the interim.

2. Jaspert, Berry and Johnson, *Encyclopedia of Type Faces*, 40.

Declaration of Causes, Spanish

(Streeter 88)

Thomas Streeter describes the Declaration of Causes for taking up arms against Mexico as "one of the fundamental Texas documents, second only in importance to the Declaration of Independence of 1836."[1] Indeed, the chief question facing the delegates to the consultation in November 1835, was whether to declare independence in recognition of the fact that hostilities had already begun, or to declare adherence to the Mexican Federal Constitution of 1824 and fight for status as an independent state within

Mexico. This status was threatened by Santa Anna and a decree of the Mexican Congress, dated October 3rd, that reduced the Mexican states to mere departments with no legislative authority. Stephen F. Austin described the situation in an editorial in the *Telegraph and Texas Register* for December 3, 1835:

> The general consultation of Texas was elected at a time when the country was distracted by popular excitements, produced by the diversity of opinions which naturally resulted from the disbelief of some that the federal system would be destroyed, or was even attacked, the excited and intemperate zeal of others, and the general want of certain information in all. It could not be reasonably expected that a body elected under such circumstances, would be entirely free from the conflicting opinions that prevailed amongst their constituents, or that a clear and positively definite position would be taken by it. The majority of Texas, so far as an opinion can be formed, from the acts of the people at their primary meetings, was decidedly in favor of declaring in positive, clear and unequivocal terms, for the federal constitution of 1824, and for the organization of local government, either as a state of the Mexican confederation, or provisionally, until the authorities of the state of Coahuila and Texas could be restored. This measure was absolutely necessary to save the country from anarchy; for it was left without any government at all, owing to the dispersion and imprisonment of the executive and legislative authorities, by the unconstitutional intervention of the military power [i.e., Santa Anna]. Some individuals were also in favor of independence, though no public meeting whose proceedings I have seen, expressed such an idea.

Austin's last statement is not quite accurate; a vote was taken on the issue of independence at the consultation and was defeated: 15 for, 33 against. Eugene Barker described the text finally adopted as

> a strategic document, designed on the one hand to justify the war in the eyes of Texas and of an impartial world, and on the other to convince the Mexican Federalists that the Texans desired only to preserve from destruction the republican constitution of 1824. At the

same time it represents a compromise between the war party which desired an outright declaration of independence, and the conservatives, who believed that the time for that had not arrived.[2]

Austin was not sanguine about the effectiveness of this compromise. In the editorial of December 3rd he continued:

> We have seen the consequence of these conflicting opinions, in the declaration made by the consultation, on the 7th of last month. It is not entirely positive and definite in its character. Whether or not the crisis in which Texas is now placed, can be met and sufficiently provided for, by a position which admits of construction in its application, is a matter of opinion; as for myself, I believe it cannot.

In the end, Noah Smithwick may have best summarized the events: "Some were for independence; some for the constitution of 1824; and some for anything, just so it was a row."[3]

On November 8, 1835, two days after the Declaration of Causes was adopted, the consultation voted to ask Lorenzo de Zavala "to translate into Spanish the declaration for a provisional government . . . for distribution among our Mexican fellow citizens." Baker and Bordens printed one thousand copies each of the Spanish and the English editions.[4]

Streeter lists the Spanish edition first (in his alphabetically arranged bibliography *declaración* precedes *declaration*), but the English version was set and printed first. Among the names of municipalities in the Spanish edition, "Municipality of Bevil" remains in English, having been overlooked when the various place names were reset in Spanish and placed among the names of the signers. The prior printing of the English version is also indicated by Baker and Bordens' bill,[5] which charged $63 for printing one thousand copies of the English version but only $40 for the same number in Spanish—a difference accounted for by the fact that the names of the signers (almost half of the document) and the decorative border did not need to be reset for the Spanish version.

It is not surprising that the surviving copies of Spanish and English versions of the Declaration of Causes have often ended up as pairs. Streeter had a pair, now at Yale; the University of Texas at Austin had a pair (its copy of the Spanish version is missing). According to an inventory of the

Eberstadt's Texas Collection as it was acquired by John Jenkins, that collection also contained a pair, probably duplicates from the Yale collection (Streeter 88) and Streeter's collection (Streeter 89). There are also pairs at the University of Texas at San Antonio and in the Texas Collection at Baylor University. These last, however, share a problem: at the University of Texas at San Antonio the Spanish version is genuine, the English version is fake; at Baylor the English version is genuine, the Spanish version fake. The copies at the University of Texas at San Antonio were received with the collection of John Peace, who probably acquired them from either John Jenkins or Ray Walton.[6] The copies at Baylor were received as a gift, accompanied by a letter of appraisal from John Jenkins which states that the donor acquired the documents from Ray Walton in payment of a debt.

There is another connection between these pairs: the forgery of the Spanish edition at Baylor is simply a photocopy on old paper;[7] the original used to make the forgery is the copy now in the Peace Collection at the University of Texas at San Antonio. There are two ink marks on the penultimate line of text in that copy that obscure three letters. In the Baylor photocopy, one of these letters has been touched up, and an *i* has been re-dotted; the third has been left alone. Another small flaw in line 9 of the text has disappeared, and a flaw in the rule between the list of names has been modified. Apparently, a preliminary copy was made and those flaws that would look unnatural, and that could be repaired, were fixed. Then a copy of this retouched copy was made on the old paper. This hypothesis is further supported by the considerable loss of definition in the details of the ornaments surrounding the text, which can be accounted for by its being a second-generation photocopy. It's a rather poor forgery —but who looks a gift horse in the mouth?

Census

Genuine copies:

1. Yale University, Beinecke Library. Received with a collection from Henry R. Wagner, c. 1920.
2. Library of Congress. Purchased on January 6, 1904, from the dealer Francis Harper of New York, for $2.50. This may well be the same copy noted by Streeter (Part I, 1:90) as appearing in Francis Edwards' catalogue 265 in July 1905 for four shillings. While the library acquired the copy eighteen months before Edwards' listing, it is not uncommon for booksellers to catalogue items that have been sold, either

accidentally or by design. Beyond that, the Library of Congress copy has a pencilled price of four shillings in the upper left corner. I am inclined to believe they are the same copy—unless, of course, Edwards had more than one.

3. Texas State Library, Lamar Papers. Acquired by purchase in 1909.
4. University of Texas at Austin, Vandale Collection. Now missing.
5. University of Texas at San Antonio. Received as part of the gift of the John Peace Collection c. 1974. This document (along with the companion English version, Streeter 89) was purchased by Peace between July and December of 1973, according to a list prepared by Mr. Peace for gift appraisal purposes. From a letter from Peace to Ray Walton, of December 6, 1973, now in the files of the university, it can be reasonably inferred that this pair of documents was purchased from either Ray Walton or John Jenkins.

Forgeries:

1. Baylor University, Texas Collection. Received as a gift on December 30, 1977. The donor acquired the document from Ray Walton. Photocopy, made from copy no. 5 above.

Untraced copies:

1. Yale University, Beinecke Library. Released as a duplicate, probably to the Eberstadts, subsequent to the acquisition of the Streeter Collection in 1957. An inventory of Streeter Texas imprints in the Eberstadt's Texas Collection prior to its sale to John Jenkins in 1975 lists a copy of this item. It may have been this copy; it cannot presently be located.

Notes

1. Streeter, *Bibliography*, Part I, 1:88.
2. Barker, "The Texas Declaration of Causes," 185.
3. Smithwick, *The Evolution of a State*, 102.
4. Binkley, *Official Correspondence*, 1:112–113.
5. Ibid.
6. Peace was known to have bought most of his material from these two dealers, and there is evidence that this was the case with these two documents (see note to genuine copy no. 5 in census).
7. The paper is a laid paper watermarked "W. Laflin"; although the Laflin mill in Massachusetts was making paper at this time (see Gravell and Miller, *A Catalogue of American Watermarks*, 188), there is no evidence that Baker and Bordens used it. All of the Baker and Bordens imprints I have examined are on unwatermarked wove paper.

Declaration of Causes, English

(Streeter 89)

If the single located forgery of the Spanish version of the Declaration of Causes is notable for its casualness, the forgeries of the English version are remarkable for their audacity. As accurate reproductions, they are failures. But a forgery need not be good to be convincing. The forgery of this document at the University of Texas at San Antonio, for example, *looks* good: the paper is appropriately worn, torn, and aged; it has a roughened patina that is convincing to an unschooled eye. It gives the impression of being real, especially in the grand morocco slipcase made to house it and its Spanish companion.

A close look, however, reveals problems that are so obvious it is hard to believe anyone accepted the document as real. Virtually every word in the lower half of the document, which contains the names of fifty-seven men printed in capitals and small capitals, plus eleven place names and a date printed in italic, has been extensively retouched or even entirely re-created in facsimile of the original.

The original used to make the forgery—the top half of it, anyway—appears to be the copy now in the Jenkins Garrett Collection at the University of Texas at Arlington. An ink inscription on the reverse of that copy has bled through the paper, severely obscuring letters in fourteen lines vertically, and across approximately one-third of two lines horizontally. The forged document has altered letters in its text that correspond exactly to these defects in the original. But the bottom half of the original is intact and essentially perfect, and would have required little retouching, much less complete re-creation (and the maker of the forgery had to have an original of the bottom of the document before him, in order to copy it).

As we have seen, this forger did not mind making whimsical changes in his creations—the needless misspelling of *denies* in the Declaration of Independence, for example—but there had to have been more than whimsy involved in re-creating half of a document. This remained a puzzle until I made a visit to the Garrett Collection, where I was shown a halftone facsimile of the genuine document made by Waco dealer Bill Morrison before he sold it to Jenkins Garrett in the mid-1960s. There is no evidence that Dorman David owned the original document before Morrison; but there *is* evidence that David liked to use reproductions of genuine documents to make forgeries—he had done it in at least four other cases (Streeter 11, 64.1, 150, 1246). If he had used Morrison's facsimile, rather than the original, as his source, the negative would have been a second-generation image, which would have tended to blur the sharp edges of the small and rather delicate type. Unless the photograph were carefully prepared—and David was anything but careful—it is quite possible that enough detail could have been lost to require extensive retouching. (The most likely cause for this occurring on half of the document is that the original was not perfectly flat when photographed, putting a portion of it slightly out of focus.) Whatever the cause, a touch of whimsy does remain: in the forgery, the thin rule running between the two columns of names has been left out entirely.

Census

Genuine copies:

1. Yale University, Beinecke Library, Streeter Collection. This copy bears on the reverse an inscription, "Forwarded by R. R. Royall / To the Committee of / New Orleans." Royall was a delegate to the consultation when this document was adopted. Yale reproduced this copy as a Christmas keepsake in 1977.
2. University of Texas at Austin, Barker Texas History Center. Source unknown.
3. Baylor University, Texas Collection. Signed on the back, "G. W. Smith / District Bevil / Texas." Received as a gift on December 29, 1976; donor acquired it from Ray Walton (Walton's price is still faintly visible on the upper right corner). This was Thomas W. Streeter's copy, with his pencilled date on the upper left corner. Streeter apparently had another copy as well–see no. 1 above. (He also had more than one copy of the Declaration of Independence.) Either Streeter himself, or Yale after it acquired his collection (if Streeter left both copies in the collection), may have sold or traded this one to the Eberstadts–there was a copy in their collection, according to the previously mentioned inventory.
4. University of Texas at Arlington. Received as a gift from Jenkins Garrett. Garrett purchased it from Bill Morrison, a Texas dealer now deceased, in the early 1970s. This (or the halftone facsimile made from it) was the copy used to make the forgeries.

Forgeries:

1. University of Texas at San Antonio. Received as part of the gift of the John Peace Collection c. 1974.
2. Private Collection, Texas. Purchased from John Jenkins between March and October of 1987. Photocopy of another forgery.
3. Private Collection, Dallas. Purchased from and returned to John Jenkins sometime around July 1987.
4. Private Collection, Houston. Purchased from Dorman David on April 10, 1973, according to a bill of sale signed by David.

The Town of Houston

(Revised Streeter 112.1)

On August 30, 1836, a lengthy advertisement with the heading "The Town of Houston" appeared in the *Telegraph and Texas Register*. Signed by Augustus C. Allen and John K. Allen, land speculating brothers who had arrived in Texas from New York in 1832, the ad extolled the virtues of their fledgling town:

> The town of Houston is located at a point on the river which must ever command the trade of the largest and richest portion of Texas. . . . When the rich lands of this country shall be settled, a trade will flow to it, making it, beyond all doubt, the great interior commercial emporium of Texas. . . .
>
> The town of Houston must be the place where arms, amunitions [sic] and provisions for the government will be stored, because, situated in the very heart of the country, it combines security and the means of easy distribution, and a national armory will no doubt very soon be established at this point.
>
> There is no place in Texas more healthy, having an abundance of excellent spring water, and enjoying the sea breeze in all its freshness. . . .
>
> . . . It is handsome and beautifully elevated, salubrious and well watered, and now in the very heart or centre of population, and will be so for a length of time to come. . . .

Their selection of a name for the town was not accidental: Sam Houston was running for president of the republic, expected to win, and the brothers reasoned that, if elected, he might be inclined to agree with them that "nature appears to have designated this place for the future seat of Government." By January 1837, they were able to amend their advertisement by adding "The Seat of Government" below "The Town of Houston."[1]

As the seat of government, Houston was notable for its lack of governance. Francis Lubbock remembers it as a town known for "drinking, dissipation, gambling and fighting."[2] He gives a memorable account of one immigrant's first encounter with life on the frontier:

Charles Hedenberg, of the firm of Hedenberg & Vedder, commission merchants, had induced an uncle of his to come out from New Jersey with the view of establishing a carriage manufactory. Arriving very early in the morning, his trunks were taken to the business house of Hedenberg & Vedder. About 10 o'clock of that day Hedenberg suggested to his uncle that the Congress of the Republic was then in session, and that if he would go up to the capitol he might be entertained, and after a while they would go to the house. The Jersey man proceeded to the capitol after a short time, and while seated in the Senate chamber rapid firing took place in the hall of the building, which caused everyone to leave the chamber. Repairing to the hall to see what was going on, he (Hedenberg) witnessed the bearing off of Algernon Thompson, badly shot by one Brashear, both clerks in the Senate. He probably had never shot a pistol or seen the effects of a shot before, and immediately left the building, going down Main Street on the west side. After traveling very fast and walking several blocks, in passing the Round Tent Saloon a soldier who was shot by one Seevey nearly fell upon him. He at once with a double quick rushed across to the east side of the street, and just as he got over and directly in front of John Carlos' Saloon a party rushed out of the door, almost running against him, with his bowels protruding from an immense bowie knife wound inflicted by a discharged soldier. His steps were again quickened and he hastened to the store of his nephew nearby, out of breath, and gasped . . . "Charley, I have seen enough. I wish to return home immediately. I do not wish to see any more of Texas."[3]

Another town that hoped to boom, but never did, was Magnolia, founded in 1840 ten miles west of Palestine in East Texas.[4] Its proprietors hired A. W. Canfield, a printer in San Augustine, to produce a broadside headed "Town of Magnolia," proclaiming that "To the Emigrant, the Merchant, and the Agriculturist, it offers greater inducements than any other point above Galveston Bay." The bottom half of the broadside announces "A Public Sale of Lots in Magnolia," scheduled for the 1st of September 1840. A copy of this broadside was first discovered around 1955, just as Streeter was finishing his bibliography, and it is entered "from a privately owned copy."[5] Apparently a small batch of them was discovered, because there are now copies at Yale and the DeGolyer Library at Southern Methodist University.

Dorman David also had a copy. It appears on page 14 of the inventory of material seized by police in the raid of his premises in 1972.[6] And on page 47 of that inventory is a possibly related entry: "No. 4 Document (1) Clipping entitled 'The Town of Houston' dated Aug. 30, 1836." Could it have occurred to Dorman David, with the newspaper clipping for "The Town of Houston" in one hand, and the broadside for the "Town of Magnolia" in the other, that the enterprising Allen brothers really should have printed a broadside announcing their more famous town? It is an interesting speculation; but whatever the inspiration, there is no doubt that at some point such a broadside was made, and was duly entered in the revised edition of Streeter, also "from a copy privately owned."

In the process of checking for copies of every entry that was new in the revised Streeter, I encountered not one but two copies of this item in the University of Houston library. One was in a group of documents from the 1840s that had apparently once belonged to Washington County. They were received as a gift, through William Simpson, in 1985. The other was from an unknown source. The types in the broadside looked comfortably similar to Bodoni types used by the *Telegraph and Texas Register* and most other newspapers of the period. Similar, but not identical—a close inspection revealed that the types were in fact 18-point Linotype Bodoni Bold for the text, 18-point Linotype Bodoni Black for the headline, and 12-point Century for the Allens' signatures. Since the types are modern, the broadsides had to be modern as well, apparently inspired by an entrepreneurial spirit that the Allen brothers undoubtedly would have admired.

Census

Fabrications:

1. "Entered from a copy privately owned" reads the entry in the revised edition of Streeter. I have been unable to discover to whom this refers.
2. University of Houston (copy 1). Received as part of a gift in 1985; appraised by and acquired by donor from William Simpson.
3. University of Houston (copy 2). Source unknown; acquired before 1980.
4. Star of the Republic Museum, Washington-on-the-Brazos. Purchased from William Simpson on July 30, 1978.

5. Bob Medlar, a dealer and collector in San Antonio. Acquired from John N. Rowe, a Dallas dealer.

Notes

1. The capital was moved to Austin in 1839.
2. Lubbock, *Six Decades in Texas*, 54–55.
3. Ibid., 55.
4. At one time Magnolia had a population of eight hundred, but when the railroad went through Palestine, it declined rapidly and is now a ghost town. (Webb, *Handbook*, 2:129).
5. Streeter 1640. It is listed in the revised edition as 393.1.
6. "No. 34 Document (1) Broadside describing town of Magnolia and announcing an auction for lots Sept. 1, 1840 (Streeter no. 1640)."

Pagés Wanted Poster

(Revised Streeter 119.1)

A vexing question facing the government of Texas following the Battle of San Jacinto was what to do with its most illustrious prisoner of war, Antonio López de Santa Anna. He lived "amidst the insolent hisses of the Texans who loudly called for [his] death,"[1] some even suggesting that he be sent to Goliad and shot in the same spot where Fannin's troops were massacred. It is clear, however, that Santa Anna was determined to live. By a tortuous path of grandiloquent rhetoric, he relates in his *Manifesto* how he reached a simple, happy conclusion—"I did not believe the loss of my life was indispensible to the welfare of my country"[2]—and thus comforted, proceeded to sign whatever was necessary to secure his release.

He was aided in his efforts by a group of prominent Texans—most notably Sam Houston, Stephen F. Austin, and David G. Burnet, president of the new republic—who considered Santa Anna much more useful alive than dead. Having extracted the desired concessions from him by the Treaties of Velasco on May 14, 1836, these cooler heads were content to send the general on his way, confident that his return to Mexico would stir up enough internal strife to prevent any attempt to re-take Texas.

At four o'clock on June 1, 1836, Santa Anna was put on board the schooner *Invincible* at Velasco.[3] But before it could sail, Thomas J. Green arrived at the port with 130 volunteers from New Orleans, surly adventurers in need of action.[4] Green and his men succeeded in preventing

Santa Anna's departure, and it was only with some effort that the general and his retinue—consisting of Colonel Nuñez, Colonel Almonte, and Ramón Martinez Caro—were moved to nearby Quintana. Green has left left an amusing (if unreliable) account of Santa Anna during this little crisis:

> This great Napolean the second, in his debarkation from on board the *Invincible*, at one time threatening suicide by taking or pretending to take, large doses of opium; at other times sobbing, blubbering, and weeping, lest the people should devour or tear him piecemeal, when he landed, and when assured . . . 'that there was not a Texian on Velasco beach cowardly enough to assault him'; he became one of the happiest men in the world, no bridegroom ever rivalled the joy that this hero experienced. . . .[5]

After three days they returned to Velasco under the guard of Captain Patton,[6] where they were lodged "in the second story of a house whose first floor was a restaurant."[7] It was while they were in residence above the restaurant, relates Martínez Caro, who was Santa Anna's secretary, that "a certain Bartolomé Pagés, a young Spaniard who had a wine shop in the place, came and expressed a desire of speaking with His Excellency. This he succeeded in doing during one of the moments the guard was not watching. He explained his plan of going to New Orleans and, if he were given the necessary funds there, of arranging for our escape upon his return."[8]

Pagés must have appeared ready for intrigue. He was described as "of ordinary size, light make, black hair and eyes, light complexion, diffident in his manners, supposed to be under twenty-five years of age, has a peculiar blinking of the eyes when put in fear, is in the habit of wearing his coat with the collar thrown back. . . .[9] He spoke English badly.

His recollection of events differed from that of Martínez Caro. In a deposition given on August 23, 1836, to Judge B. C. Franklin in Columbia, he stated that:

> When on the point of opening a Grog-shop in Velasco, the place of imprisonment of General Santa Anna, and Suite, he went one day accompanied by Capn. Woods to visit the family of Deaf Smith. He

> was subsequently introduced by them to Santa Anna, and the latter in conjunction with Don Ramon Martinez Caro, his Secretary, pressed him to repeat his visits frequently, and made enquiries concerning his circumstances. Caro drawing him aside told him that he might improve his fortune by getting up a plot for Santa Anna's liberation by bringing out a Vessel & Cargo with that object, and then reveal the affair to the Texians, by which means they [Martínez Caro & Pagés] would obtain that property. . . .[10]

Martínez Caro agrees that Pagés had no real intent to liberate Santa Anna, but does not offer himself as a co-conspirator. He states that Pagés was secretly given letters from Santa Anna to the Mexican consul in New Orleans with which to obtain funds, but concludes that:

> When he asked for the above mentioned letters from General Santa Anna, Pagés had no other idea in mind save the acquisition of money by this means, his plan being to go to New Orleans, secure 5,000 *pesos*, buy a schooner and a small cargo and, without any plan for the liberation of the prisoners, return as he did to a country where no one could ask him to give an account, and to enjoy there the fruit of the lack of foresight and caution on the part of those who gave him the documents with which he acquired the capital he desired.[11]

Pagés' deposition before Judge Franklin is the sole authority for his activities while in New Orleans. He was to bring out a boat with two guns and armed men and a bottle drugged with opium to administer to Santa Anna's guards. Acquiring boat and drugs proved complicated:

> In consequence of this arrangement the deponent was handed two letters of credit and recommendations for the Lisardis Mercts of New Orleans and for the Mexican Consul there, Don Francisco Pisarro Martinez by which said Pagés was authorized to draw for what sums he might require. On the deponent's arrival at New Orleans he applied to said Consul for the funds, who referred him to the Lisardis & after a delay of 10 or 12 days he obtained from the latter Four thousand five Hundred dollars. . . .[12]

> Moreover the deponent declared that when he informed the Mexican Consul of the delay or repugnance, in the Lisardis, to let him have the money, & that he did not intend going any more to see them on the subject, the Consul told him not to give it up for that he would speak to those Gentlemen & communicate the importance of the affair. The deponent believes he did, for the Lisardis paid him the money altho' up to that time he is not aware they had any knowledge of the plot. When he mentioned to the Consul about making use of opium the latter said at first that he would purchase it, but afterwards said no for it might be discovered & he be exposed. Then the deponent undertook to buy it which he did by means of a person whose name he forgets, but thinks he is called Raffall. He does not know at what apothecarys the opium was bought.
>
> On receiving the funds from Lisardis he went with Don Gabriel Avelez, an . . . American Citizen residing in New Orleans (who is known innocent of the plot), & bought the schooner Passaic for Two thousand five hundred dollars. He had her put in the name of Avelez because he (the deponent) is not an American Citizen. The cargo cost Two thousand dollars. Neither the Captain, crew, nor Capt Sovereign (alias Portuguese Joe) had any participation in the plot. . . .[13]

The one surviving copy of Pagés' deposition breaks off here in mid-sentence, and for the remainder of the story we are chiefly dependent on Martínez Caro's account, which picks up on August 14th, more than a month after Pagés had departed for New Orleans. There were visitors at the Phelps' home, Orozimbo,[14] where Santa Anna had been moved, and the secretary declared, "Imagine our surprise upon seeing Pagés among our visitors! We took a seat, Colonel Almonte sitting down by the ladies, while I found a place next to Pagés."[15] Although forbidden to speak Spanish, Martínez Caro did manage to discover from Pagés what had supposedly happened: " 'I was unable to do anything because they took away the crew I had secured for the schooner which I bought for 5,000 *pesos* given to me in New Orleans. Furthermore, the distance at which you now are from the seashore would preclude any hope of an escape even if I had the means for the attempt.' "[16]

A sergeant overheard this conversation and "rudely dragged Pagés from his seat and began abusing him with a thousand epithets. . . ."[17] When informed of this conversation by Martínez Caro, Santa Anna had one concern: his five thousand *pesos*. When Captain Patton heard of it from the sergeant, he had other concerns, and closely questioned Martínez Caro and Pagés. Patton had apparently been warned from New Orleans that something was amiss on the schooner *Passaic*,[18] and when, during questioning, he discovered that Pagés was carrying a safe conduct pass from the Mexican consul in New Orleans, he decided to arrest Pagés and everyone else who had arrived on the schooner.[19]

The arrest of Pagés occasioned another contemporary account of this incident. In the journal of Ammon Underwood it is recounted that on August 17th:

> The officers and crew of Schooner Passaic which arrived here a few days since were this day arrested as prisoners of war. Documents were discovered against them bearing strong evidence that said schooner Passaic had been procured and dispatched by the Mexican consul and other friends of Santa Anna in New Orleans to effect the release of Santa Anna and his Suit. Don [Bartolomé Pagés] the principal of the expidition [sic] was arrested by Maj W H Patton, and Mr John Scags and myself were placed as guard over him, commanded to see that he moved not nor destroyed any papers. More of this anon.[20]

Underwood never wrote "more of this" in his journal, but from Martínez Caro's account we learn that:

> The following day [August 18] a judge [Benjamin C. Franklin] from Colombia [sic] came, and after three more days spent in taking declarations, making investigations, and inspecting all the papers of the ship's captain, exhausting every imaginable means for bringing out testimony to reveal the accomplices of Pagés, they were all set at liberty, except the latter who was detained as a prisoner because of the aforesaid safe conduct.[21]

A brief note in the *Telegraph and Texas Register* relates that Pagés' trial was scheduled for September 9 before Judge Franklin in Brazoria, but also that "the evening previous he contrived to make his escape."[22] Apparently Underwood and Scags had failed to see that he "moved not," and it was up to Sheriff R. J. Calder to apprehend the escaped prisoner.[23] A reward poster, the first ever issued in Texas, was set up at the *Telegraph* office, with "$200 Reward" at the top in large, bold wood type.[24] Pagés was back in custody by the 13th, and the *Telegraph* reported, "His case will soon be disposed of." Unfortunately there is no record of the disposition of the case, and no way of knowing whether Pagés really had intended to help Santa Anna escape or was simply cheating him. The only thing that can be said with certainty is that Pagés did not get to enjoy the fruits of his mischief—his schooner *Passaic*, bought with Santa Anna's much lamented five thousand *pesos*, was apparently confiscated and put into service as a supply ship by the Texas government.[25]

And Pagés himself was still being detained in December 1836 (by which time Santa Anna was a free man, on his way to Washington for an audience with Andrew Jackson), suffering from maltreatment that prompted him to write a pitiful letter to Sam Houston:

> Most Excellent Señor General and President of the Republic of Tejas.
> Most Excellent Sir:
>
> [I] Bartolomé Pagés [have been] a prisoner in this [town] of Velasco for a period of five months and [five?] days, suffering the greatest discomforts, particularly during this winter season because of the cold. I can barely sleep, as much for the chains on my feet as for the manacles which they put on my hands each night, such that they hinder me from even performing my bodily needs. To this I must add that the hut where I stay has such poor flooring that every night, with my hands manacled, the insects that thrive there deprive me of my only rest, which is sleep. As a result of all this which I have stated, I fell quite seriously ill, whereupon the doctor ordered that I be taken to the hospital, where I remained for a month. I had not recovered (or better said) I was dying, when a soldier grabbed me by the arm and dragged me to the hut with no more consideration than for a negro, or a dog. I did not expect such treatment from these gentlemen under whose custody I remain. And for what is stated above,

I beseech Your Excellency to please to order (through your kind heart for those in misfortune) that I be given some relief in my imprisonment, because I doubt that I shall survive long if I continue in this situation. I would be overjoyed were Your Excellency to see me in this condition, one which you could not witness without experiencing unprecedented emotion in your magnanimous breast and ordering that I be given different treatment from that which I now receive. Witnesses to this are several individuals who are here as well as at Brazoria, and even your distinguished brother was an eyewitness when he had the goodness to visit me while passing through this town, and made to feel the same sensation as would Your Excellency in the same situation.

God keep Your Excellency the many years hoped for you by this most humble supplicant, who wishes with all his heart to see you.

Velasco,

December 6, 1836.

Bartolomé Pagés

P.S. Coincidentally this very day, in the presence of the captain in command of this post, a soldier dared to strike me on the head with a hammer, just because he felt like it. Immediately, as one would expect, I made a protest (in my own manner and always omitting nothing) to said captain. So as to mock my protest, he personally tied me to a post and draped a blanket over my head. As much from shortness of breath as from weakness, I fell in a faint. Despite seeing me in this miserable and fallen state, he would not have let me go had not some privates and sergeants urged him to do so, perhaps out of pity.

It is very painful for me, after suffering such a long and dreadful imprisonment, to find myself in this situation, knowing nothing, not even when I am to be freed. But at least I know to whom I turn in my misfortune, and I do not know what heavenly foreboding tells me that this, my plea, will have in the hands and heart of the president and general of the Republic of Tejas—the Most Excellent Señor Samuel Houston—the results which it seeks.[26]

With this lamentation Pagés fades from the historical record—but it was not the last time his name was to be associated with larceny.

In early 1955, Morris Cook, an Austin book collector and sometime dealer, was in a bookshop in San Antonio—he cannot now recall which one—where he was shown a copy of the poster announcing the reward for the capture of Pagés. He promptly bought it, and showed it to Llerena Friend, librarian at the Barker Texas History Center. On May 24, 1955, Ms. Friend sent a photostat of the document to Thomas W. Streeter, who was in the final stages of preparing his bibliography.[27] Streeter made a careful transcription, returned the photostat, and, being the collector that he was, immediately contacted Cook himself: "If you have any wish to sell this little broadside I would appreciate your getting in touch with me about it. Seventy-five dollars would be about my limit on this."[28] By now Cook knew that his was the only known copy of this reward poster, and he politely declined Streeter's offer.[29]

Nine years later, in early 1964, Cook got a more satisfactory offer, this time from Dorman David, who had opened his establishment, The Bookman, in Houston the year before.[30] The recently acquired Pagés wanted poster appeared on the cover of his catalogue 9, with "DORMAN DAVID" stripped into the place occupied by Pagés' name on the original. This was to prove prophetic—David was charged with receiving stolen books in 1972 (another of his catalogues was entitled "Books from a Recent Robbery").

But in 1964 he was flying high, and one of his better customers was E. B. Taylor, an enthusiastic collector of Texana in Dickinson, Texas. Taylor apparently bought the Pagés poster from David, because it is prominently featured in a *Houston Post* article that appeared on August 2, 1964, describing Taylor's collection. There can be no question that this is the same copy illustrated by Dorman David on the cover of his catalogue, because an ink stain near the right end of the rule at the top of the document that appears on David's catalogue is clearly visible in the illustration in the newspaper article. However, when the University of Houston acquired the Taylor collection in December 1964,[31] the Pagés poster was not mentioned among its highlights in another *Houston Post* story,[32] and there is no copy of it at the University of Houston today. Taylor may have parted with the item between August and December, but it seems more likely that he retained it as a souvenir of his collection when he sold the bulk of it to the University of Houston. When the Pagés poster next appeared, it was owned by John Jenkins, who sold it before 1969 to Jenkins Garrett.

By 1977, unbeknownst to Garrett, his copy of the poster was no longer "the only known copy"—Yale University purchased a copy from Ray Walton in that year, although Walton cannot remember from whom he acquired it. Garrett, however, distinctly recalls when he learned of a second copy. He was at a William Simpson auction in 1984 or 1985, and Simpson was proudly holding aloft and touting "the only known copy" of the Pagés poster. Garrett, deciding that he really should buy *this* "only known copy" to go with *his* "only known copy," bid on and bought it for $200—$1,400 less than he had paid Jenkins for the first "only known copy." A bemused Garrett took his new prize home. When he examined it, he doubted its authenticity but figured the story alone was worth what he paid for it.

It certainly is a peculiar document. Stained and baked to a brittle-edged condition,[33] it is printed on obviously modern paper—Fabriano watercolor paper, to be precise. It also shares with the Yale copy—and another copy, received by Baylor as a gift from John N. Rowe in 1987—certain characteristics first noticed by comparing the Yale copy with the careful transcription made by Streeter in 1955. Where the transcription calls for a "thick-thin rule" (i.e., a double rule, one thick, one thin) between the headlines and the rest of the text, there is only a thick rule; and where the transcription calls for a "thin rule" above the imprint, there is no rule at all.[34] This is reminiscent of the forgery of the English Declaration of Causes (Streeter 89), in which the forger left out the rule between two columns of names. The Pagés poster also shares with several other forgeries a discrepancy between the measurements of the type area of the forged document and those of a genuine copy (even though in this case he had the genuine document to work from). The presumably genuine copy—the Morris Cook / Dorman David / E. B. Taylor / John Jenkins / Jenkins Garrett copy—measures 283 mm from the top of "$200" to the baseline of the imprint. The forgeries measure 271 mm. Finally, there is a rather amusing problem with the copy at Yale, which is not apparent unless one is looking for problems. The document, printed on pleasingly old paper, was folded in thirds, and along the two folds are symmetrical water stains that give a convincing aura of age to the item. However, upon reflection one realizes that it is impossible to stain the folds of a document folded in thirds without at the same time staining the ends of the document. The stains must have been artificially created—perhaps while the Fabriano paper was gently baking in the oven.

Census

Genuine copies:

1. University of Texas at Arlington. Received as a gift from Jenkins Garrett. Garrett purchased it from John Jenkins before 1969. Previously it had been owned by E. B. Taylor, who purchased it from Dorman David in 1964; David had purchased it from Morris Cook, who purchased it from a San Antonio bookstore in 1955.

Forgeries:

1. University of Texas at Arlington. Received as a gift from Jenkins Garrett. Garrett purchased it at a William Simpson auction in 1984 or 1985.
2. Yale University, Beinecke Library. Purchased from Ray Walton in 1977. Walton cannot remember from whom he acquired it.
3. Baylor University, Texas Collection. Received as part of a gift of 167 items from Dallas dealer John N. Rowe on December 21, 1987.
4. Private Collection, Dallas. Bought from and returned to the Jenkins Company c. 1986.

Notes

1. Santa Anna, "Manifesto," 5.

2. Ibid., 87.

3. Martínez Caro, "A True Account," 133.

4. Thomas Jefferson Green had first come to Texas in early 1836, but returned almost immediately to the United States to raise volunteers for the Revolution (Webb, *Handbook*, 1:728). David Burnet said of these late-arriving volunteers, "Their minds had been often and long inflamed by reports of the barbarous atrocities, practiced by our enemies, and their indignation against Santa Anna, partook of fanaticism" (*Telegraph and Texas Register*, September 20, 1836).

5. *Telegraph and Texas Register*, November 19, 1836.

6. William H. Patton immigrated to Brazoria County in 1828. He served in the Battle of Velasco in 1832 and the siege of Bexar in 1835, and was aide-de-camp to General Houston at the Battle of San Jacinto. He accompanied Santa Anna to Washington upon the general's release, then returned to Texas, where he resided until he was murdered in 1842 (Webb, *Handbook*, 2:346).

7. Martínez Caro, "A True Account," 134.

8. Ibid.

9. "$200 Reward . . ." broadside reward poster for apprehension of Bartolomé Pagés (Revised Streeter 119.1).

10. Bartolomé Pagés' Declaration in Regard to his Acquisition of the Schooner *Passaic*, August 23, 1836. *Papers of Mirabeau Buonaparte Lamar*, vol. 1, no. 440, 441. This passage

is not an exact transcription of Pagés' deposition; punctuation and grammar have been regularized for clarity's sake.

11. Martínez Caro, "A True Account," 142.

12. The Lisardis were Cuban commission merchants who occupied the buildings at 527–533 Royal Street, which now house the Historic New Orleans Collection. They purchased the building in 1832 and sold it in 1857.

13. Pagés' Declaration, 442. Transcription is modified; see note 10 above.

14. Orozimbo was one of the earliest plantations in Texas, established by James A. E. Phelps in 1822. Santa Anna was held there from July to December of 1836. In his *Journal of the Texian Expedition Against Mier* (page 287), Thomas J. Green described an incident that was to greatly benefit the Phelps family later: "When [Santa Anna] was confined a prisoner at Orozimbo, in Texas, the seat of Dr. Phelps, in 1836, and failed in his attempt to poison his guards, he was ironed by Captain Patton, the officer in charge of him. This threw such a gloom over his destiny, that in a fit of despondence he determined to drink the poison prepared for his guards. Dr. Phelps succeeded in pumping it from his stomach and restoring him, for which he generously released his son [Orlando Phelps], and furnished him means to return home." Orlando Phelps had been captured with Green during the ill-fated Mier Expedition into Mexico in 1842.

15. Martínez Caro, "A True Account," 136.

16. Ibid., 136–137.

17. Ibid., 137.

18. Ibid., 138.

19. Among those arrested were F. C. Gray, printer of the Brazoria *Texas Republican*, and his wife. According to A. C. Gray (no relation) in his "History of the Texas Press" contained in Wooten's *Comprehensive History of Texas, 1685–1897* (page 369), "Gray's wife was accused of intriguing to effect the escape of Santa Anna after the Battle of San Jacinto, and Gray himself fell under suspicion. His influence therefore was destroyed, and his paper died in consequence. He afterwards went to California. . . ."

20. *Southwestern Historical Quarterly*, vol. 32, no. 2, 146–147. Underwood arrived in Velasco in 1834, served in the Texas army, and lived in Columbia until his death in 1887 (Webb, *Handbook*, 2:817–818).

21. Martínez Caro, "A True Account," 140.

22. *Telegraph and Texas Register*, September 13, 1836.

23. Calder, who had come to Texas from Kentucky in 1832, was captain of K Company at the Battle of San Jacinto. He was appointed Marshal of Texas by President David G. Burnet in 1836 (Webb, *Handbook*, 1:267).

24. Revised Streeter 119.1.

25. Letter from F. A. Sawyer, "acting sec. of War and of the Navy," to "James D. Boylan, Commanding Schr. Passaic," September 3, 1836: "I do not wish the Passaic called the 'Sam'l. Houston,' she is too small—call her what you please" (Jenkins, *Papers*, 8:380, no. 4139).

26. A. J. Houston Papers, Texas State Library. Original in Spanish.

27. Typed note on transcription of Revised Streeter 119.1. Streeter Collection, Beinecke Library, Yale University.

28. Letter from Thomas W. Streeter to Morris G. Cook, May 26, 1955. Streeter Collection, Beinecke Library, Yale University.

29. Letter from Morris G. Cook to Thomas W. Streeter, June 3, 1955. Streeter Collec-

tion, Beinecke Library, Yale University.

30. For an account of Dorman David, see Curtis, *Texas Monthly*, 104.

31. Now known as the Bates Collection, after Colonel W. B. Bates, chairman of the board of Anderson, Clayton, & Co., which donated $34,000 to acquire the collection.

32. *Houston Post*, December 23, 1964.

33. "A former secretary and companion of one of David's best customers recalls going with her boss to see David in the mid-sixties. They found him baking paper in an oven. Without hesitating David volunteered that he was trying to make the paper look older" (Curtis, *Texas Monthly*, 181).

34. Both rules appear correctly on the copy illustrated on the cover of David's catalogue 9.

Important News

(Streeter 136)

John Sharp immigrated to Texas in 1835, and by December was involved in the hostilities with Mexico as a participant in the seige of Bexar in December of that year.[1] In this less well-known prelude to the Alamo, the Texans were victorious, defeating the numerically superior force of General Cós in a four-day house-to-house assault. Cós surrendered and, ceding all his army's property to the Texans, returned to Mexico. For a brief period—from December 1835 until March 1836—Texans were in control of Bexar.

In February, the Mexican army returned with a vengeance, this time under Santa Anna, and John Sharp became a first lieutenant in Robert J. Calder's K Company on the 24th of the following month.[2] On the 27th he was in Brazoria, "having just returned on express forty hours from camp." This, according to the handbill headed "Important News," written by Sharp in an attempt to reassure Texans that the army had matters well in hand despite the news from the Alamo. The text of the handbill is full of optimistic misinformation—most notably that "our army now encamped at and near Beason's on the Colorado, consists of from 1,000 to 1,200 men, and reinforcements hourly coming in, they are all well armed, with plenty of provisions, ammunition, &c, are in good spirits, and have perfect confidence in themselves and their officers."

In fact, Houston's force consisted of approximately eight hundred men, with more deserting or leaving on furlough for their family's sake than were arriving. They were ill-provisioned, in foul spirits, and two company commanders, Wiley Martin and Moseley Baker, were refusing to follow Houston's orders, having no confidence at all in his willingness to engage the Mexican army.[3]

Sharp continued: "Circumstances rendered it necessary that we should retreat from Gonzales, but our army now will never leave the Colorado, but to go westward, & every day will bring news of a fresh victory." What every day actually brought was news of grim retreats, eastward from the Colorado, and Brazoria itself was abandoned within two weeks of the printing of this handbill. It is the last recorded piece of printing done by F. C. Gray before his work was interrupted for two months by the war.

The only copy of this handbill recorded by Streeter is at the Barker Texas History Center at the University of Texas at Austin. There is a forgery of it at the Star of the Republic Museum at Washington-on-the-Brazos, received as a gift in 1975. It is an amateurish piece of work—there is extensive, crudely done retouching to the text. In fact, even the person preparing the inventory of material seized in the 1972 search of Dorman David's premises was not fooled: he recorded that, "Document (2) Appears to be printings of recent [date] on old paper, entitled 'Important News'." From this listing it is also clear that there was more than one copy of this forgery made, but another one has yet to surface.

Census

Genuine copies:

1. University of Texas at Austin, Barker Texas History Center, Austin Papers. Received as a gift in 1902.

Forgeries:

1. Star of the Republic Museum, Washington-on-the-Brazos. Received as a gift in 1975. Donor purchased the document from William Simpson.

Notes

1. Dixon and Kemp, *The Heroes of San Jacinto*, 284. In 1837 Sharp was a passenger on board the schooner *Julius Caesar* when it was captured by a Mexican squadron. He was in prison in Matamoros for a time and died at Velasco on August 17, 1840 (Webb, *Handbook*, 2:597).

2. This is the same Calder who later signed the Pagés wanted poster as sheriff (Revised Streeter 119.1).

3. Tolbert, *The Day of San Jacinto*, 50–52.

Army Orders

(Streeter 150)

Sam Houston arrived at the convention at Washington-on-the-Brazos on February 29, 1836. According to William Fairfax Gray, his arrival "created more sensation than that of any other man. He is evidently the people's man, and seems to take pains to ingratiate himself with everybody. He is much broken in appearance, but has still a fine person and courtly manners; will be forty-three years old on the 3rd of March—looks older. . . ."[1] Houston's birthday was actually March 2nd, the day Texas' Declaration of Independence was read and approved. But there were no fanfares, fireworks, or celebrations for either event, and Houston had good reason to look worn. His force was scattered and undisciplined and faced a much larger and better equipped Mexican army. This broadside was Houston's first order to his army, and the text gives a grim assessment of the situation. As he correctly noted, declaring independence was one thing, maintaining it quite another.

In a defense of his conduct as commander-in-chief, written in 1859, Houston described his feelings in more detail:

> When he assumed the command what was his situation? Had he aid and succor? He had conciliated the Indians by treaty whilst he was superseded by the unlawful edicts of the council. He had conciliated thirteen bands of Indians, and they remained amicable throughout the struggle of the revolution. Had they not been conciliated, but turned loose upon our people, the women and children would have perished in their flight arising from panic. After treaty with the Indians he attended the convention, and acted in the deliberations of that body, signing the declaration of independence, and was there elected. When he started to the army, the only hope of Texas remained then at Gonzales. Men, with martial spirit, with well-nerved arms and gallant hearts, had hastily rallied there as the last hope of Texas. The Alamo was known to be in siege. Fannin was known to be embarrassed. Ward, also, and Morris and Johnson, destroyed. All seemed to bespeak calamity of the most direful character. It was under those circumstances that the general started; and what was his escort? A general-in-chief, you would suppose, was at least sur-

> rounded by a staff of gallant men. It would be imagined that some prestige ought to be given to him. He was to produce a nation; he was to defend a people; he was to command the resources of the country, and he must give character to the army. He had, sir, two aides-de-camp, one captain, and a youth. This was his escort in marching to the headquarters of the army, as it was called.[2]

The *Telegraph and Texas Register* noted in its issue of March 12, 1836, "No general has ever had more to do. . . ." The editors concluded with the hope that "our citizens at home will not presume to give orders to our army in the field, or lay out plans for the commander-in-chief. Let us suppose that *he*, on the spot, knows better the plan of attack than those in the chimney corner."

I did not discover this forgery until November 1989, while examining a private collection in Houston. Since then three more copies have surfaced, the last one at the University of Texas at Austin. I had located the genuine copy there earlier and determined that the forgery must have been made from the reproduction of this copy in Walter Lord's *A Time to Stand*. Later, a chance perusal of an elaborate "prospectus" describing the Eberstadt Collection, published by the University of Texas Board of Regents in 1977, revealed another copy of this broadside, prominently illustrated in the section devoted to the "Texas Revolution." The caption accompanying the illustration disarmingly notes it as "a variant of the one described in Thomas B. [sic] Streeter's *Bibliography of Texas*" (the one there described being the genuine copy at the University of Texas).

There is yet another "variant" of this broadside. In the sale of the Robert E. Davis collection in 1967 (discussed in Chapter One), a copy was sold as lot 113 for $1,300. It is illustrated in the catalogue on the page opposite the description of the lot. Although it superficially resembles a genuine copy—the size and arrangement of typographic material is similar—a second look discloses that it is nothing more than a modern resetting: all of the typefaces are different, the rule below the heading is different, and the dateline is set in all caps rather than caps and small caps. As a final touch, an exclamation mark rather than a period terminates Houston's postscript. The copy in the Davis sale is the only forgery of this variety that I have encountered, and I do not know its present location (it was purchased at the sale by someone named Coronel).

Census

Genuine copies:

1. University of Texas at Austin, Barker Texas History Center, Austin Papers. Received as a gift in 1902.

Forgeries:

1. Private Collection, Houston. Purchased from Dorman David on October 22, 1971, according to an invoice signed by David.
2. Star of the Republic Museum, Washington-on-the-Brazos. Received as a gift on August 11, 1972, accompanied by an appraisal by William Simpson.
3. University of Texas at San Antonio. Received as part of the gift of the John Peace Collection c. 1974. Source unknown.
4. University of Texas at Austin. Purchased from John Jenkins as part of the Eberstadt Collection in 1975.

Forgery from modern type:

1. Robert E. Davis, Waco. Sold as lot 113 at the sale of his collection at Parke-Bernet Galleries in New York, November 21, 1967. Present location unknown.

Notes

1. Gray, *From Virginia to Texas*, 121.

2. *Speech of General Sam Houston, of Texas, Refuting Calumnies Produced and Circulated Against His Character as Commander-in-Chief of the Army of Texas; delivered in the Senate of the United States, February 28, 1859* (Washington: Printed at the Congressional Globe Office, 1859), 5.

Declaration of Independence

(Streeter 165)

The historical circumstances surrounding the original printing of the Texas Declaration of Independence, and the process involved in the discovery of the forgeries of that document, have been discussed already in Chapters One and Two. It is worth noting, however, that the various forged copies of this document exhibit variations in ink, paper, and technique of printing that suggest they were not all printed at the same time, or by the same method. I am not inclined to inquire too closely as to why these variations exist or how they were produced, since the effort required to answer such inquiries would be out of proportion to the value of the information acquired. In the end, it makes little difference. The chief lesson that can be learned from discussing the variations among the forged copies—how obvious and often careless they are—is that unless one has a reason to believe that a document is bogus, the assumption of its genuineness, and indeed the desire that it should be genuine, is sufficient to overcome many observable physical characteristics that would ordinarily lead to doubt.

For instance, every one of the forgeries, except the copy at the University of Texas at San Antonio, exhibits printing that is grey, mottled, and over-inked. The copy at San Antonio is printed clearly, evenly, and with an ink that is uniformly black. Close examination reveals minute splatterings of ink around many letters in the document, which do not appear on any other forged copy of the Declaration of Independence. I cannot at present account for the fact that that copy is so different from the others.

Another variation occurs in the registration of the headline material above the main text. On most of the copies, it is properly centered, with the ornament directly above the margin between columns two and three of the text. However, on a few copies the entire headline is shifted 5 mm to the left, indicating that two zinc blocks were probably used to create the forgery. It is unclear whether the two blocks were printed at the same time but out of registration, or the text and the headline were printed separately and out of registration.

The copy at the University of Houston arrived there in two pieces. The university retained a restorer to put the two pieces together again, but in the process the restorer did not notice or comment on what now seems obvious—the two pieces of paper are significantly different. They had never formed a single document. In similar fashion, the copy acquired by the Dallas Public Library was sent to the Lakeside Press Bindery for restoration. There the document was painstakingly examined, and where lines of text had been destroyed by folds they were carefully reconstructed using letterforms selected from other parts of the document to create a facsimile of the original text. Even after examining the document in such minute detail, the restorers never noticed or commented on the distorted letters and words that were eventually to reveal this copy and the others like it as forgeries. This is not to criticize either restorer; it is simply to point out that a flawed forgery may not attract skepticism if there is no basis for it aside from the physical evidence presented by the document.

Census

Genuine copies:

1. Alamo Museum, San Antonio. Received as a gift from Billy Lasater Fish in November 1979. On the reverse is the following: "W. H. Scheffelin Esq / N. York / From C. B. Stewart." In a different hand (Scheffelin's?): "Declaration of Independence of Texas–forwarded at the time by one of the signers. Rec'd April 11, 1836." Stewart was a delegate from Austin.
2. Paul Burns, Austin. Purchased from Dorman David by H. P. Kraus in October 1973; purchased by W. Thomas Taylor on behalf of Paul Burns in 1981. It was subsequently sold from the Dorothy Sloan catalogue of the Burns Collection to Steve Ivy in 1988. This was the copy used to produce the forgeries.
3. Private Collection, Texas. Purchased as lot 354 at the sale of the Streeter Collection at Parke-Bernet Galleries, October 26, 1966, by Kenneth Nebenzahl, a dealer in Chicago.
4. Private Collection, Texas. In the Streeter bibliography there is a damaged copy listed as being at Yale. When Streeter's own collection was purchased by Yale in 1957, it contained genuine copy number 12, and this copy was apparently exchanged as a duplicate, most likely to the Eberstadts, since this was the general practice of the library at the time. There is a letter from Lindley Eberstadt to Waco dealer Bill Morrison written in 1962 in which Eberstadt says he owns a "slightly damaged" copy. And according to the inventory of the Eberstadt Texas material before it arrived in Texas, a copy of this document was present. In March 1989 I received a call from Ray Walton, asking how to tell a genuine from a fake Declaration of Independence–the widow of a collector to whom he had sold the document was curious after reading about the forgeries in the March 1989 *Texas Monthly*. Walton has now examined that document and assures me that it is genuine, and was purchased by him from the Eberstadt stock shortly after it arrived in Austin. If this is true, this is probably the Yale duplicate. (It is noteworthy that the University of Texas at Austin did not get this Declaration of Independence–or other Texas documents of great importance, such as the Spanish and English Declaration of Causes, included in the Eberstadt's Texas Collection at the time of its purchase by John Jenkins–when they purchased the Eberstadt Collection from Jenkins in 1975 for $1.5 million.)
5. Southern Methodist University, DeGolyer Library. Purchased from Indianapolis dealer William Sutfin (son of Waco dealer Bill Morrison) in April 1984; has signature "G. M. Patrick / New Washington" on reverse. Patrick, a physician, came to Texas in 1827. The Texas army camped at his home after the Battle of San Jacinto, and David G. Burnet's cabinet met there as well. He died in Grimes County in 1889. This copy was once in Thomas Streeter's collection, one of three he owned at various times (see nos. 3 and 12). He exchanged it with Goodspeed's Bookshop for cataloguing services, and Goodspeed's subsequently sold it to the private collector who owned it when it was sold to the DeGolyer Library through Sutfin.
6. University of Texas at Austin, Texas Memorial Museum. This copy came to the University of Texas library as part of the gift of the Stephen F. Austin Papers in 1902. It has been on loan to the museum since the 1940s.

7. Texas State Library. From the papers of Mirabeau B. Lamar, first vice president of the Republic of Texas; acquired from his daughter in 1909.
8. University of Texas at Arlington. Received as a gift from Jenkins Garrett. Originally from the family of George Smyth, a signer of the Declaration, with a long note in his hand on the reverse describing events at the 1836 convention. Jenkins Garrett purchased it from Bill Morrison, who had acquired it from an estate in Nacogdoches.
9. University of Texas at Austin, Barker Texas History Center (copy 1). Part of the Vandale Collection; acquired by purchase in the 1940s.
10. University of Texas at Austin, Barker Texas History Center (copy 2). Incomplete; acquired as part of the Maury Maverick, Sr., Papers.
11. University of Texas at Austin, Barker Texas History Center (copy 3). Defective; source unknown.
12. Yale University, Beinecke Library. Purchased as part of the Streeter Collection in 1957. On the back is a letter from Asa Brigham, a delegate to the convention, dated March 9, 1836, addressed to his brother and sister at Marlborough, Massachusetts. This is the earliest provenance of any copy of the Declaration of Independence.

Forgeries:

1. William Clements, former governor of Texas. Purchased c. 1978 from Fred White, Jr., a Bryan, Texas, dealer, who acquired it from John Jenkins.
2. Dallas Public Library. Purchased from W. Thomas Taylor and presented to the library by a group of citizens in the summer of 1978; Taylor purchased the document in the summer of 1977 from Ray Walton, who acquired it from John Jenkins. Previous to this, a copy with a complicated history: In the early 1970s a copy of the Declaration of Independence was on loan to the Star of the Republic Museum from William Simpson, who claimed it belonged to a collector; in 1975 he retrieved the document, saying his client wanted it. Simpson appeared in 1976 with another copy (forgery no. 7), which he offered to the library for $5,000, plus a $15,000 tax deduction. The museum accepted this apparently generous offer. Meanwhile, what had become of the copy originally on loan to the museum? While on loan, it had been photographed by Time-Life Books and appears on page 117 of *The Texans*. It is obvious from flaws in the document that this copy is the same one illustrated as item 111 in W. Thomas Taylor's catalogue 21 (summer 1977) and subsequently purchased by the Dallas Public Library.
3. Private Collection, Houston. Purchased from Dorman David on October 22, 1971, according to an invoice signed by David. This copy bears the forged signature of William Motley, one of the original signers of the document, who was killed at the Battle of San Jacinto.
4. Private Collection, Dallas. Sold by John Jenkins to the collector in 1986; returned in July 1987 because of doubts as to its authenticity; damaged in second Jenkins Company fire in September 1987 and represented as genuine in insurance claim.
5. John N. Rowe, Dallas. Acquired from William Simpson in 1987.
6. San Jacinto Monument Museum, Houston. Purchased from W. Thomas Taylor in 1980; Taylor purchased it from Ray Walton a few months previous; Walton acquired it from John Jenkins c. 1979.

7. Star of the Republic Museum, Washington-on-the-Brazos. Purchased from William Simpson in 1976.
8. University of Houston. Received as a gift in 1984; donor acquired it from William Simpson.
9. University of Texas at San Antonio. Received as part of the gift of the John Peace Collection c. 1974. Purchased by Peace from Ray Walton between January 1972 and July 1973. Walton says he was acting as agent for a woman who claimed it had been in her family for generations, and provided a letter to Peace to that effect. The letter can no longer be located.
10. University of Texas, Barker Texas History Center. Purchased from John Jenkins as part of the Eberstadt Collection in 1975.

Untraced copies:

1. For an article appearing in the *Maine Antique Digest* in January 1989, John Jenkins provided a receipt for a copy of the Declaration of Independence purchased from William Simpson on October 21, 1971, for an investor group formed by Jenkins called India, Inc. However, the earliest copy of a forged Declaration of Independence sold by Jenkins that I can locate was sold to the University of Texas in 1975.
2. John Jenkins, Austin. In catalogue 85, "Rare Texana" (a single sheet printed on both sides), a copy of the Declaration of Independence is listed, with no further description, as item 137. This "catalogue" is undated, but was probably issued in late 1974 or early 1975.

Other copies:

1. Fred White, Jr., Bryan, Texas. In White's catalogue 38, item 565 is a copy described as the John Henry Brown copy. Although this is not a genuine copy, its origin is unrelated to the David forgeries. It is a replica–in similar, but not identical, type and style–done at the press at the State Fair in Dallas some years ago. White apparently mistook it for a genuine document (it was framed at the time) and sold it to the University of North Texas, which soon discovered the error and returned the document.

Travis' Victory or Death Letter

(Streeter 185)

On February 24, 1836, one day after the arrival of the Mexican vanguard in Bexar, William Barret Travis dispatched Albert Martin to San Felipe with this famous appeal, ordering him to travel "by Express night and day."[1] The text is brief and to the point:

Commandancy of the Alamo
Bejar, Fby 24th 1836—

To the People of Texas & all Americans *in the World*—

Fellow citizens & compatriots—

I am besieged, by a thousand or more of the Mexicans under Santa Anna—I have sustained a continual Bombardment & cannonade for 24 hours & have not lost a man—The enemy has demanded a surrender at discretion, otherwise, the garrison are to be put to the sword, if the fort is taken—I have answered the demand with a cannon shot, & our flag still waves proudly from the walls—*I shall never surrender or retreat. Then*, I call on you in the name of Liberty, of patriotism & every thing dear to the American character, to come to our aid, with all dispatch—The enemy is receiving reinforcements daily & will no doubt increase to three or four thousand in four or five days. If this call is neglected, I am determined to sustain myself as long as possible & die like a soldier who never forgets what is due to his own honor & that of his country—

Victory or Death
William Barret Travis
Lt. Col. comdt

With Mexican cannon thundering behind him, Martin rode to Gonzales, where the letter was given to another courier, Lancelot Smithers, for delivery to its final destination. Smithers rushed to San Felipe, and a meeting of citizens was held on the morning of February 27. The situation was grim. The broadside account of the meeting was not designed to promote calm:

> The undersigned a committee appointed by a meeting held in the town of San Felipe, on this day, present you with the accompanying letter from the comandant of Bejar. You must read and act in the same moment, or Texas is lost. You must rise from your lethargy, and march without a moment's delay to the field of war, or the next Western breeze that sweeps over your habitations, will bring with it the shrieks and wailings of the women and children of Guadaloupe and Colorado; and the last agonized shriek of liberty will follow.
>
> Citizens of the Colorado and Brazos, your country is invaded—your homes are about to be pillaged, your families destroyed, yourselves to be enslaved. . . .[2]

Travis' letter was printed for the first time at the end of this broadside; two hundred copies were printed.

Shortly thereafter, another printing of this broadside appeared (Streeter 132A), amended to include at the end "The Latest News," which was scarcely less alarming than Travis' appeal:

> The whole Mexican army, amounting to not less than eight thousand men, are on our frontier. The inhabitants of Power's and McMullen's colonies have abandoned their homes, and are flocking into the colonies, giving up their stocks of all sorts. In ten days, the people of the Colorado and Brazos will share the same fate, unless all turn out, to conquer or die.

As was usual, the type from this broadside was kept standing, and its entire contents were reprinted in the *Telegraph and Texas Register* for March 5, 1836.

At roughly the same time that the Travis letter first appeared at the end of the broadside account of the town meeting, a separate printing of the letter was also prepared. To save labor, it was set up to be printed on the right-hand side of a sheet on which was also imposed a proclamation by Governor Henry Smith, headed "Texas Expects Every Man to do His Duty." Three hundred copies were ordered printed, and the two texts, printed side by side, were to be cut apart. Corroboration of this can be found in Baker and Bordens' bill to the government for July 1836, which does not list a separate printing for either item, noting only the joint printing of three hundred copies.[3]

By an accident of history, there is no copy known of either Travis' letter or Governor Smith's proclamation in the form that was ultimately intended.[4] The only genuine copy of this printing of Travis' letter that can be located—originally in the Lamar Papers at the Texas State Library, exchanged to Thomas W. Streeter in December 1953, and now in his collection at Yale—is still side by side with the Governor Smith proclamation (Streeter 145) on a single sheet. It is clear that there was at one time another paired set of Streeter 145 and Streeter 185 in the Public Printing Papers at the State Library. Streeter's description of no. 145 is unambiguous on the point:

> This proclamation is undated, but it appears from my copy *and the copy in the "Public Printing" files at the Texas State Library* [italics mine] that it was printed at the left of a single sheet measuring 25.2 x 39 cm. . . .[5]

The copies of the documents in the Public Printing Papers had originally been used by the printers as vouchers, with notations on the back recording the number of copies printed and the amount billed. Thus it would be logical for Baker and Bordens to have presented an undivided copy to the government for this purpose. There is evidence that this was indeed the case. E. W. Winkler made photostats of many documents in the State Library, which are now preserved at the Barker Texas History Center. The photostat of Streeter 145/185 was made from the Lamar copy, but on an accompanying sheet Winkler has written: "Another copy in Tx State Library Public Printing 15 1/16 x 9 7/8 'E / Proclamation / of Henry Smith / with Travis Letter / 300 copies — / $30.00 / Febr. 28th 1836.'" The text within single quotes is a transcription of the printer's notation—the "E" corresponds to the entry for the July 1836 bill presented to the government by Baker and Bordens—and the measurements can only refer to a sheet on which both Governor Smith's proclamation and the Travis letter were printed.

The existence of this copy in the Public Printing Papers explains why the State Library exchanged the (duplicate) Lamar copy of these documents to Thomas Streeter in 1953. Every other located copy of the printed Travis letter—a total of twelve—is fake. There is only one known copy that could have been used to make the forgeries—the missing State Library copy from the Public Printing Papers. One wonders if it is still attached to Governor Smith's proclamation, and what has become of it.

CENSUS

Genuine copies:

1. Texas State Library, Public Printing Papers. Now missing.
2. Yale University, Beinecke Library, Streeter Collection. According to a note on the document in Streeter's hand, this copy was acquired by exchange from the Texas State Library in December 1953 (from the Lamar Papers, which the state had purchased in 1909).

Forgeries:

1. Private Collection, Texas. Acquired from John Jenkins.
2. Dallas Public Library. Purchased from W. Thomas Taylor in 1974; he purchased it from Ray Walton; Walton cannot remember from whom he acquired it.
3. Private Collection, Texas. Purchased from John Jenkins on August 14, 1984.
4. Private Collection, Texas. Acquired from Dorman David in the early 1970s.
5. Private Collection, Texas. Purchased from John Jenkins in late 1985. Returned to Jenkins because of doubts as to its authenticity.
6. John Jenkins. Sold to Gary Hendershott, a dealer in Little Rock, Arkansas, who offered the document to H. Ross Perot, who returned it after confirming that it was fake, in January 1986.
7. John Jenkins. Damaged and listed in fire claim September 1987. May be identical to copy 5; it is *not* the same as copy 6, because in his letter to the insurance adjustor he mentioned that he had copy 6 at home, in his "private collection."
8. Private Collection, Texas. Ray Walton states that he sold this copy to the same collector to whom he sold the duplicate Yale copy of the Declaration of Independence, but he cannot remember from whom he acquired it.
9. San Jacinto Monument Museum, Houston. Received as a gift; the donor acquired the document from William Simpson.
10. University of Texas at Austin, Barker Texas History Center. Purchased by the University of Texas from John Jenkins in 1976.
11. University of Texas at San Antonio. Received as part of the gift of the John Peace Collection c. 1974. Purchased for John Peace, then Chairman of the University of Texas Board of Regents, by Ray Walton at Parke-Bernet Galleries (now Sotheby's) in New York, sale of October 30, 1973, lot 67. Sotheby's will not release the name of the consignor.
12. Private Collection. California. Purchased in 1983 from John N. Rowe, who acquired it from John Jenkins.

Untraced copy:

1. William Simpson Galleries, Houston. In a catalogue dated August 10, 1980, a copy was offered as lot 856. It is described as being from the Beauregard Bryan Collec-

tion and marked (not signed) "M. Austin Bryan" on the reverse. Beauregard Bryan (1862–1918) was Moses Austin Bryan's son. If this provenance is genuine, so is the document–but this cannot be taken for granted–see forged copy no. 3 of the Declaration of Independence.

Notes

1. Green, "To the People of Texas," 483–508.
2. "Meeting of the Citizens of San Felipe," Streeter 132 and 132A.
3. "Provisional Government of Texas to Baker and Bordens," July 6, 1836. Ms., Secretary of State Papers, 2–9/41 no. 5, Texas State Archive, Austin.
4. E. W. Winkler, in a note accompanying the photostat of the copy that was in the Lamar Papers, notes a copy of Governor Smith's proclamation (Streeter 145) in a private collection; however, it cannot presently be located.
5. Streeter, *Bibliography*, Part I, 1:145.

Austin's Grant Application

(Streeter 1082)

This permit was the first piece of printing associated with Stephen F. Austin's colonization effort in Texas. It was printed in New Orleans in the fall of 1821, after Austin's return from his survey of Texas in the summer of that year. There were several regulations listed, basically requiring that each settler be of good character (written recommendations were advisable), swear allegiance to the Mexican government, pay Austin 12.5 cents per acre for his services, and furnish a list of his family. One prospective settler, in writing to a friend for a recommendation to Austin, discovered a particular asset in his family: "I shall expect to bring in family as follows—a wife and child (by the by—I did not tell you what a fine daughter I have—yes one that shall make many a heart tremble in the Province). . . ."[1] Given the acute shortage of single women in the colony, he was undoubtedly correct.

On November 23, 1835, Austin sent James Bryan, his brother-in-law in Missouri, a copy of the form for his use, and prepared to return to Texas. In the letter to Bryan accompanying the form he bade farewell to his family:

> I leave here the day after tomorrow, and the vessel sails the same day —it will probably be one year before I return to the U[nited] States,

> in the mean time take care of our Dear Mother, and make no calculations on me, or Texas until I get better underway in that country—send on as many settlers of good character as you can—I have no doubt of success and think all who join me will do well, but I advice [sic] no one to come, no man shall reproach me for leading him into difficulty should things result badly—[2]

Streeter describes this as "a choice bit of Texana," and with only two located copies in 1955 (Streeter's own, and one at the University of Texas at Austin), a rare one as well. Thus it came as some surprise to find not one, not two, but three copies of this document at the University of Houston, all received as gifts since 1977. One copy had on its reverse Dorman David's glyph-like cost code. Comparing this copy with the other two, the familiar pattern emerged: where words or letters in the copy bearing David's code were damaged or obscured, the other two copies showed evidence of retouching before printing. Here, in one place, were the genuine original and two forgeries made from it.

The easiest way to determine if a copy of this document is a David forgery is to look at the word *slave* at the end of a line in the main text. After it is a semi-colon, which in the forged copies looks more like an equal sign. However, this is overall a convincing forgery, and were it not for the convenient accumulation of copies at the University of Houston, it might well have gone undiscovered.

Census

Genuine copies:

1. University of Houston. Received as a gift in 1982; appraised for donor by William Simpson. At one time owned by Dorman David (his cost code is on the reverse). This is the copy used to make the forgeries.
2. University of Texas at Austin, Barker Texas History Center. Source unknown.
3. University of Texas at Austin, Barker Texas History Center (another copy). Source unknown.
4. Yale University, Beinecke Library, Streeter Collection.

Forgeries:

1. Private Collection, Houston. Acquired from John Jenkins.
2. Private Collection, Texas. Purchased from John Jenkins between March and October 1987.
3. Private Collection, Dallas. Acquired from John N. Rowe, who acquired it from, and returned it to, John Jenkins. (Jenkins claimed a copy of this document as a total loss in his September 1987 fire claim.)

4. Ben Pingenot, Brackettville, Texas. Purchased at the 1981 Texas State Historical Association auction; it had been donated by a Houston collector, who acquired it from William Simpson.
5. University of Houston (copy 1). Received as part of a gift in 1985; appraised by and probably acquired from William Simpson.
6. University of Houston (copy 2). Received as a gift in 1977. Source unknown; donor is now deceased.
7. University of Texas at Arlington, Garrett Library. Received as a gift from Jenkins Garrett. Garrett apparently purchased it from John Jenkins on an unknown date. There is a price, cost code, and reference to this Streeter number in Jenkins' hand on a note Garrett kept with the document.

Notes

1. James Fort Muse to William W. Little, December 1, 1821, *Austin Papers*, 1:439.
2. Stephen F. Austin to James Bryan, *Austin Papers*, 1:434–435.

New Orleans Recruiting Poster

(Streeter 1246)

The city of New Orleans was the fundamental source of support for the Texas Revolution in terms of men, money, and morale. During the entire course of the hostilities, meetings were held there, money raised, editorials written, and men recruited for the struggles. Broadsides, much more dramatic typographically than those printed in Texas, appeared regularly, with bold headings such as "To the Brave and Generous!" "To the Friends of Liberty Throughout the World!" "Texas, Official!!" "Texas Forever!!" "To the Friends of Civil Liberty!" These broadsides must have put a strain on the printers' fonts of exclamation marks.

A broadside headed simply "Texas!!" appeared on April 23, 1836, two days after the Battle of San Jacinto had been fought and won. The news of the victory had not yet arrived in New Orleans, and when it did arrive, hotheads like Thomas Jefferson Green were still eagerly seeking volunteers. While Sam Houston sent word to "tell them to come on and let the people plant corn," Green wanted to "complete our glorious success" by pursuing the Mexican army south of the Rio Grande.[1]

Thus the lure of adventure—and the "fortune in land" promised to the soldier emigrants on this broadside—continued to swell the ranks of the Texas army while the original "Army of San Jacinto" (which consisted primarily of old settlers) had largely disbanded as the men returned to their homes. These latter-day adventurers were a thorn in the side of Sam

Houston until May 18, 1837, when he furloughed the entire army save six hundred men.[2]

In April 1988, I was asked to examine this document by a dealer who was concerned about its authenticity. I took it to the Barker Texas History Center at the University of Texas, which had the only copy recorded by Streeter. It was immediately obvious that the dealer's copy was fake, since the type area was considerably smaller than that of the genuine copy. (The length of the ornament of the genuine copy is 250 mm; of the forgery, 186 mm.) There was a second copy at the Barker Center, acquired as a part of the Eberstadt Collection in 1975. It, too, is fake, and there is evidence to suggest that it was not in the Eberstadt Collection when the trucks arrived in Austin from New Jersey.[3]

As was the case before (Streeter 11, 150), without an original at hand the forger could only guess at the correct size to make the forgery. His source for this item was undoubtedly Walter Lord's book on the Alamo, *A Time to Stand*. The New Orleans broadside is reproduced there, credited to the University of Texas Library.

Census

Genuine copies:

1. University of Texas at Austin, Barker Texas History Center. Source unknown.

Forgeries:

1. Private Collection, Texas. Purchased from John Jenkins, September 1985.
2. John N. Rowe, Dallas. Acquired from William Simpson.
3. University of Texas at Austin, Barker Texas History Center. Purchased from John Jenkins in 1975 as part of the Eberstadt Collection.
4. Star of the Republic Museum, Washington-on-the-Brazos. Received as a gift in 1975. Donor apparently acquired the document from William Simpson.

Notes

1. Streeter 1238 (*Bibliography*, Part III, 1:225).
2. James, *The Raven*, 285.
3. According to an inventory of Eberstadt holdings of Streeter Texas imprints, there was no copy of this document present.

A Public Meeting

(Not in Streeter)

Captain Joseph Taylor was a prominent early citizen of Galveston, noted for his hospitality. His house, erected on the south side of Market Street, was described as "a house of public entertainment."[1] His ship, the brig *Elbe*, provided accommodations of another kind: in the absence of a jail, a portion of the hull was set aside to house local prisoners.[2] One can only imagine what it was like to be incarcerated in the hull of a small ship in Galveston Bay in the middle of August.

At his more congenial quarters, in a more pleasant season, Taylor hosted "a large and respectable meeting of the citizens of Galveston" for the purpose of raising money to erect a church—none existed in Galveston at the time. The meeting, held on Sunday, April 8, 1838, was "regarded as a full-dress occasion, as the Colonel [Yard] states that he felt it obligatory to wear a white shirt, and that it was the first time since his debarkation that he had indulged in this appurtenance of civilization."[3] It began with a worship service, followed by election of officers, then the formulation of an unusual approach to building a church. Money would be raised, the building erected, and it would then be available for use by any "preacher in regular standing."[4] However, the building was also to be for sale, the object being to find a denomination to acquire it. The subscribers to the building fund were then to be reimbursed for their contributions.[5] Details of the meeting, including all of the resolutions, appeared in the Houston (formerly San Felipe) *Telegraph and Texas Register* for April 18, 1838.

On page 14 of the police inventory of Dorman David's stock seized in the 1972 raid is the following entry: "No. 28 Newspaper (1) Telegraph, Houston (April 18, 1838, Vol. III, No. 19)." In 1986, fourteen years after the raid, the Harris County Heritage Society acquired from William Simpson a collection of 1,750 items relating to the history of Galveston. On page 47 of the inventory of *that* collection is the following entry:

> Galveston's First Church is
> Organized in a rare broadside
> Located in only the present copy

Actually, the church was organized in Captain Taylor's house; but there is a problem with this description aside from syntax. The broadside is a fake—a crude fake, made by stripping up the original article from the newspaper into two columns instead of one, moving the date line from the beginning to the end, and photocopying the result onto pleasantly old-looking paper.

I first saw this document after the Heritage Society retained Dorothy Sloan to inspect and appraise the collection. It is still unclear whether the society's concern was foremost to discover if the collection contained stolen and forged documents, or to simply use this as a pretext for returning a collection they could not pay for in any case.[6] According to Simpson, "What we arranged was a fair and equitable way of getting the Heritage (Society) out of debt and for me to get my collection back."[7] He denied that any of the collection was fake—although this broadside obviously is—and also denied that two documents from the Samuel May Williams Collection at the Rosenberg Library in Galveston were stolen. He claimed they were copies, and told the library, "In time, you're going to find your originals, and when you do, I want my copies back."[8] But he did take the collection back, and the society got back some of its money. Whether there were more stolen documents in the collection remains a question; nevertheless, Simpson had no trouble selling the collection again within a year.

Census

Fabrications:

1. Private Collection, Houston. Acquired from William Simpson in 1989.

Notes

1. Hayes, *Galveston*, 310.
2. Ibid., 336.
3. Ibid., 310.
4. Ibid.
5. Ibid. This church building was purchased by the Presbyterians, who used it until 1877, when it was moved and put into use by the Methodist Episcopal Church, a black congregation.
6. Tutt, "Dealer Repurchases Rare Texas Documents," *Houston Chronicle*, A-29.
7. Ibid.
8. Ibid.

ILLUSTRATIONS

Please note that the quality of several illustrations suffers from being made from a slide, xerox, or other inadequate source, originals not being available at the time of publication.

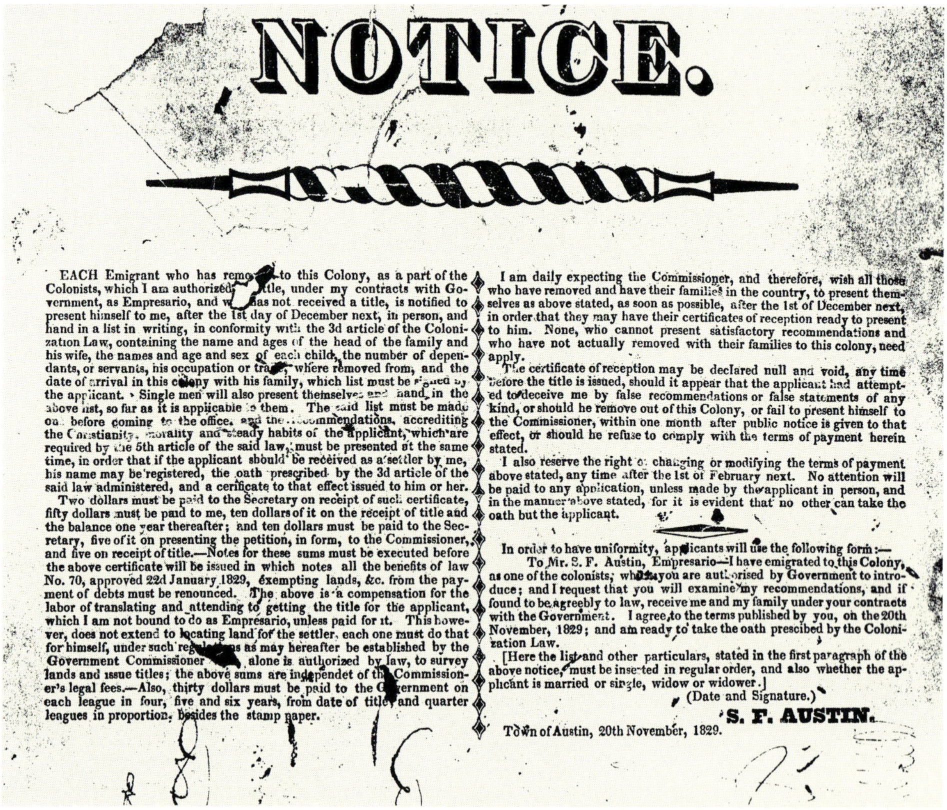

NOTICE.

EACH Emigrant who has remo[illegible] to this Colony, as a part of the Colonists, which I am authorized [illegible]tle, under my contracts with Government, as Empresario, and w[illegible]as not received a title, is notified to present himself to me, after the 1st day of December next, in person, and hand in a list in writing, in conformity with the 3d article of the Colonization Law, containing the name and ages of the head of the family and his wife, the names and age and sex of each child, the number of dependants, or servants, his occupation or tra[illegible], where removed from, and the date of arrival in this colony with his family, which list must be signed by the applicant. Single men will also present themselves and hand in the above list, so far as it is applicable to them. The said list must be made out before coming to the office, and the [illegible]commendations, accrediting the Christianity, morality and steady habits of the applicant, which are required by the 5th article of the said law, must be presented at the same time, in order that if the applicant should be received as a settler by me, his name may be registered, the oath prescribed by the 3d article of the said law administered, and a cerificate to that effect issued to him or her.

Two dollars must be paid to the Secretary on receipt of such certificate, fifty dollars must be paid to me, ten dollars of it on the receipt of title and the balance one year thereafter; and ten dollars must be paid to the Secretary, five of it on presenting the petition, in form, to the Commissioner, and five on receipt of title.—Notes for these sums must be executed before the above certificate will be issued in which notes all the benefits of law No. 70, approved 22d January 1829, exempting lands, &c. from the payment of debts must be renounced. The above is a compensation for the labor of translating and attending to getting the title for the applicant, which I am not bound to do as Empresario, unless paid for it. This however, does not extend to locating land for the settler, each one must do that for himself, under such reg[illegible]s as may hereafter be established by the Government Commissioner [illegible] alone is authorized by law, to survey lands and issue titles; the above sums are independet of th[illegible] Commissioner's legal fees.—Also, thirty dollars must be paid to the G[illegible]ernment on each league in four, five and six years, from date of title, and quarter leagues in proportion, besides the stamp paper.

I am daily expecting the Commissioner, and therefore, wish all those who have removed and have their families in the country, to present themselves as above stated, as soon as possible, after the 1st of December next, in order that they may have their certificates of reception ready to present to him. None, who cannot present satisfactory recommendations and who have not actually removed with their families to this colony, need apply.

The certificate of reception may be declared null and void, any time before the title is issued, should it appear that the applicant had attempted to deceive me by false recommendations or false statements of any kind, or should he remove out of this Colony, or fail to present himself to the Commissioner, within one month after public notice is given to that effect, or should he refuse to comply with the terms of payment herein stated.

I also reserve the right of changing or modifying the terms of payment above stated, any time after the 1st of February next. No attention will be paid to any application, unless made by the applicant in person, and in the manner above stated, for it is evident that no other can take the oath but the applicant.

In order to have uniformity, applicants will use the following form:—

To Mr. S. F. Austin, Empresario—I have emigrated to this Colony, as one of the colonists, wh[illegible] you are authorised by Government to introduce; and I request that you will examine my recommendations, and if found to be agreebly to law, receive me and my family under your contracts with the Government. I agree to the terms published by you, on the 20th November, 1829; and am ready to take the oath prescibed by the Colonization Law.

[Here the list and other particulars, stated in the first paragraph of the above notice, must be inserted in regular order, and also whether the applicant is married or single, widow or widower.]

(Date and Signature.)

S. F. AUSTIN.

Town of Austin, 20th November, 1829.

Plate 13. Austin's Notice to Colonists (Streeter 11). Genuine copy (19.5 x 24.5 cm). *Texas General Land Office, Austin.*

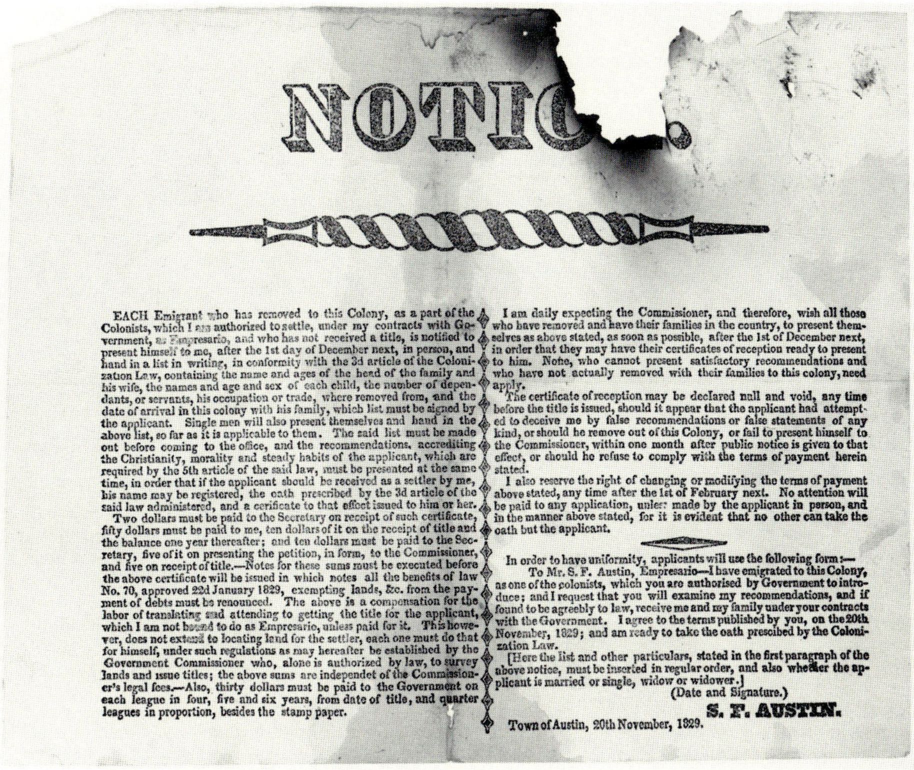

NOTIC[illegible].

EACH Emigrant who has removed to this Colony, as a part of the Colonists, which I am authorized to settle, under my contracts with Government, as Empresario, and who has not received a title, is notified to present himself to me, after the 1st day of December next, in person, and hand in a list in writing, in conformity with the 3d article of the Colonization Law, containing the name and ages of the head of the family and his wife, the names and age and sex of each child, the number of dependants, or servants, his occupation or trade, where removed from, and the date of arrival in this colony with his family, which list must be signed by the applicant. Single men will also present themselves and hand in the above list, so far as it is applicable to them. The said list must be made out before coming to the office, and the recommendations, accrediting the Christianity, morality and steady habits of the applicant, which are required by the 5th article of the said law, must be presented at the same time, in order that if the applicant should be received as a settler by me, his name may be registered, the oath prescribed by the 3d article of the said law administered, and a cerificate to that effect issued to him or her.

Two dollars must be paid to the Secretary on receipt of such certificate, fifty dollars must be paid to me, ten dollars of it on the receipt of title and the balance one year thereafter; and ten dollars must be paid to the Secretary, five of it on presenting the petition, in form, to the Commissioner, and five on receipt of title.—Notes for these sums must be executed before the above certificate will be issued in which notes all the benefits of law No. 70, approved 22d January 1829, exempting lands, &c. from the payment of debts must be renounced. The above is a compensation for the labor of translating and attending to getting the title for the applicant, which I am not bound to do as Empresario, unless paid for it. This however, does not extend to locating land for the settler, each one must do that for himself, under such regulations as may hereafter be established by the Government Commissioner who, alone is authorized by law, to survey lands and issue titles; the above sums are independet of the Commissioner's legal fees.—Also, thirty dollars must be paid to the Government on each league in four, five and six years, from date of title, and quarter leagues in proportion, besides the stamp paper.

I am daily expecting the Commissioner, and therefore, wish all those who have removed and have their families in the country, to present themselves as above stated, as soon as possible, after the 1st of December next, in order that they may have their certificates of reception ready to present to him. None, who cannot present satisfactory recommendations and who have not actually removed with their families to this colony, need apply.

The certificate of reception may be declared null and void, any time before the title is issued, should it appear that the applicant had attempted to deceive me by false recommendations or false statements of any kind, or should he remove out of this Colony, or fail to present himself to the Commissioner, within one month after public notice is given to that effect, or should he refuse to comply with the terms of payment herein stated.

I also reserve the right of changing or modifying the terms of payment above stated, any time after the 1st of February next. No attention will be paid to any application, unless made by the applicant in person, and in the manner above stated, for it is evident that no other can take the oath but the applicant.

In order to have uniformity, applicants will use the following form:—

To Mr. S. F. Austin, Empresario—I have emigrated to this Colony, as one of the colonists, which you are authorised by Government to introduce; and I request that you will examine my recommendations, and if found to be agreebly to law, receive me and my family under your contracts with the Government. I agree to the terms published by you, on the 20th November, 1829; and am ready to take the oath prescibed by the Colonization Law.

[Here the list and other particulars, stated in the first paragraph of the above notice, must be inserted in regular order, and also whether the applicant is married or single, widow or widower.]

(Date and Signature.)

S. F. AUSTIN.

Town of Austin, 20th November, 1829.

Plate 14. Austin's Notice to Colonists. Forgery. The type on the forgery is 14 percent larger than on a genuine copy—the decorative rule on a forged copy measures 15.7 cm. The burn damage on this copy is from the Jenkins Company fire in September, 1987.

COLUMBIA JOCKEY CLUB

The Races over the Columbia Turf will take place on the 4th Monday in May ensuing, in the town of Columbia. Weights according to the rules of the Turf:

The 1st day.—A sweep stake for one mile, free for any horse, mare or gelding in the Province.—Entrance	$100.00
The 2nd day.—One mile and repeat	$100.00
The 3rd day.—Two miles and repeat	$100.00
The 4th day.—Three mile heats	$125.00
The 5th day.—One mile heats, 3 best in 5	$150.00

The liberality of the public spirited proprietors has rendered this one of the pleasantest, and most eligible situations in Texas for the sports of the Turf. It is anticipated by the Club, that the races contemplated will be among the most interesting ever holden in Texas. —Their fine horses are already entered.

Gentlemen at a distance wising to enter horses, and procure stables, will do well to address the proprietor J. H. Bell, Esg. or the Secretary of the Club.
By order of the C. J. Club:

A. C. AINSWORTH, Sec'y

Columbia, April 11, 1835.

Plate 15. Columbia Jockey Club (Revised Streeter 64.1). Fabrication (23.5 x 13.5 cm).
Beinecke Rare Book and Manuscript Library, Yale University.

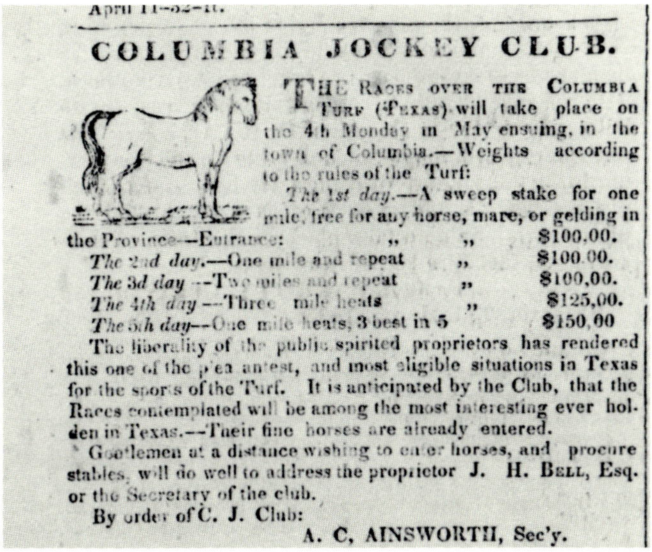

April 11–52–tf.

COLUMBIA JOCKEY CLUB.

THE RACES OVER THE COLUMBIA TURF (TEXAS) will take place on the 4th Monday in May ensuing, in the town of Columbia.—Weights according to the rules of the Turf:

The 1st day.—A sweep stake for one mile, free for any horse, mare, or gelding in the Province—Entrance: " " $100.00.

The 2d day.—One mile and repeat " $100.00.

The 3d day --Two miles and repeat " $100,00.

The 4th day ---Three mile heats " $125,00.

The 5th day--One mile heats, 3 best in 5 $150,00

The liberality of the public spirited proprietors has rendered this one of the pleasantest, and most eligible situations in Texas for the sports of the Turf. It is anticipated by the Club, that the Races contemplated will be among the most interesting ever holden in Texas.--Their fine horses are already entered.

Gentlemen at a distance wishing to enter horses, and procure stables, will do well to address the proprietor J. H. BELL, Esq. or the Secretary of the club.

By order of C. J. Club:

A. C, AINSWORTH, Sec'y.

Plate 16. Ad for the Columbia Jockey Club races from the April 11, 1835, issue of the Brazoria *Texas Republican.* The text of this ad, slightly modified, was used for the fabrication.

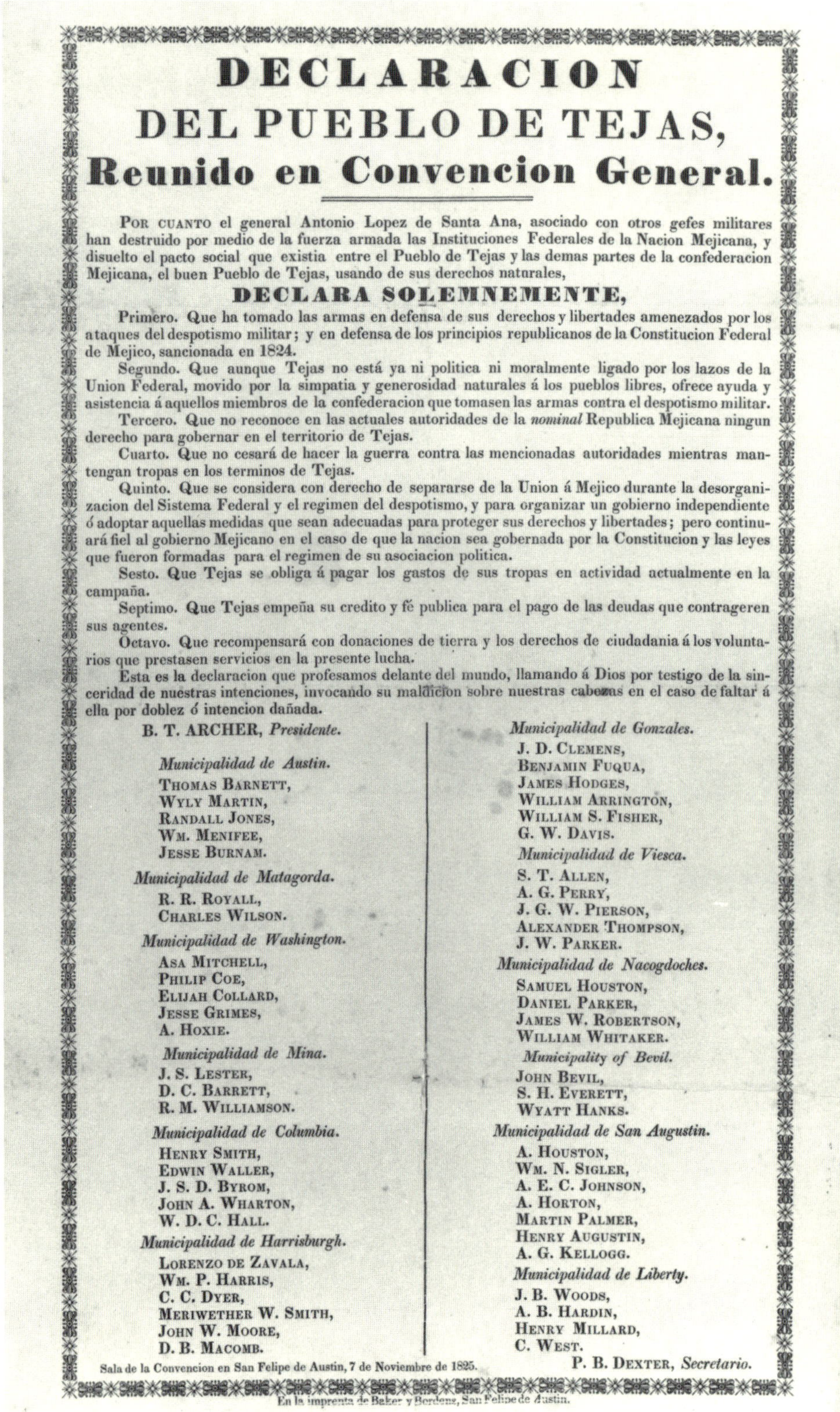

DECLARACION
DEL PUEBLO DE TEJAS,
Reunido en Convencion General.

POR CUANTO el general Antonio Lopez de Santa Ana, asociado con otros gefes militares han destruido por medio de la fuerza armada las Instituciones Federales de la Nacion Mejicana, y disuelto el pacto social que existia entre el Pueblo de Tejas y las demas partes de la confederacion Mejicana, el buen Pueblo de Tejas, usando de sus derechos naturales,

DECLARA SOLEMNEMENTE,

Primero. Que ha tomado las armas en defensa de sus derechos y libertades amenezados por los ataques del despotismo militar; y en defensa de los principios republicanos de la Constitucion Federal de Mejico, sancionada en 1824.

Segundo. Que aunque Tejas no está ya ni politica ni moralmente ligado por los lazos de la Union Federal, movido por la simpatia y generosidad naturales á los pueblos libres, ofrece ayuda y asistencia á aquellos miembros de la confederacion que tomasen las armas contra el despotismo militar.

Tercero. Que no reconoce en las actuales autoridades de la *nominal* Republica Mejicana ningun derecho para gobernar en el territorio de Tejas.

Cuarto. Que no cesará de hacer la guerra contra las mencionadas autoridades mientras mantengan tropas en los terminos de Tejas.

Quinto. Que se considera con derecho de separarse de la Union á Mejico durante la desorganizacion del Sistema Federal y el regimen del despotismo, y para organizar un gobierno independiente ó adoptar aquellas medidas que sean adecuadas para proteger sus derechos y libertades; pero continuará fiel al gobierno Mejicano en el caso de que la nacion sea gobernada por la Constitucion y las leyes que fueron formadas para el regimen de su asociacion politica.

Sesto. Que Tejas se obliga á pagar los gastos de sus tropas en actividad actualmente en la campaña.

Septimo. Que Tejas empeña su credito y fé publica para el pago de las deudas que contrageren sus agentes.

Octavo. Que recompensará con donaciones de tierra y los derechos de ciudadania á los voluntarios que prestasen servicios en la presente lucha.

Esta es la declaracion que profesamos delante del mundo, llamando á Dios por testigo de la sinceridad de nuestras intenciones, invocando su maldicion sobre nuestras cabezas en el caso de faltar á ella por doblez ó intencion dañada.

B. T. ARCHER, *Presidente.*

Municipalidad de Austin.
THOMAS BARNETT,
WYLY MARTIN,
RANDALL JONES,
WM. MENIFEE,
JESSE BURNAM.

Municipalidad de Matagorda.
R. R. ROYALL,
CHARLES WILSON.

Municipalidad de Washington.
ASA MITCHELL,
PHILIP COE,
ELIJAH COLLARD,
JESSE GRIMES,
A. HOXIE.

Municipalidad de Mina.
J. S. LESTER,
D. C. BARRETT,
R. M. WILLIAMSON.

Municipalidad de Columbia.
HENRY SMITH,
EDWIN WALLER,
J. S. D. BYROM,
JOHN A. WHARTON,
W. D. C. HALL.

Municipalidad de Harrisburgh.
LORENZO DE ZAVALA,
WM. P. HARRIS,
C. C. DYER,
MERIWETHER W. SMITH,
JOHN W. MOORE,
D. B. MACOMB.

Municipalidad de Gonzales.
J. D. CLEMENS,
BENJAMIN FUQUA,
JAMES HODGES,
WILLIAM ARRINGTON,
WILLIAM S. FISHER,
G. W. DAVIS.

Municipalidad de Viesca.
S. T. ALLEN,
A. G. PERRY,
J. G. W. PIERSON,
ALEXANDER THOMPSON,
J. W. PARKER.

Municipalidad de Nacogdoches.
SAMUEL HOUSTON,
DANIEL PARKER,
JAMES W. ROBERTSON,
WILLIAM WHITAKER.

Municipality of Bevil.
JOHN BEVIL,
S. H. EVERETT,
WYATT HANKS.

Municipalidad de San Augustin.
A. HOUSTON,
WM. N. SIGLER,
A. E. C. JOHNSON,
A. HORTON,
MARTIN PALMER,
HENRY AUGUSTIN,
A. G. KELLOGG.

Municipalidad de Liberty.
J. B. WOODS,
A. B. HARDIN,
HENRY MILLARD,
C. WEST.

Sala de la Convencion en San Felipe de Austin, 7 de Noviembre de 1835.

P. B. DEXTER, *Secretario.*

En la imprenta de Baker y Bordens, San Felipe de Austin.

Plate 17. Declaration of Causes, Spanish edition (Streeter 88). Genuine copy (32.5 x 19.5 cm).

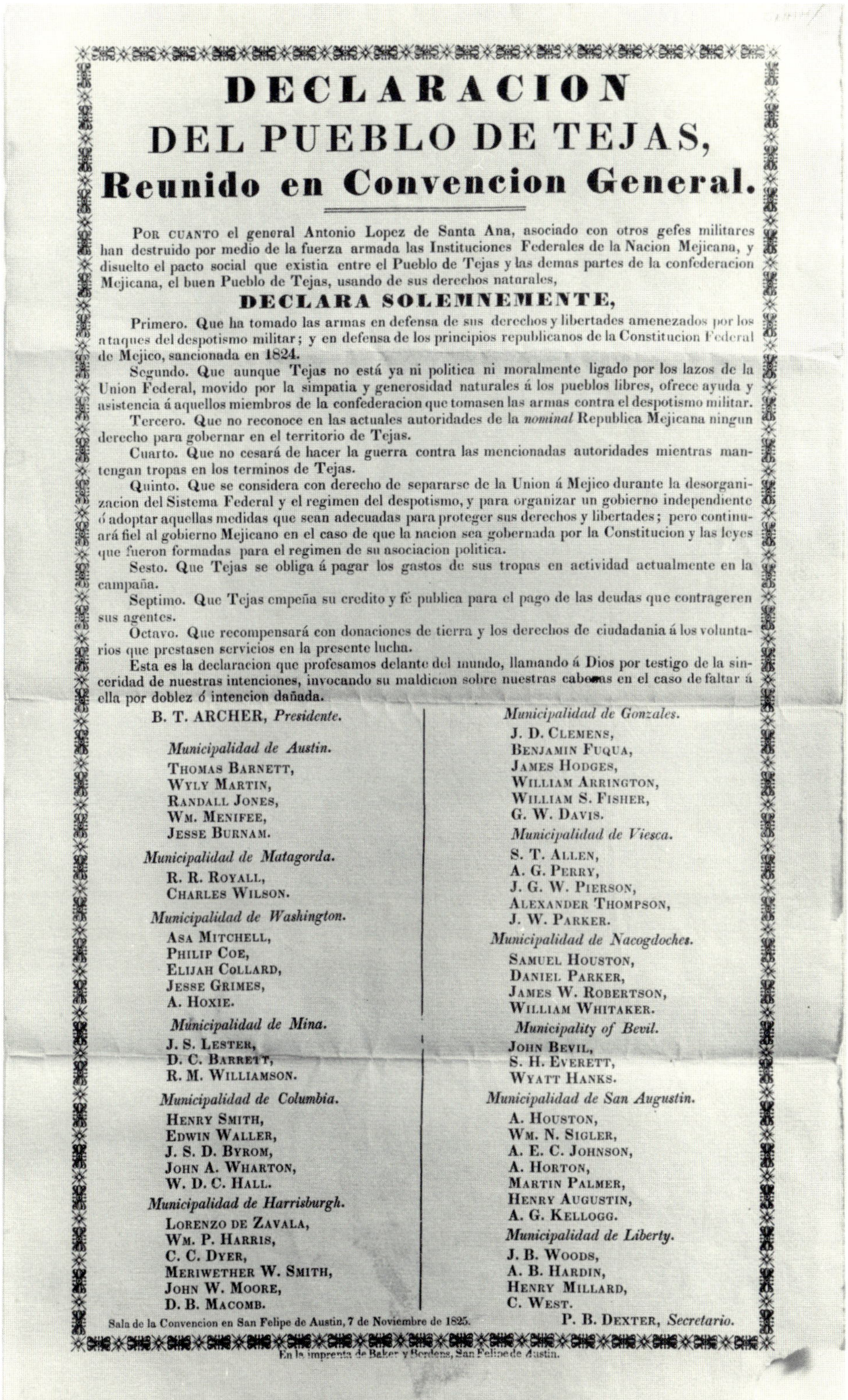

DECLARACION
DEL PUEBLO DE TEJAS,
Reunido en Convencion General.

Por cuanto el general Antonio Lopez de Santa Ana, asociado con otros gefes militares han destruido por medio de la fuerza armada las Instituciones Federales de la Nacion Mejicana, y disuelto el pacto social que existia entre el Pueblo de Tejas y las demas partes de la confederacion Mejicana, el buen Pueblo de Tejas, usando de sus derechos naturales,

DECLARA SOLEMNEMENTE,

Primero. Que ha tomado las armas en defensa de sus derechos y libertades amenezados por los ataques del despotismo militar; y en defensa de los principios republicanos de la Constitucion Federal de Mejico, sancionada en 1824.

Segundo. Que aunque Tejas no está ya ni politica ni moralmente ligado por los lazos de la Union Federal, movido por la simpatia y generosidad naturales á los pueblos libres, ofrece ayuda y asistencia á aquellos miembros de la confederacion que tomasen las armas contra el despotismo militar.

Tercero. Que no reconoce en las actuales autoridades de la *nominal* Republica Mejicana ningun derecho para gobernar en el territorio de Tejas.

Cuarto. Que no cesará de hacer la guerra contra las mencionadas autoridades mientras mantengan tropas en los terminos de Tejas.

Quinto. Que se considera con derecho de separarse de la Union á Mejico durante la desorganizacion del Sistema Federal y el regimen del despotismo, y para organizar un gobierno independiente ó adoptar aquellas medidas que sean adecuadas para proteger sus derechos y libertades; pero continuará fiel al gobierno Mejicano en el caso de que la nacion sea gobernada por la Constitucion y las leyes que fueron formadas para el regimen de su asociacion politica.

Sesto. Que Tejas se obliga á pagar los gastos de sus tropas en actividad actualmente en la campaña.

Septimo. Que Tejas empeña su credito y fé publica para el pago de las deudas que contrageren sus agentes.

Octavo. Que recompensará con donaciones de tierra y los derechos de ciudadania á los voluntarios que prestasen servicios en la presente lucha.

Esta es la declaracion que profesamos delante del mundo, llamando á Dios por testigo de la sinceridad de nuestras intenciones, invocando su maldicion sobre nuestras cabe[illegible]as en el caso de faltar á ella por doblez ó intencion dañada.

B. T. ARCHER, *Presidente.*

Municipalidad de Austin.
Thomas Barnett,
Wyly Martin,
Randall Jones,
Wm. Menifee,
Jesse Burnam.

Municipalidad de Matagorda.
R. R. Royall,
Charles Wilson.

Municipalidad de Washington.
Asa Mitchell,
Philip Coe,
Elijah Collard,
Jesse Grimes,
A. Hoxie.

Municipalidad de Mina.
J. S. Lester,
D. C. Barrett,
R. M. Williamson.

Municipalidad de Columbia.
Henry Smith,
Edwin Waller,
J. S. D. Byrom,
John A. Wharton,
W. D. C. Hall.

Municipalidad de Harrisburgh.
Lorenzo de Zavala,
Wm. P. Harris,
C. C. Dyer,
Meriwether W. Smith,
John W. Moore,
D. B. Macomb.

Municipalidad de Gonzales.
J. D. Clemens,
Benjamin Fuqua,
James Hodges,
William Arrington,
William S. Fisher,
G. W. Davis.

Municipalidad de Viesca.
S. T. Allen,
A. G. Perry,
J. G. W. Pierson,
Alexander Thompson,
J. W. Parker.

Municipalidad de Nacogdoches.
Samuel Houston,
Daniel Parker,
James W. Robertson,
William Whitaker.

Municipality of Bevil.
John Bevil,
S. H. Everett,
Wyatt Hanks.

Municipalidad de San Augustin.
A. Houston,
Wm. N. Sigler,
A. E. C. Johnson,
A. Horton,
Martin Palmer,
Henry Augustin,
A. G. Kellogg.

Municipalidad de Liberty.
J. B. Woods,
A. B. Hardin,
Henry Millard,
C. West.

Sala de la Convencion en San Felipe de Austin, 7 de Noviembre de 1835.

P. B. Dexter, *Secretario.*

En la imprenta de Baker y Bordens, San Felipe de Austin.

Plate 18. Declaration of Causes, Spanish edition. Forgery (32.4 x 19.9 cm). This is a photocopy on old paper, most easily detected by the poor quality of reproduction of the ornaments surrounding the text. *Texas Collection, Baylor University.*

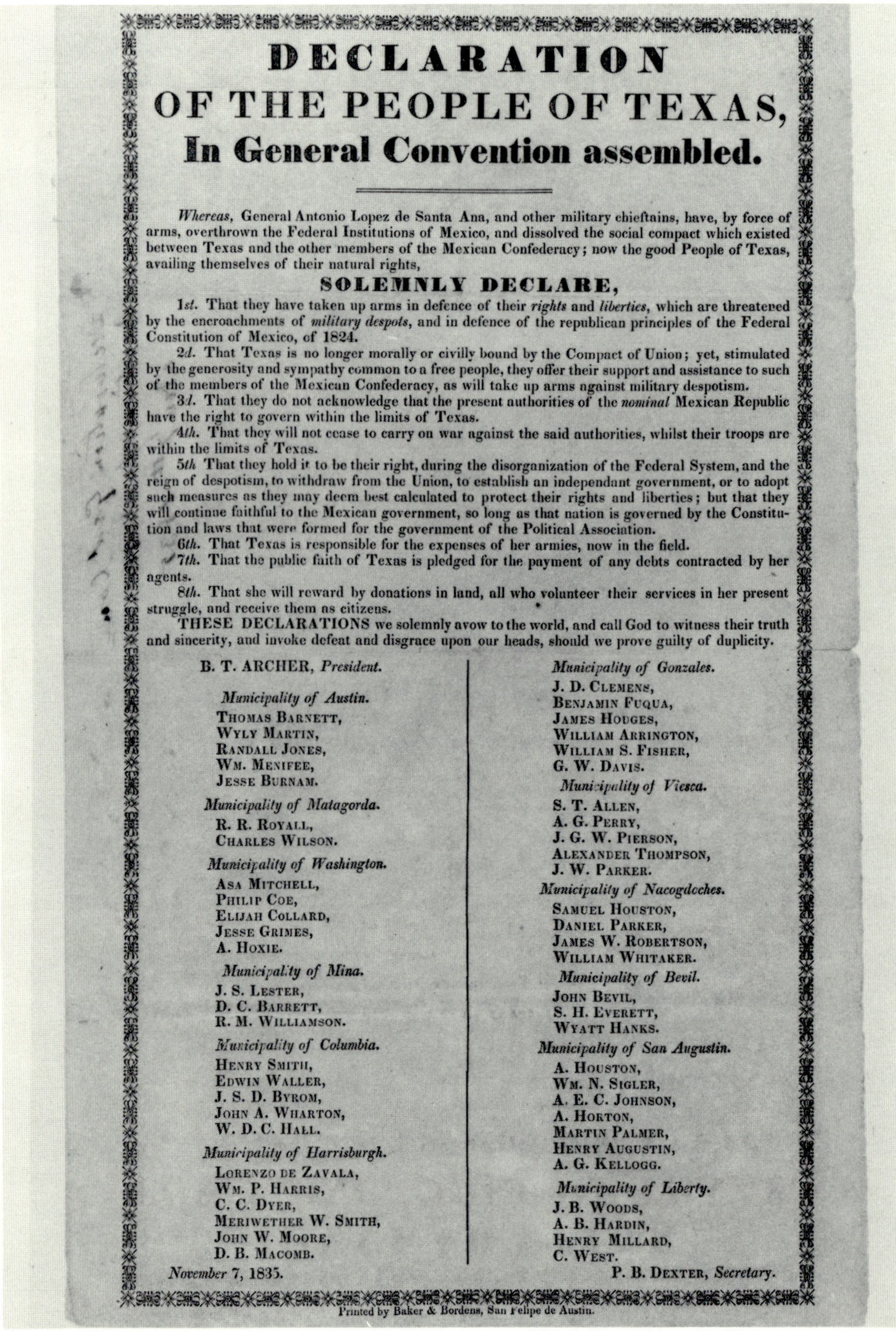

DECLARATION
OF THE PEOPLE OF TEXAS,
In General Convention assembled.

Whereas, General Antonio Lopez de Santa Ana, and other military chieftains, have, by force of arms, overthrown the Federal Institutions of Mexico, and dissolved the social compact which existed between Texas and the other members of the Mexican Confederacy; now the good People of Texas, availing themselves of their natural rights,

SOLEMNLY DECLARE,

1st. That they have taken up arms in defence of their *rights* and *liberties,* which are threatened by the encroachments of *military despots,* and in defence of the republican principles of the Federal Constitution of Mexico, of 1824.

2d. That Texas is no longer morally or civilly bound by the Compact of Union; yet, stimulated by the generosity and sympathy common to a free people, they offer their support and assistance to such of the members of the Mexican Confederacy, as will take up arms against military despotism.

3d. That they do not acknowledge that the present authorities of the *nominal* Mexican Republic have the right to govern within the limits of Texas.

4th. That they will not cease to carry on war against the said authorities, whilst their troops are within the limits of Texas.

5th That they hold it to be their right, during the disorganization of the Federal System, and the reign of despotism, to withdraw from the Union, to establish an independant government, or to adopt such measures as they may deem best calculated to protect their rights and liberties; but that they will continue faithful to the Mexican government, so long as that nation is governed by the Constitution and laws that were formed for the government of the Political Association.

6th. That Texas is responsible for the expenses of her armies, now in the field.

7th. That the public faith of Texas is pledged for the payment of any debts contracted by her agents.

8th. That she will reward by donations in land, all who volunteer their services in her present struggle, and receive them as citizens.

THESE DECLARATIONS we solemnly avow to the world, and call God to witness their truth and sincerity, and invoke defeat and disgrace upon our heads, should we prove guilty of duplicity.

B. T. ARCHER, *President.*

Municipality of Austin.
THOMAS BARNETT,
WYLY MARTIN,
RANDALL JONES,
WM. MENIFEE,
JESSE BURNAM.

Municipality of Matagorda.
R. R. ROYALL,
CHARLES WILSON.

Municipality of Washington.
ASA MITCHELL,
PHILIP COE,
ELIJAH COLLARD,
JESSE GRIMES,
A. HOXIE.

Municipality of Mina.
J. S. LESTER,
D. C. BARRETT,
R. M. WILLIAMSON.

Municipality of Columbia.
HENRY SMITH,
EDWIN WALLER,
J. S. D. BYROM,
JOHN A. WHARTON,
W. D. C. HALL.

Municipality of Harrisburgh.
LORENZO DE ZAVALA,
WM. P. HARRIS,
C. C. DYER,
MERIWETHER W. SMITH,
JOHN W. MOORE,
D. B. MACOMB.

Municipality of Gonzales.
J. D. CLEMENS,
BENJAMIN FUQUA,
JAMES HODGES,
WILLIAM ARRINGTON,
WILLIAM S. FISHER,
G. W. DAVIS.

Municipality of Viesca.
S. T. ALLEN,
A. G. PERRY,
J. G. W. PIERSON,
ALEXANDER THOMPSON,
J. W. PARKER.

Municipality of Nacogdoches.
SAMUEL HOUSTON,
DANIEL PARKER,
JAMES W. ROBERTSON,
WILLIAM WHITAKER.

Municipality of Bevil.
JOHN BEVIL,
S. H. EVERETT,
WYATT HANKS.

Municipality of San Augustin.
A. HOUSTON,
WM. N. SIGLER,
A. E. C. JOHNSON,
A. HORTON,
MARTIN PALMER,
HENRY AUGUSTIN,
A. G. KELLOGG.

Municipality of Liberty.
J. B. WOODS,
A. B. HARDIN,
HENRY MILLARD,
C. WEST.

November 7, 1835.

P. B. DEXTER, *Secretary.*

Printed by Baker & Bordens, San Felipe de Austin.

Plate 19. Declaration of Causes, English edition (Streeter 89). Genuine copy (31.5 x 19.3 cm). *Barker Texas History Center, University of Texas at Austin.*

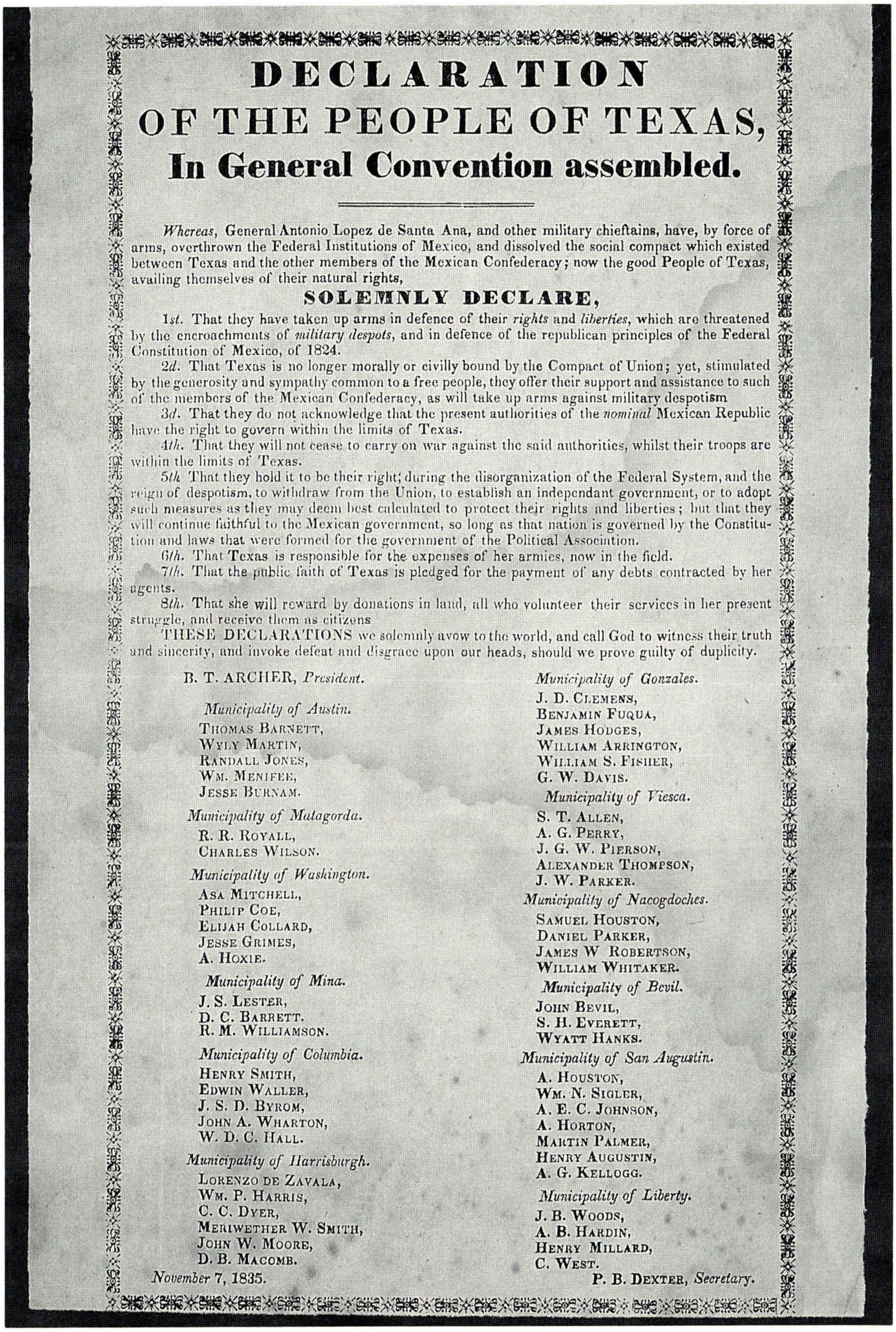

DECLARATION
OF THE PEOPLE OF TEXAS,
In General Convention assembled.

Whereas, General Antonio Lopez de Santa Ana, and other military chieftains, have, by force of arms, overthrown the Federal Institutions of Mexico, and dissolved the social compact which existed between Texas and the other members of the Mexican Confederacy; now the good People of Texas, availing themselves of their natural rights,

SOLEMNLY DECLARE,

1st. That they have taken up arms in defence of their *rights* and *liberties,* which are threatened by the encroachments of *military despots,* and in defence of the republican principles of the Federal Constitution of Mexico, of 1824.

2d. That Texas is no longer morally or civilly bound by the Compact of Union; yet, stimulated by the generosity and sympathy common to a free people, they offer their support and assistance to such of the members of the Mexican Confederacy, as will take up arms against military despotism

3d. That they do not acknowledge that the present authorities of the *nominal* Mexican Republic have the right to govern within the limits of Texas.

4th. That they will not cease to carry on war against the said authorities, whilst their troops are within the limits of Texas.

5th That they hold it to be their right; during the disorganization of the Federal System, and the reign of despotism, to withdraw from the Union, to establish an independant government, or to adopt such measures as they may deem best calculated to protect their rights and liberties; but that they will continue faithful to the Mexican government, so long as that nation is governed by the Constitution and laws that were formed for the government of the Political Association.

6th. That Texas is responsible for the expenses of her armies, now in the field.

7th. That the public faith of Texas is pledged for the payment of any debts contracted by her agents.

8th. That she will reward by donations in land, all who volunteer their services in her present struggle, and receive them as citizens

THESE DECLARATIONS we solemnly avow to the world, and call God to witness their truth and sincerity, and invoke defeat and disgrace upon our heads, should we prove guilty of duplicity.

B. T. ARCHER, *President.*

Municipality of Austin.
THOMAS BARNETT,
WYLY MARTIN,
RANDALL JONES,
WM. MENIFEE,
JESSE BURNAM.

Municipality of Matagorda.
R. R. ROYALL,
CHARLES WILSON.

Municipality of Washington.
ASA MITCHELL,
PHILIP COE,
ELIJAH COLLARD,
JESSE GRIMES,
A. HOXIE.

Municipality of Mina.
J. S. LESTER,
D. C. BARRETT.
R. M. WILLIAMSON.

Municipality of Columbia.
HENRY SMITH,
EDWIN WALLER,
J. S. D. BYROM,
JOHN A. WHARTON,
W. D. C. HALL.

Municipality of Harrisburgh.
LORENZO DE ZAVALA,
WM. P. HARRIS,
C. C. DYER,
MERIWETHER W. SMITH,
JOHN W. MOORE,
D. B. MACOMB.

Municipality of Gonzales.
J. D. CLEMENS,
BENJAMIN FUQUA,
JAMES HODGES,
WILLIAM ARRINGTON,
WILLIAM S. FISHER,
G. W. DAVIS.

Municipality of Viesca.
S. T. ALLEN,
A. G. PERRY,
J. G. W. PIERSON,
ALEXANDER THOMPSON,
J. W. PARKER.

Municipality of Nacogdoches.
SAMUEL HOUSTON,
DANIEL PARKER,
JAMES W ROBERTSON,
WILLIAM WHITAKER.

Municipality of Bevil.
JOHN BEVIL,
S. H. EVERETT,
WYATT HANKS.

Municipality of San Augustin.
A. HOUSTON,
WM. N. SIGLER,
A. E. C. JOHNSON,
A. HORTON,
MARTIN PALMER,
HENRY AUGUSTIN,
A. G. KELLOGG.

Municipality of Liberty.
J. B. WOODS,
A. B. HARDIN,
HENRY MILLARD,
C. WEST.

November 7, 1835.

P. B. DEXTER, *Secretary.*

Plate 20. Declaration of Causes, English edition. Forgery (30.7 x 19.6 cm). *Private Collection.*

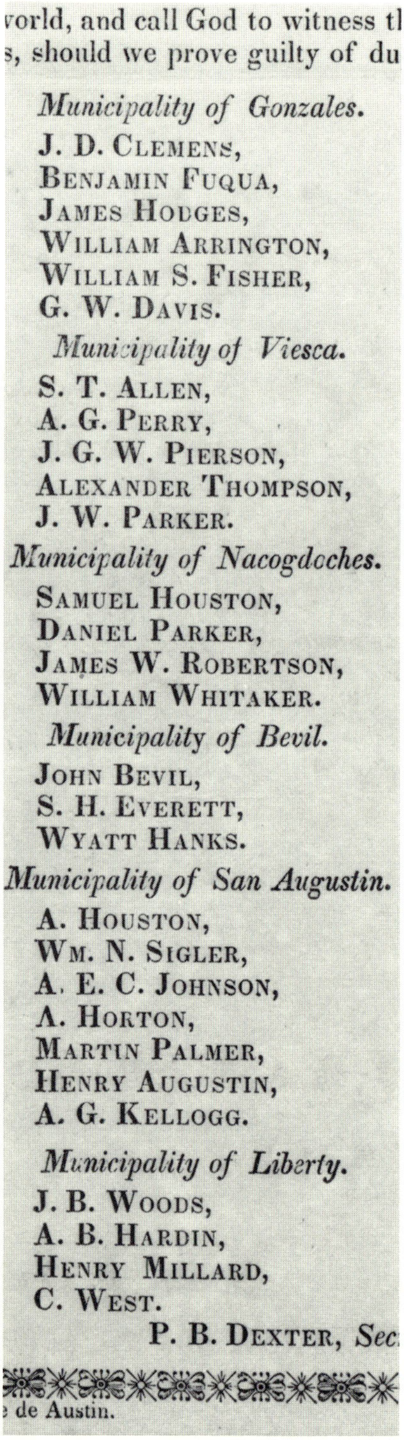

world, and call God to witness t
s, should we prove guilty of du

Municipality of Gonzales.

J. D. CLEMENS,
BENJAMIN FUQUA,
JAMES HODGES,
WILLIAM ARRINGTON,
WILLIAM S. FISHER,
G. W. DAVIS.

Municipality of Viesca.

S. T. ALLEN,
A. G. PERRY,
J. G. W. PIERSON,
ALEXANDER THOMPSON,
J. W. PARKER.

Municipality of Nacogdoches.

SAMUEL HOUSTON,
DANIEL PARKER,
JAMES W. ROBERTSON,
WILLIAM WHITAKER.

Municipality of Bevil.

JOHN BEVIL,
S. H. EVERETT,
WYATT HANKS.

Municipality of San Augustin.

A. HOUSTON,
WM. N. SIGLER,
A. E. C. JOHNSON,
A. HORTON,
MARTIN PALMER,
HENRY AUGUSTIN,
A. G. KELLOGG.

Municipality of Liberty.

J. B. WOODS,
A. B. HARDIN,
HENRY MILLARD,
C. WEST.

P. B. DEXTER, *Sec.*

e de Austin.

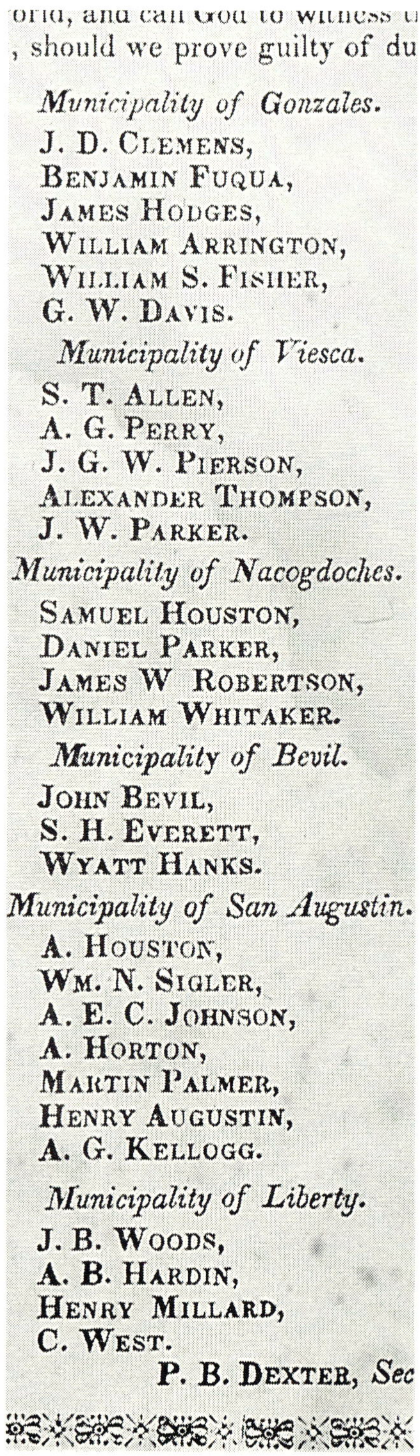

orld, and call God to witness t
, should we prove guilty of du

Municipality of Gonzales.

J. D. CLEMENS,
BENJAMIN FUQUA,
JAMES HODGES,
WILLIAM ARRINGTON,
WILLIAM S. FISHER,
G. W. DAVIS.

Municipality of Viesca.

S. T. ALLEN,
A. G. PERRY,
J. G. W. PIERSON,
ALEXANDER THOMPSON,
J. W. PARKER.

Municipality of Nacogdoches.

SAMUEL HOUSTON,
DANIEL PARKER,
JAMES W ROBERTSON,
WILLIAM WHITAKER.

Municipality of Bevil.

JOHN BEVIL,
S. H. EVERETT,
WYATT HANKS.

Municipality of San Augustin.

A. HOUSTON,
WM. N. SIGLER,
A. E. C. JOHNSON,
A. HORTON,
MARTIN PALMER,
HENRY AUGUSTIN,
A. G. KELLOGG.

Municipality of Liberty.

J. B. WOODS,
A. B. HARDIN,
HENRY MILLARD,
C. WEST.

P. B. DEXTER, *Sec*

Plate 21. *Left:* Detail from genuine copy. *Right:* Detail from forgery, showing extensive retouching of letters.

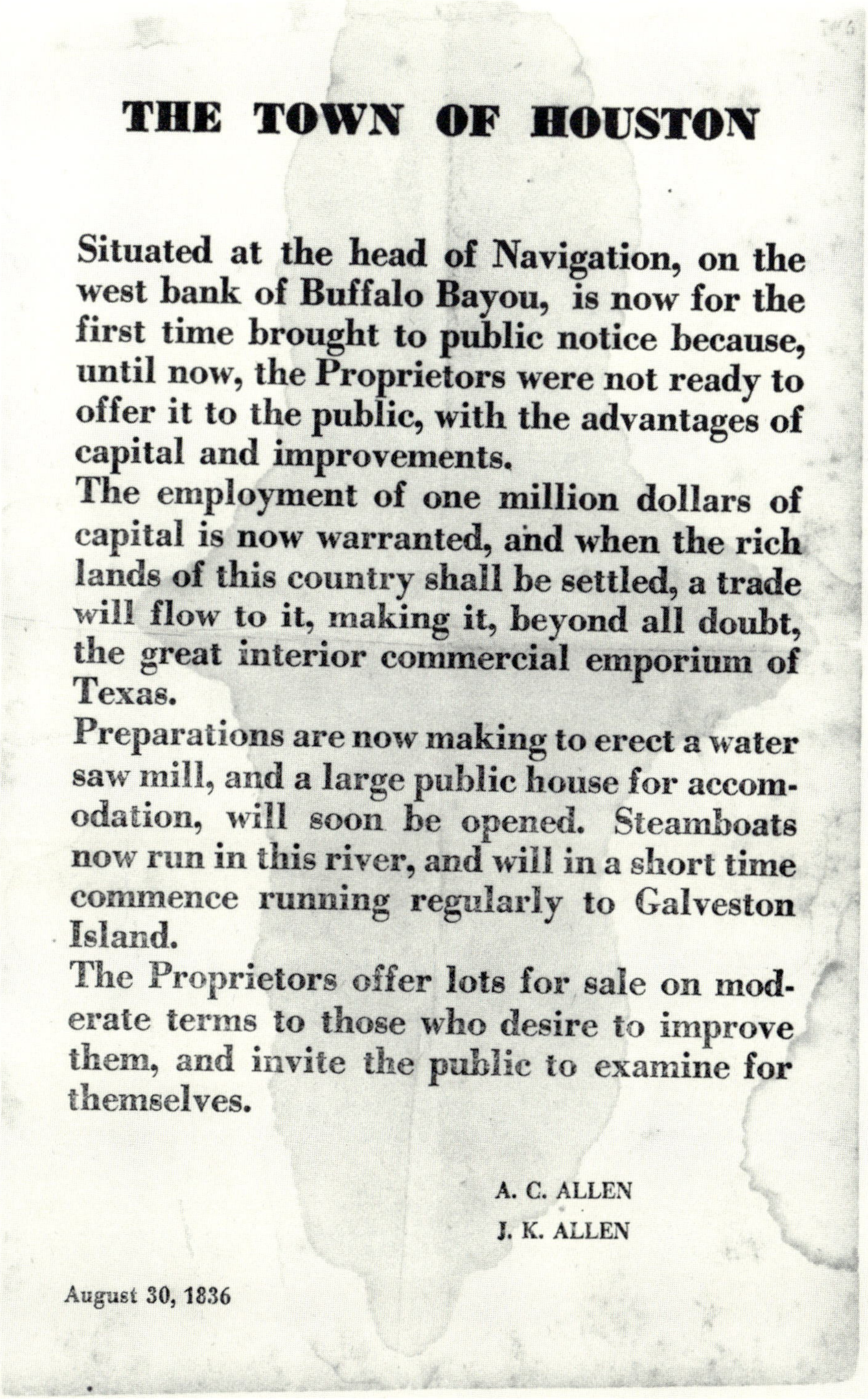

THE TOWN OF HOUSTON

Situated at the head of Navigation, on the west bank of Buffalo Bayou, is now for the first time brought to public notice because, until now, the Proprietors were not ready to offer it to the public, with the advantages of capital and improvements.

The employment of one million dollars of capital is now warranted, and when the rich lands of this country shall be settled, a trade will flow to it, making it, beyond all doubt, the great interior commercial emporium of Texas.

Preparations are now making to erect a water saw mill, and a large public house for accomodation, will soon be opened. Steamboats now run in this river, and will in a short time commence running regularly to Galveston Island.

The Proprietors offer lots for sale on moderate terms to those who desire to improve them, and invite the public to examine for themselves.

A. C. ALLEN

J. K. ALLEN

August 30, 1836

Plate 22. The Town of Houston (Revised Streeter 112.1). Fabrication (23 x 14 cm). *Star of the Republic Museum, Washington-on-the-Brazos.*

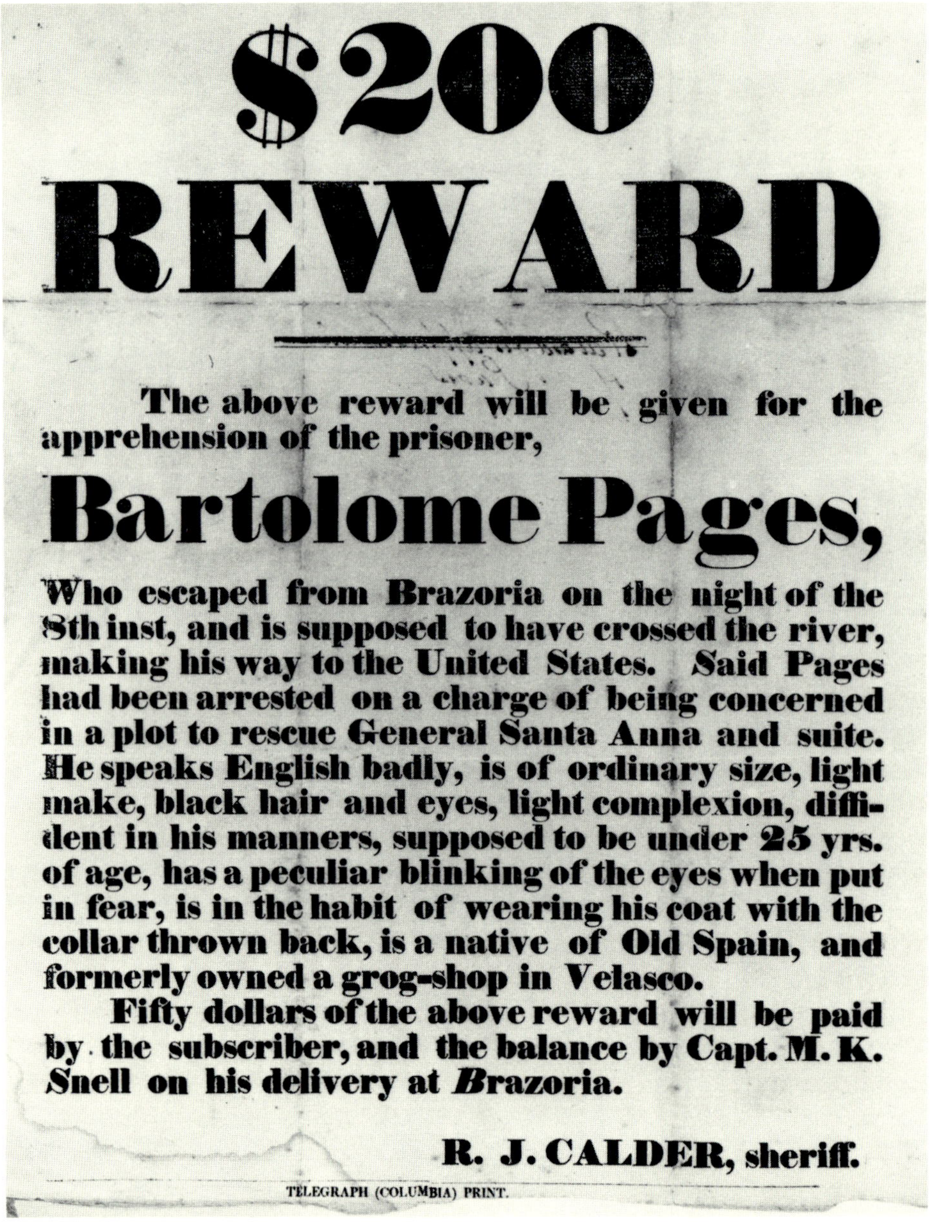

Plate 23. Pagés Wanted Poster (Revised Streeter 119.1). Genuine copy (31 x 26 cm). *Jenkins Garrett Library, Special Collections, University of Texas at Arlington.*

$200
REWARD

The above reward will be given for the apprehension of the prisoner,

Bartolome Pages,

Who escaped from Brazoria on the night of the 8th inst, and is supposed to have crossed the river, making his way to the United States. Said Pages had been arrested on a charge of being concerned in a plot to rescue General Santa Anna and suite. He speaks English badly, is of ordinary size, light make, black hair and eyes, light complexion, diffident in his manners, supposed to be under 25 yrs. of age, has a peculiar blinking of the eyes when put in fear, is in the habit of wearing his coat with the collar thrown back, is a native of Old Spain, and formerly owned a grog-shop in Velasco.

Fifty dollars of the above reward will be paid by the subscriber, and the balance by Capt. M. K. Snell on his delivery at Brazoria.

R. J. CALDER, sheriff.

TELEGRAPH (COLUMBIA) PRINT.

Plate 24. Pagés Wanted Poster. Forgery (31.8 x 25.4 cm). The thin rules are missing below the word *Reward*, and between the sheriff's name and the imprint. Also, while the staining on this forgery is convincing, it is impossible to produce naturally: if the document had actually been stained while folded in thirds, the *ends* would have to be stained, as well as the folds. *Beinecke Rare Books and Manuscript Library, Yale University*.

IMPORTANT NEWS.

BRAZORIA, MARCH 27, 1836.

HAVING just returned on express forty hours from camp, and finding great alarm prevailing among the people, many of them flying with their families to the United States, and being called upon by the Committee of Safety and Vigilance in this place, to give a statement of facts, in relation to our army, and what its movements are, &c.: I take this method of informing them, that there is no cause for the excitement now prevailing in this part of the country. Our army, now encamped at and near Beason's on the Colorado, consists of from 1,000 to 1,200 men, and reinforcements hourly coming in, they are all well armed, with plenty of provisions, ammunition, &c, are in good spirits, and have perfect confidence in themselves and their officers. From all the information we can gain, either through our own spies, or prisoners, taken from the enemy, they cannot have more than from six to eight hundred men in the army, now encamped about five miles above us on the opposite side of the river. The prisoners say that there were but from twenty five hundred to three thousand men at Bexar after the Alamo was taken; of this number one thousand were sent to attack us at Gonzales, and the remainder were sent to retake Goliad. Of the army opposed to us at Beason's, from two to three hundred are cavalry, and the remainder infantry, with two small pieces of cannon; this body are under the command of Gen. Siezma. An attack has been made on them, I think, ere this, and if it has, who can doubt of the result? Circumstances rendered it necessary that we should retreat from Gonzales, but our army now will never leave the Colorado, but to go westward, & every day will bring news of a fresh victory, until not a Mexican Soldier, opposed to us, can be found this side of the Rio Grande! Let but the men of Texas turn out, with arms in their hands, resolved to be FREE OR DIE! and their families will be as safe here as on the other side of the Sabine.

JOHN SHARP.

P. S. On my way down I met several small companies pushing on for our camp, and those that came from the Eastward report from 300 to 500 men on their way from that quarter.

Plate 25. Important News (Streeter 136). Genuine copy (19.3 x 16.5 cm). *Barker Texas History Center, University of Texas at Austin.*

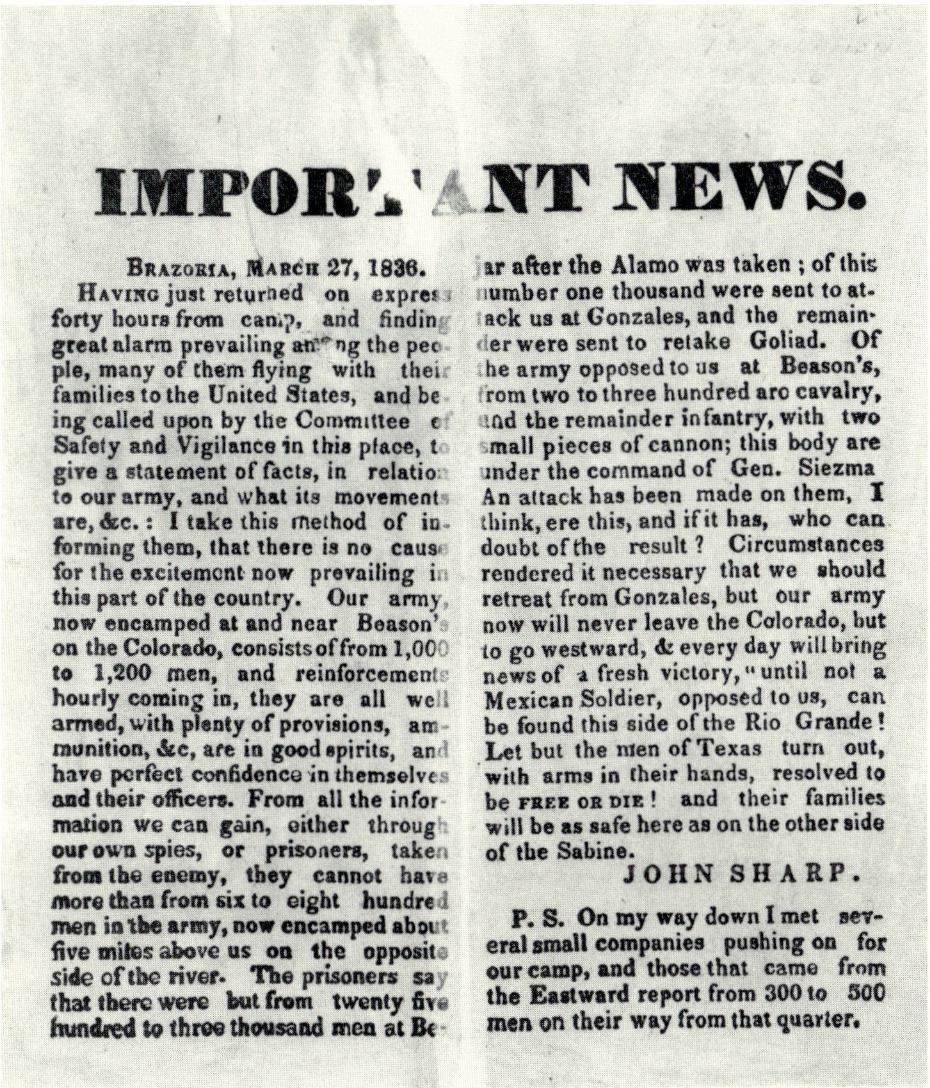

IMPOR[illegible]T NEWS.

BRAZORIA, MARCH 27, 1836.

HAVING just returned on expres[s] forty hours from camp, and findin[g] great alarm prevailing am[o]ng the peo-ple, many of them flying with thei[r] families to the United States, and be-ing called upon by the Committee o[f] Safety and Vigilance in this place, t[o] give a statement of facts, in relatio[n] to our army, and what its movement[s] are, &c. : I take this method of in-forming them, that there is no caus[e] for the excitement now prevailing i[n] this part of the country. Our army, now encamped at and near Beason'[s] on the Colorado, consists of from 1,00[0] to 1,200 men, and reinforcement[s] hourly coming in, they are all we[ll] armed, with plenty of provisions, am-munition, &c, are in good spirits, an[d] have perfect confidence in themselve[s] and their officers. From all the infor-mation we can gain, either throug[h] our own spies, or prisoners, take[n] from the enemy, they cannot hav[e] more than from six to eight hundre[d] men in the army, now encamped abou[t] five miles above us on the opposit[e] side of the river. The prisoners sa[y] that there were but from twenty fiv[e] hundred to three thousand men at Be-[y]ar after the Alamo was taken ; of this [n]umber one thousand were sent to at-[t]ack us at Gonzales, and the remain-[d]er were sent to retake Goliad. Of [t]he army opposed to us at Beason's, [f]rom two to three hundred are cavalry, [a]nd the remainder infantry, with two [s]mall pieces of cannon; this body are under the command of Gen. Siezma An attack has been made on them, I think, ere this, and if it has, who can doubt of the result ? Circumstances rendered it necessary that we should retreat from Gonzales, but our army now will never leave the Colorado, but to go westward, & every day will bring news of a fresh victory, "until not a Mexican Soldier, opposed to us, can be found this side of the Rio Grande ! Let but the men of Texas turn out, with arms in their hands, resolved to be FREE OR DIE ! and their families will be as safe here as on the other side of the Sabine.

JOHN SHARP.

P. S. On my way down I met sev-eral small companies pushing on for our camp, and those that came from the Eastward report from 300 to 500 men on their way from that quarter.

Plate 26. Important News. Forgery (14.5 x 12.5 cm). A crude piece of work—note clumsy retouching in lower left portion of document. *Star of the Republic Museum, Washington-on-the-Brazos.*

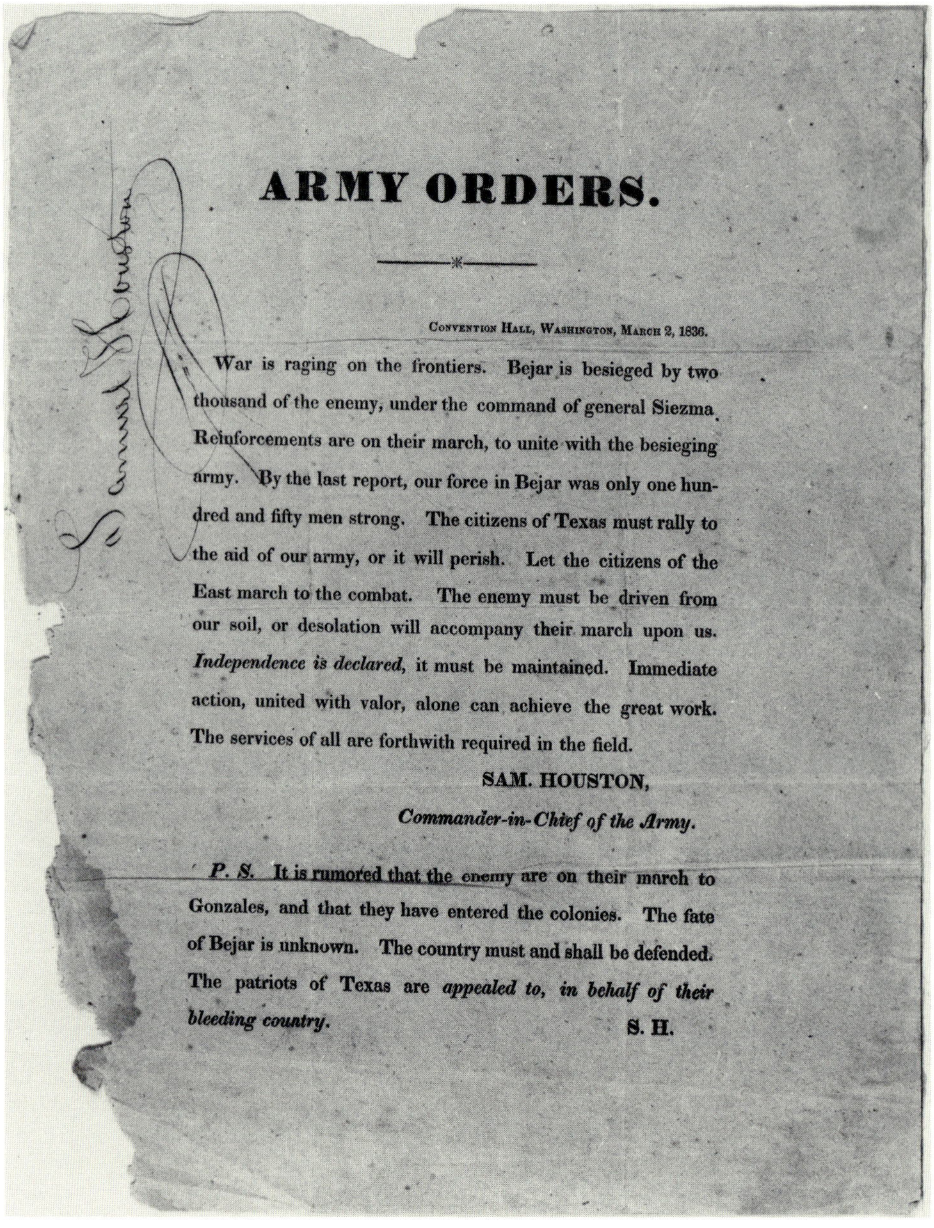

ARMY ORDERS.

CONVENTION HALL, WASHINGTON, MARCH 2, 1836.

War is raging on the frontiers. Bejar is besieged by two thousand of the enemy, under the command of general Siezma. Reinforcements are on their march, to unite with the besieging army. By the last report, our force in Bejar was only one hundred and fifty men strong. The citizens of Texas must rally to the aid of our army, or it will perish. Let the citizens of the East march to the combat. The enemy must be driven from our soil, or desolation will accompany their march upon us. *Independence is declared*, it must be maintained. Immediate action, united with valor, alone can achieve the great work. The services of all are forthwith required in the field.

SAM. HOUSTON,

Commander-in-Chief of the Army.

P. S. It is rumored that the enemy are on their march to Gonzales, and that they have entered the colonies. The fate of Bejar is unknown. The country must and shall be defended. The patriots of Texas are *appealed to, in behalf of their bleeding country.*

S. H.

Plate 27. Army Orders (Streeter 150). Genuine copy (24.8 x 19.5 cm). *Barker Texas History Center, University of Texas at Austin.*

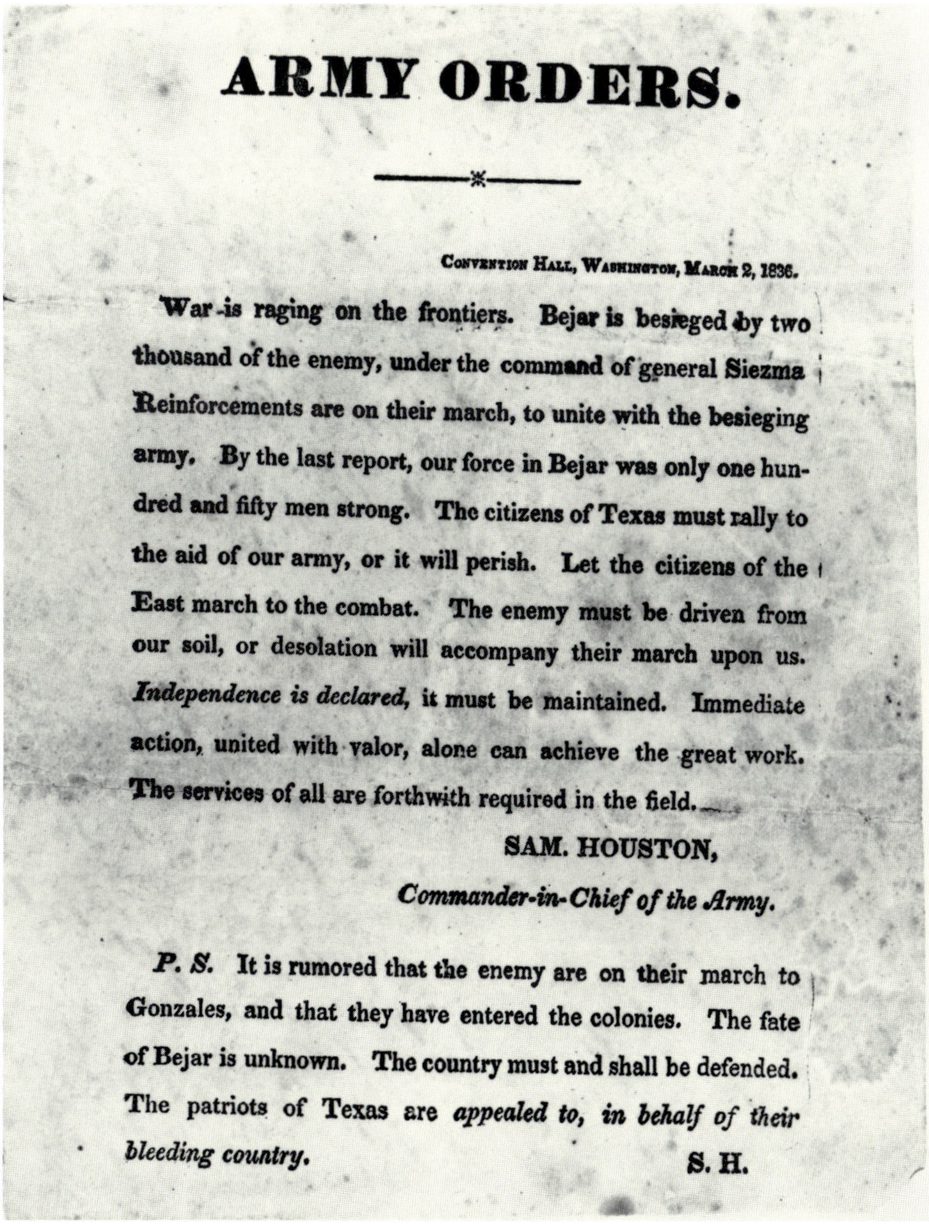

ARMY ORDERS.

CONVENTION HALL, WASHINGTON, MARCH 2, 1836.

War is raging on the frontiers. Bejar is besieged by two thousand of the enemy, under the command of general Siezma Reinforcements are on their march, to unite with the besieging army. By the last report, our force in Bejar was only one hundred and fifty men strong. The citizens of Texas must rally to the aid of our army, or it will perish. Let the citizens of the East march to the combat. The enemy must be driven from our soil, or desolation will accompany their march upon us. *Independence is declared,* it must be maintained. Immediate action, united with valor, alone can achieve the great work. The services of all are forthwith required in the field.

SAM. HOUSTON,

Commander-in-Chief of the Army.

P. S. It is rumored that the enemy are on their march to Gonzales, and that they have entered the colonies. The fate of Bejar is unknown. The country must and shall be defended. The patriots of Texas are *appealed to, in behalf of their bleeding country.*

S. H.

Plate 28. Army Orders. Forgery (20 x 15.4 cm). The plate mark from the zinc printing plate is faintly visible at intervals along the right edge of the text.

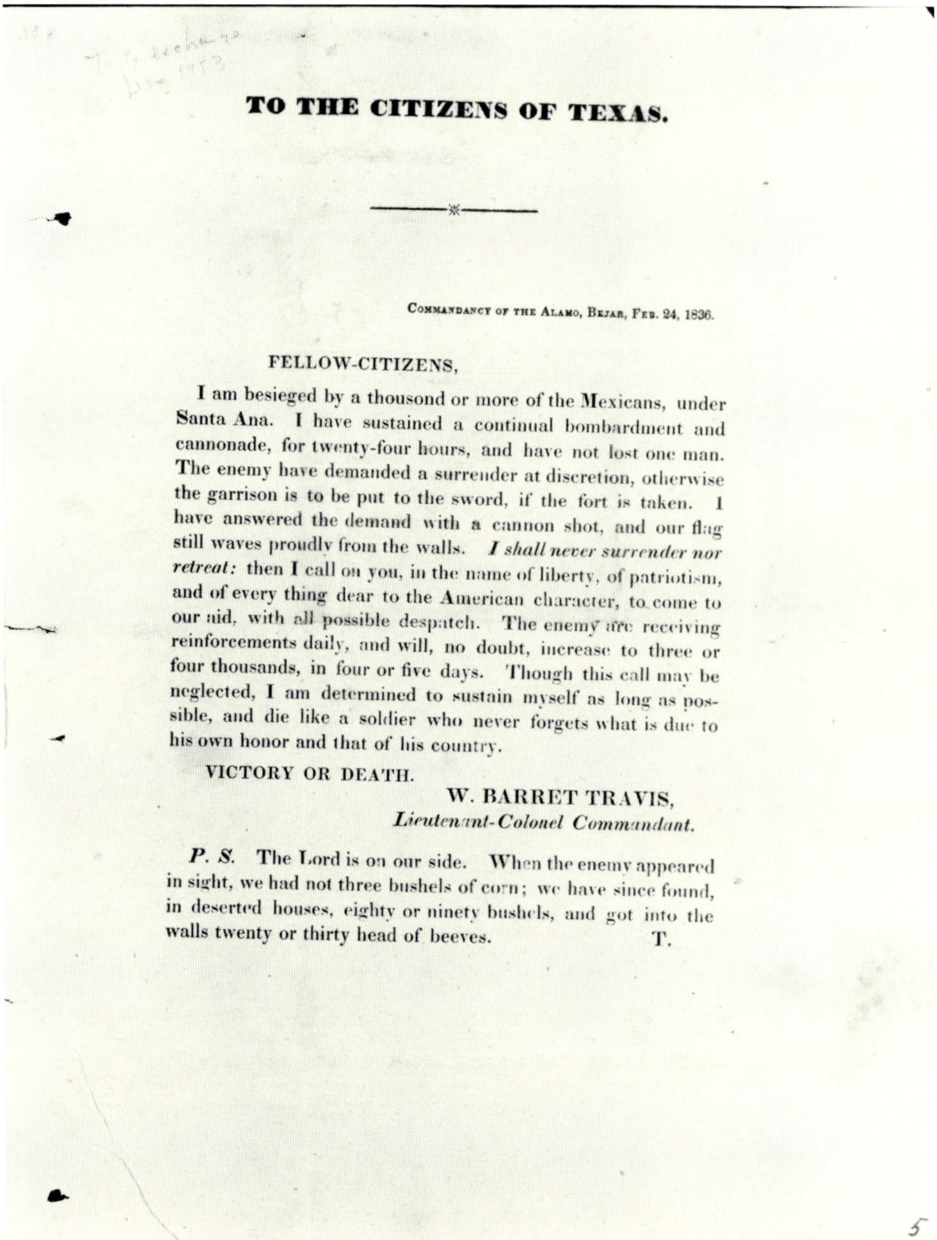

TO THE CITIZENS OF TEXAS.

COMMANDANCY OF THE ALAMO, BEJAR, FEB. 24, 1836.

FELLOW-CITIZENS,

I am besieged by a thousond or more of the Mexicans, under Santa Ana. I have sustained a continual bombardment and cannonade, for twenty-four hours, and have not lost one man. The enemy have demanded a surrender at discretion, otherwise the garrison is to be put to the sword, if the fort is taken. I have answered the demand with a cannon shot, and our flag still waves proudly from the walls. *I shall never surrender nor retreat:* then I call on you, in the name of liberty, of patriotism, and of every thing dear to the American character, to come to our aid, with all possible despatch. The enemy are receiving reinforcements daily, and will, no doubt, increase to three or four thousands, in four or five days. Though this call may be neglected, I am determined to sustain myself as long as possible, and die like a soldier who never forgets what is due to his own honor and that of his country.

VICTORY OR DEATH.

W. BARRET TRAVIS,
Lieutenant-Colonel Commandant.

P. S. The Lord is on our side. When the enemy appeared in sight, we had not three bushels of corn; we have since found, in deserted houses, eighty or ninety bushels, and got into the walls twenty or thirty head of beeves. T.

Plate 29. Travis' Victory or Death Letter (Streeter 185). Genuine copy (25.2 x 19.5 cm). This text is still attached to "Texas Expects Every Man to Do His Duty" by Henry Smith, as originally printed (see p. 108). The pencil note "Tx by exchange/Dec. 1953" is in the hand of Thomas W. Streeter. *Beinecke Rare Book and Manuscript Library, Yale University.*

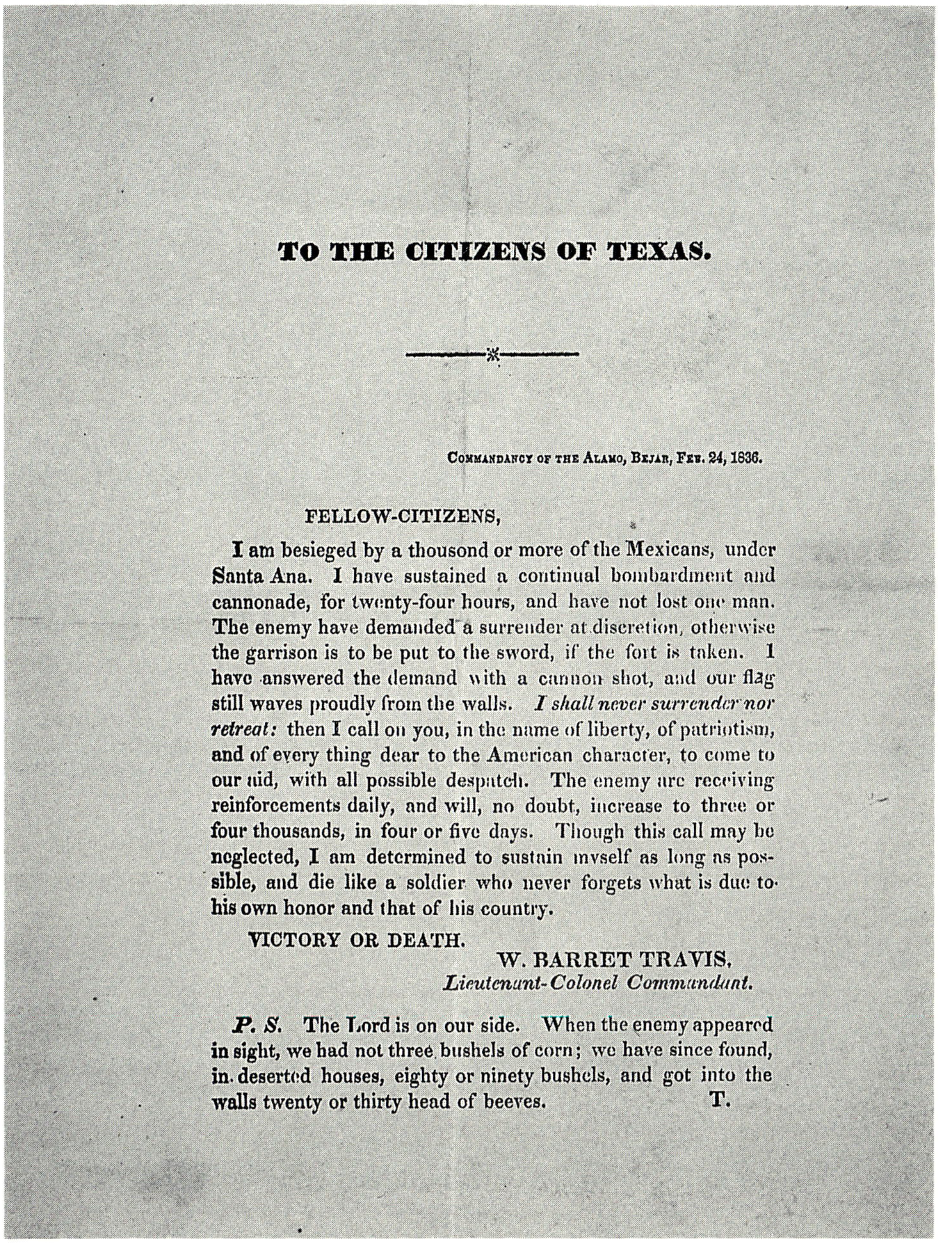

TO THE CITIZENS OF TEXAS.

COMMANDANCY OF THE ALAMO, BEJAR, FEB. 24, 1836.

FELLOW-CITIZENS,

I am besieged by a thousond or more of the Mexicans, under Santa Ana. I have sustained a continual bombardment and cannonade, for twenty-four hours, and have not lost one man. The enemy have demanded a surrender at discretion, otherwise the garrison is to be put to the sword, if the fort is taken. I have answered the demand with a cannon shot, and our flag still waves proudly from the walls. *I shall never surrender nor retreat:* then I call on you, in the name of liberty, of patriotism, and of every thing dear to the American character, to come to our aid, with all possible despatch. The enemy are receiving reinforcements daily, and will, no doubt, increase to three or four thousands, in four or five days. Though this call may be neglected, I am determined to sustain myself as long as possible, and die like a soldier who never forgets what is due to his own honor and that of his country.

VICTORY OR DEATH.

W. BARRET TRAVIS,
Lieutenant-Colonel Commandant.

P. S. The Lord is on our side. When the enemy appeared in sight, we had not three bushels of corn; we have since found, in deserted houses, eighty or ninety bushels, and got into the walls twenty or thirty head of beeves. T.

Plate 30. Travis' Victory or Death Letter. Forgery. The revealing detail is the misformed letter *a* in *flag* at the end of line 6.

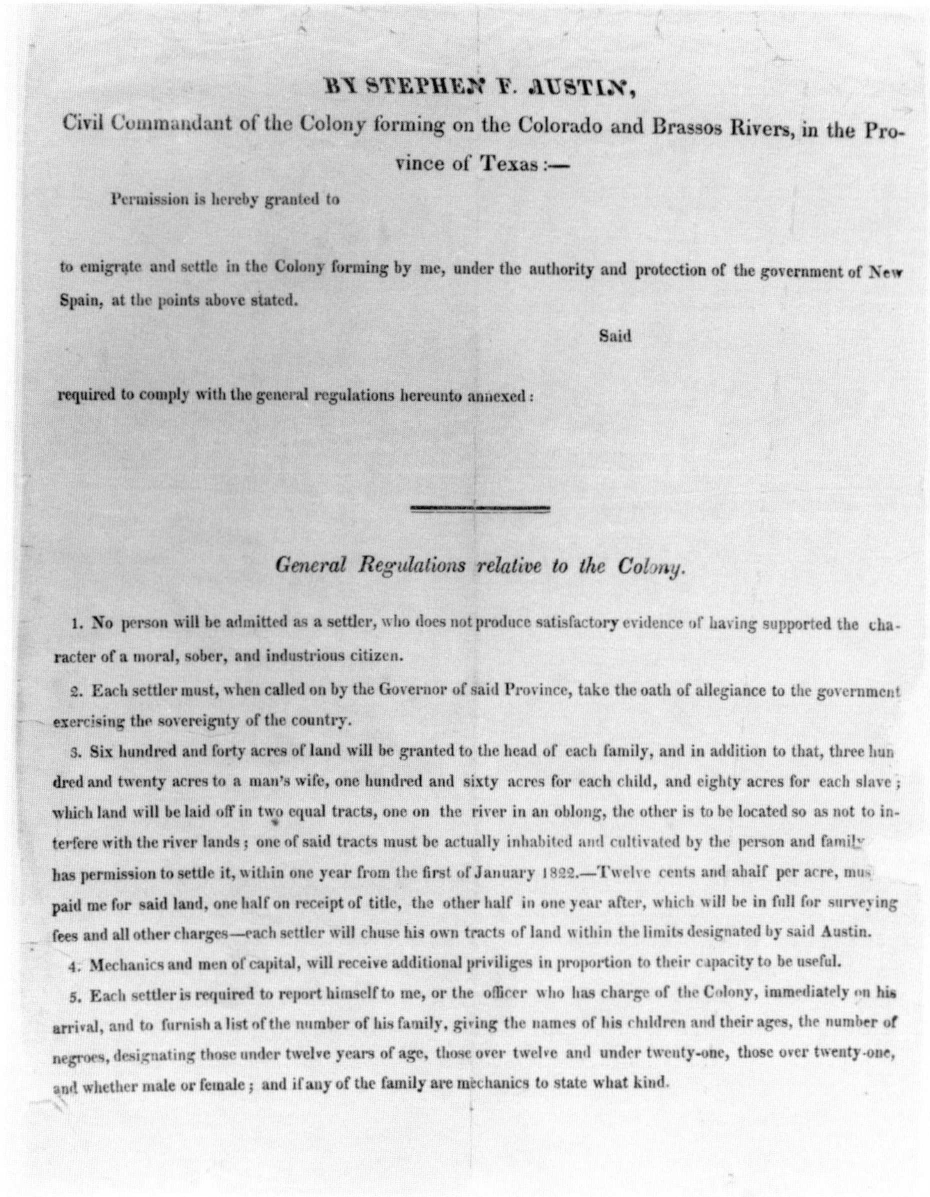

BY STEPHEN F. AUSTIN,

Civil Commandant of the Colony forming on the Colorado and Brassos Rivers, in the Province of Texas:—

Permission is hereby granted to

to emigrate and settle in the Colony forming by me, under the authority and protection of the government of New Spain, at the points above stated.

Said

required to comply with the general regulations hereunto annexed:

General Regulations relative to the Colony.

1. No person will be admitted as a settler, who does not produce satisfactory evidence of having supported the character of a moral, sober, and industrious citizen.

2. Each settler must, when called on by the Governor of said Province, take the oath of allegiance to the government exercising the sovereignty of the country.

3. Six hundred and forty acres of land will be granted to the head of each family, and in addition to that, three hun dred and twenty acres to a man's wife, one hundred and sixty acres for each child, and eighty acres for each slave; which land will be laid off in two equal tracts, one on the river in an oblong, the other is to be located so as not to interfere with the river lands; one of said tracts must be actually inhabited and cultivated by the person and family has permission to settle it, within one year from the first of January 1822.—Twelve cents and ahalf per acre, mus paid me for said land, one half on receipt of title, the other half in one year after, which will be in full for surveying fees and all other charges—each settler will chuse his own tracts of land within the limits designated by said Austin.

4. Mechanics and men of capital, will receive additional priviliges in proportion to their capacity to be useful.

5. Each settler is required to report himself to me, or the officer who has charge of the Colony, immediately on his arrival, and to furnish a list of the number of his family, giving the names of his children and their ages, the number of negroes, designating those under twelve years of age, those over twelve and under twenty-one, those over twenty-one, and whether male or female; and if any of the family are mechanics to state what kind.

Plate 31. Austin's Grant Application (Streeter 1082). Genuine copy (25 x 20 cm). *Special Collections, University of Houston Library.*

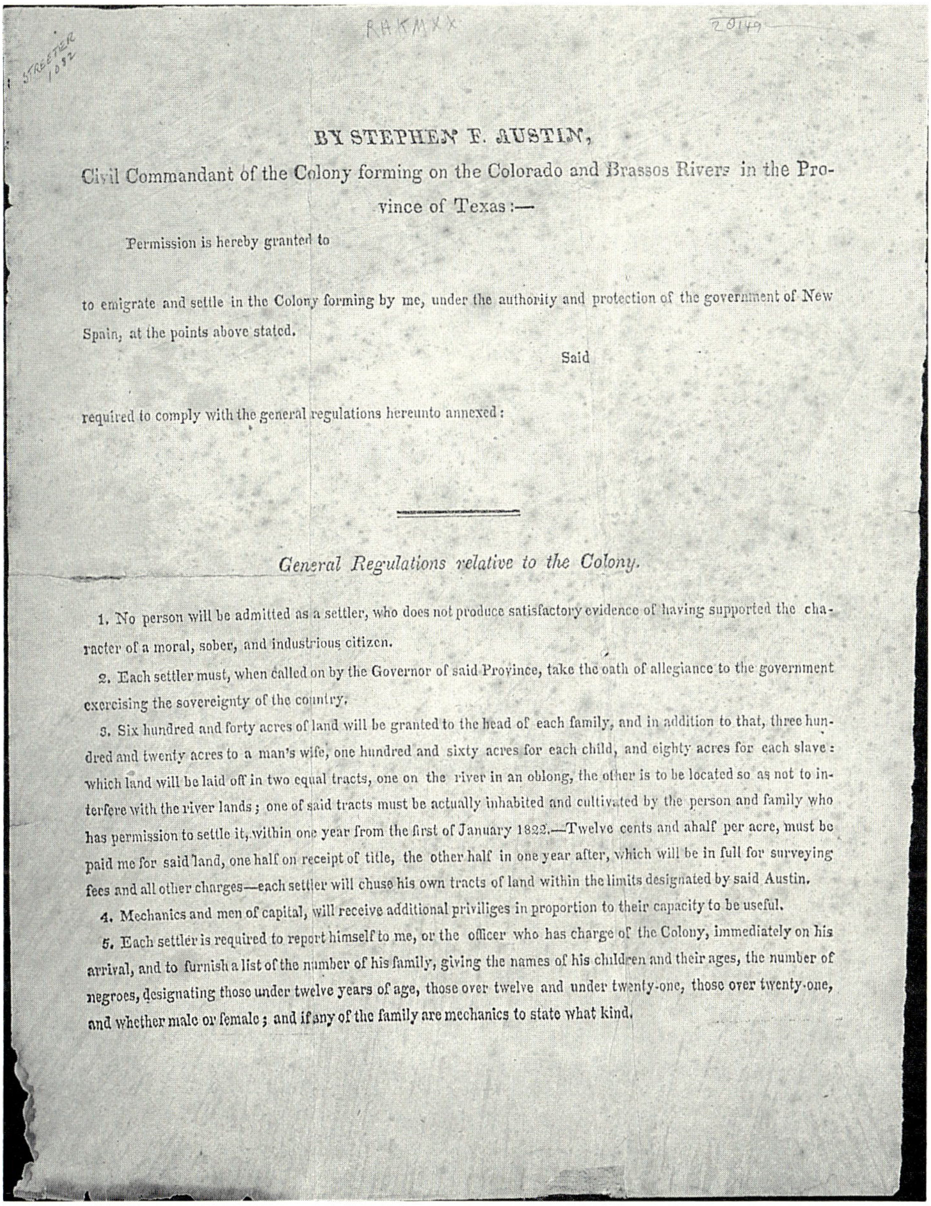
BY STEPHEN F. AUSTIN,

Civil Commandant of the Colony forming on the Colorado and Brassos Rivers in the Province of Texas:—

Permission is hereby granted to

to emigrate and settle in the Colony forming by me, under the authority and protection of the government of New Spain, at the points above stated.

Said

required to comply with the general regulations hereunto annexed:

General Regulations relative to the Colony.

1. No person will be admitted as a settler, who does not produce satisfactory evidence of having supported the character of a moral, sober, and industrious citizen.

2. Each settler must, when called on by the Governor of said Province, take the oath of allegiance to the government exercising the sovereignty of the country.

3. Six hundred and forty acres of land will be granted to the head of each family, and in addition to that, three hundred and twenty acres to a man's wife, one hundred and sixty acres for each child, and eighty acres for each slave: which land will be laid off in two equal tracts, one on the river in an oblong, the other is to be located so as not to interfere with the river lands; one of said tracts must be actually inhabited and cultivated by the person and family who has permission to settle it, within one year from the first of January 1822.—Twelve cents and ahalf per acre, must be paid me for said land, one half on receipt of title, the other half in one year after, which will be in full for surveying fees and all other charges—each settler will chuse his own tracts of land within the limits designated by said Austin.

4. Mechanics and men of capital, will receive additional priviliges in proportion to their capacity to be useful.

5. Each settler is required to report himself to me, or the officer who has charge of the Colony, immediately on his arrival, and to furnish a list of the number of his family, giving the names of his children and their ages, the number of negroes, designating those under twelve years of age, those over twelve and under twenty-one, those over twenty-one, and whether male or female; and if any of the family are mechanics to state what kind.

Plate 32. Austin's Grant Application. Forgery (24.6 x 19.2 cm). *Private Collection.*

TEXAS!!
Emigrants who are desirious of assisting Texas at this important crisis of her affairs may have a free passage and equipments, by applying at the
NEW-YORK and PHILADELPHIA HOTEL,
On the Old Levee, near the Blue Stores.
Now is the time to ensure a fortune in Land:
To all who remain in Texas during the War will be allowed 1280 Acres.
To all who remain Six Months, 640 Acres.
To all who remain Three Months, 320 Acres.
And as Colonists, 4600 Acres for a family and 1470 Acres for a Single Man.
New Orleans, April 23d, 1836.

Plate 33. New Orleans Recruiting Poster (Streeter 1246). Genuine copy (25 x 26 cm).
Barker Texas History Center, University of Texas at Austin.

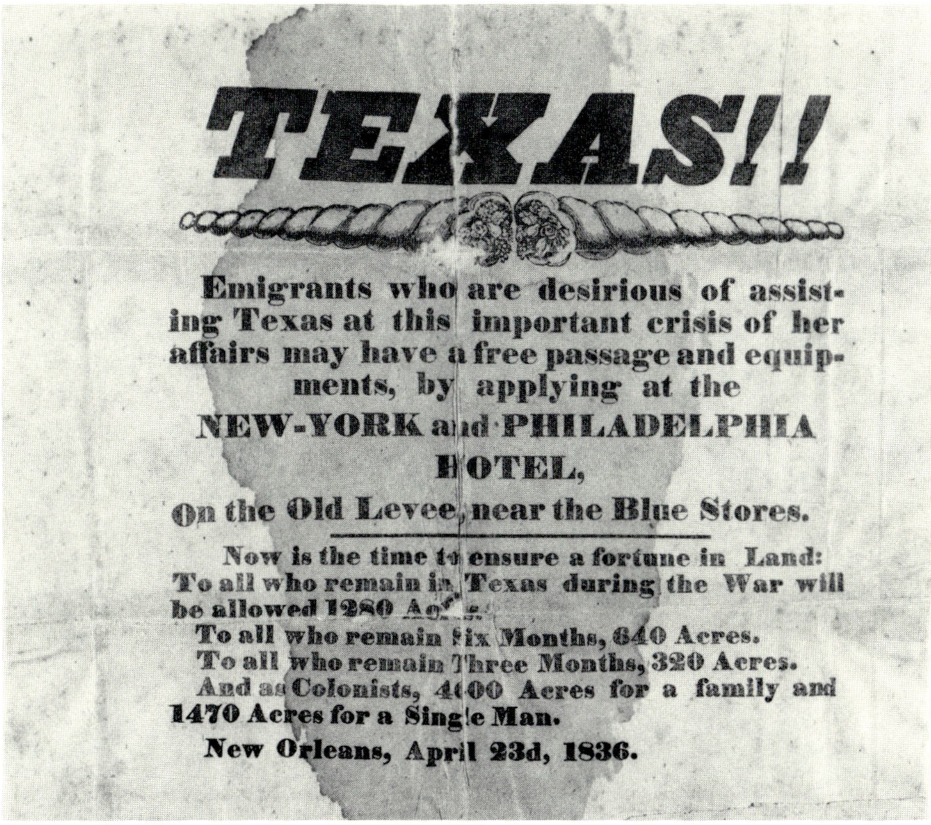
TEXAS!!
Emigrants who are desirious of assisting Texas at this important crisis of her affairs may have a free passage and equipments, by applying at the
NEW-YORK and PHILADELPHIA HOTEL,
On the Old Levee, near the Blue Stores.
Now is the time to ensure a fortune in Land:
To all who remain in Texas during the War will be allowed 1280 Acres.
To all who remain Six Months, 640 Acres.
To all who remain Three Months, 320 Acres.
And as Colonists, 4400 Acres for a family and 1470 Acres for a Single Man.
New Orleans, April 23d, 1836.

Plate 34. New Orleans Recruiting Poster. Forgery (22.3 x 26.5 cm). The type area is smaller than for a genuine copy; on a forgery the cornucopia ornaments measure 18.6 cm. *Star of the Republic Museum, Washington-on-the-Brazos.*

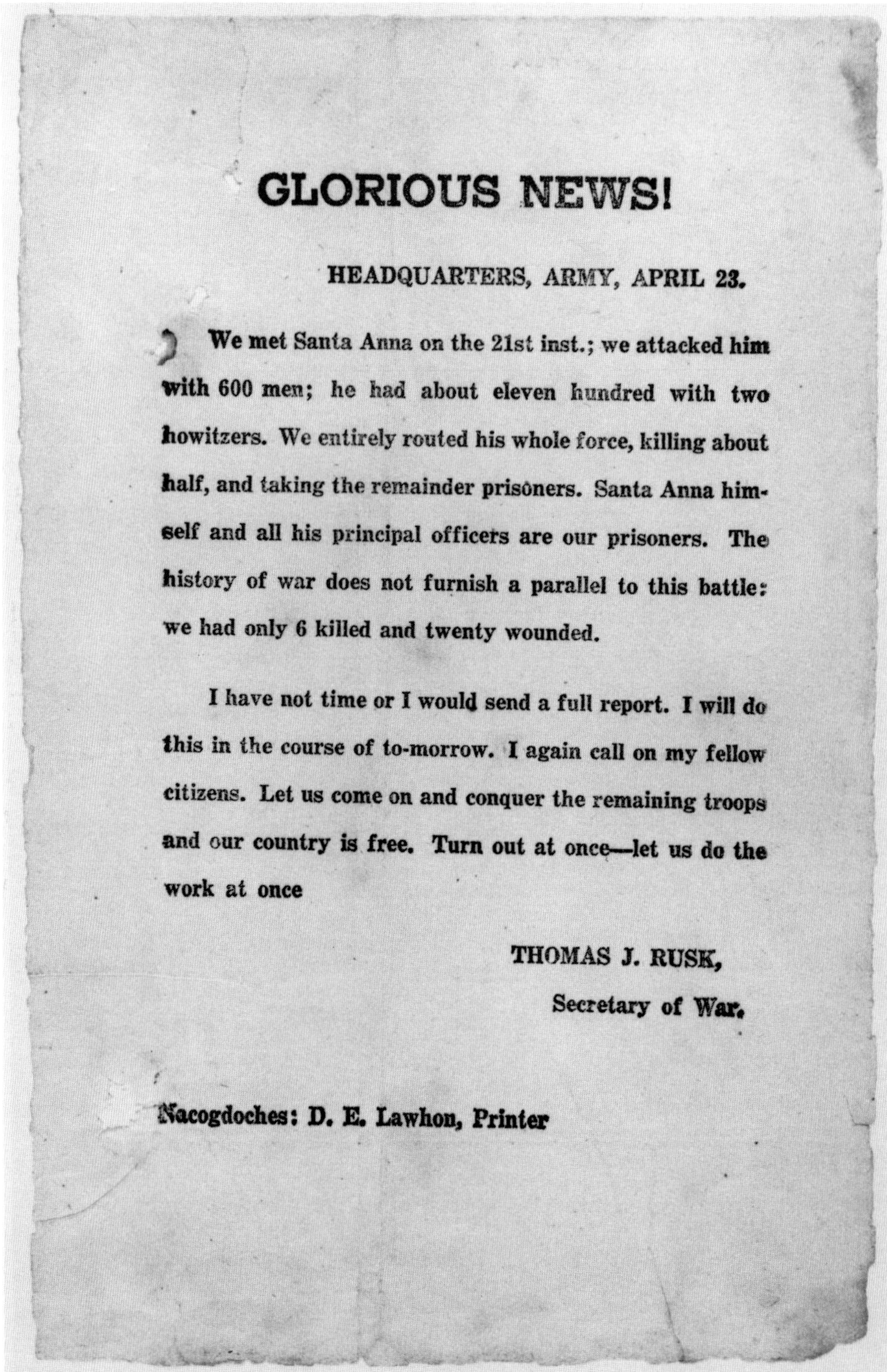

GLORIOUS NEWS!

HEADQUARTERS, ARMY, APRIL 23.

We met Santa Anna on the 21st inst.; we attacked him with 600 men; he had about eleven hundred with two howitzers. We entirely routed his whole force, killing about half, and taking the remainder prisoners. Santa Anna himself and all his principal officers are our prisoners. The history of war does not furnish a parallel to this battle: we had only 6 killed and twenty wounded.

I have not time or I would send a full report. I will do this in the course of to-morrow. I again call on my fellow citizens. Let us come on and conquer the remaining troops and our country is free. Turn out at once—let us do the work at once

THOMAS J. RUSK,
Secretary of War.

Nacogdoches: D. E. Lawhon, Printer

Plate 35. Glorious News! (Not in Streeter). Fabrication (21.3 x 14 cm). *Star of the Republic Museum, Washington-on-the-Brazos.*

G & S TYPESETTERS—This form will be held for 7 days from **3-11-88**

HEADQUARTERS, ARMY, APRIL 23.

We met Santa Anna on the 21st inst.; we attacked him with 600 men; he had about eleven hundred with two howitzers. We entirely routed his whole force, killing about half, and taking the remainder prisoners. Santa Anna himself and all his principal officers are our prisoners. The history of war does not furnish a parallel to this battle: we had only 6 killed and twenty wounded.

I have not time or I would send a full report. I will do this in the course of to-morrow. I again call on my fellow citizens. Let us come on and conquer the remaining troops and our country is free. Turn out at once—let us do the work at once

THOMAS J. RUSK,

Secretary of War.

Nacogdoches: D. E. Lawhon, Printer

Plate 36. Glorious News! The text of this fabrication is set in 12-point Century Bold Linotype by G & S Typesetters in Austin. The headline, not reproduced in this sample, is Rockwell Antique.

A PUBLIC MEETING.

At a large and respectable meeting of the citizens of Galveston and subsequent to a meeting convened for public worship, the following proceedings took place:

On motion of Col. Turner, Gail Border jr. Esq. was called to the Chair, and C. H. Winkle Esq., appointed Secretary.

The objects of the meeting were stated by A. J. Yates, Esq., after which he offered the following resolutions which were unanimously adopted.

Resolved, That a subscription be circulated in this place for the purpose of obtaining funds for the erection of a Church, for public worship in this city.

Resolved, That a committee of three be appointed to request of the directors of the Galveston City Association at their next meeting, the grant of a convenient lot in this city, for the purpose of erecting said Church thereon, and that a conveyance of the same be made to said Committee to be held in trust, or a bond given them therefor, to be conveyed to the first organized and incorporated Protestant Church established in this city, who shall pay to such of the original subscribers, their heirs or assigns, who shall subscribe with the condition of reimbursement on sale as aforesaid, the amount of their respective subscriptions in the current funds of this Republic, and that the condition of said conveyance or bond be, that the Church to be erected on said lot, be completed within one year from the date hereof, or that the sum of three thousand dollars at least be expended in the erection thereof within said period.

Resolved, That said Committee consist of Messrs. Gail Borden jr., Levi Jones and A. Turner Esqrs., and that it be their further duty to solicit subscriptions for the erection of said Church and that the same be payable to them, on or before the 1st day of July next, ensuing this date, and that said committee keep an account of all monies subscribed as free donations, and those which are subscribed for reimbursement on sale, and that when said committee shall have collected the sum of three thousand dollars, or such less sum as they shall deem sufficient, they shall authorize and employ some responsible person to contract for the preparation, shipment and delivery of said Church at this place and powered to the erection of the same so far as said funds shall extend.

Resolved, That the doors of said Church shall be opened for the performance of public worship to any denomination of Protestant Christians at any time previous to the sale thereof, who shall have a preacher in regular standing [illegible] and in case no such person be employed here, then the doors of the same shall be open to any preacher of any Protestant Christian Church, who may be temporarily here, so long as he shall continue to preach regularly in this city, until such sale of said Church as aforesaid, and not exceeding a period of six months, it being understood that when two or more transient preachers of different denominations are here at any time previous to said sale, the time shall be agreeably divided between them.

Resolved, That the care and control of said Church and its property shall be in charge of a majority of said committee under these resolutions, and that if no sale is made of the property within two years from the 1st of July next, that then the same shall be offered for sale at public auction, and the proceeds of the sale be divided *pro rata* among the subscriberr claiming reimbursement, and in case of any sale all sums remaining unclaimed for six months after said sale from subscribers claiming reimbursement, or their legal representatives shall reverted to the purchaser or purchasers thereof.

Resolved, That these resolutions be made part of the conditions of the subscription to be circulated and that the same be furnished to the Directors of the Galveston City Association for record, and that a copy of the proceedings of this meeting with the resolutions be furnished to the Texas Telegraph for publication.

Dr. Jones offered the following resolution, which was also unanimously adopted:

Resolved, That the Rev. Messrs E. A. Huntington and Rowls and Mr. Yates be appointed a committee to solicit subsriptions from our friends in the United States.

GALVESTON, Sunday, April 8th, 1838.

Plate 37. A Public Meeting (Not in Streeter). Fabrication (20.4 x 19.8 cm), made by re-stripping a genuine newspaper article into two columns, then photocopying onto old paper. *Private Collection.*

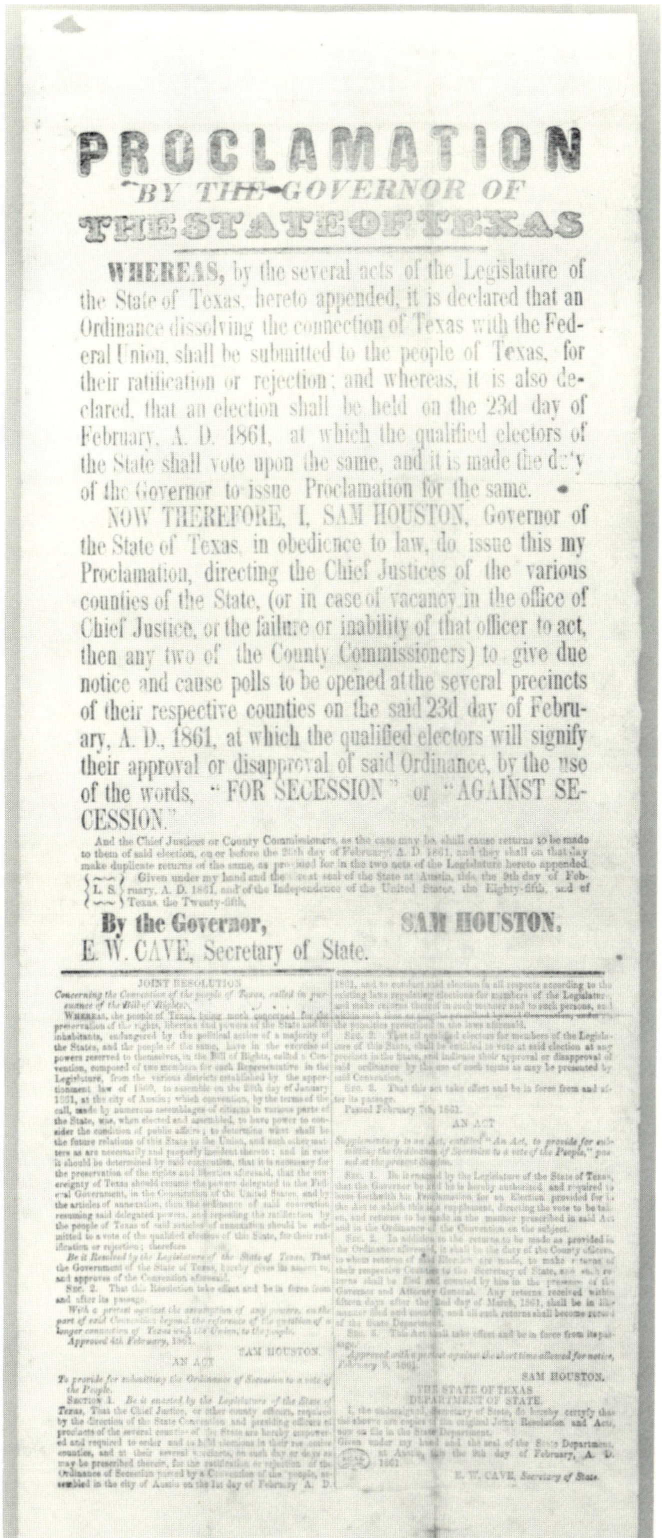
PROCLAMATION
BY THE GOVERNOR OF
THE STATE OF TEXAS

WHEREAS, by the several acts of the Legislature of the State of Texas, hereto appended, it is declared that an Ordinance dissolving the connection of Texas with the Federal Union, shall be submitted to the people of Texas, for their ratification or rejection; and whereas, it is also declared, that an election shall be held on the 23d day of February, A. D. 1861, at which the qualified electors of the State shall vote upon the same, and it is made the duty of the Governor to issue Proclamation for the same.

NOW THEREFORE, I, SAM HOUSTON, Governor of the State of Texas, in obedience to law, do issue this my Proclamation, directing the Chief Justices of the various counties of the State, (or in case of vacancy in the office of Chief Justice, or the failure or inability of that officer to act, then any two of the County Commissioners) to give due notice and cause polls to be opened at the several precincts of their respective counties on the said 23d day of February, A. D., 1861, at which the qualified electors will signify their approval or disapproval of said Ordinance, by the use of the words, "FOR SECESSION" or "AGAINST SECESSION."

And the Chief Justices or County Commissioners, as the case may be, shall cause returns to be made to them of said election, on or before the 28th day of February, A. D. 1861, and they shall on that day make duplicate returns of the same, as provided for in the two acts of the Legislature hereto appended.

{L. S.} Given under my hand and the great seal of the State at Austin, this, the 9th day of February, A. D. 1861, and of the Independence of the United States, the Eighty-fifth, and of Texas, the Twenty-fifth,

By the Governor, SAM HOUSTON.
E. W. CAVE, Secretary of State.

JOINT RESOLUTION

AN ACT

AN ACT

THE STATE OF TEXAS
DEPARTMENT OF STATE.

E. W. CAVE, Secretary of State.

Plate 38. Sam Houston Proclamation (Winkler/Friend 202). Genuine copy (54.6 x 22.4 cm); probably the one used to make the forgeries. *Special Collections, University of Houston Library.*

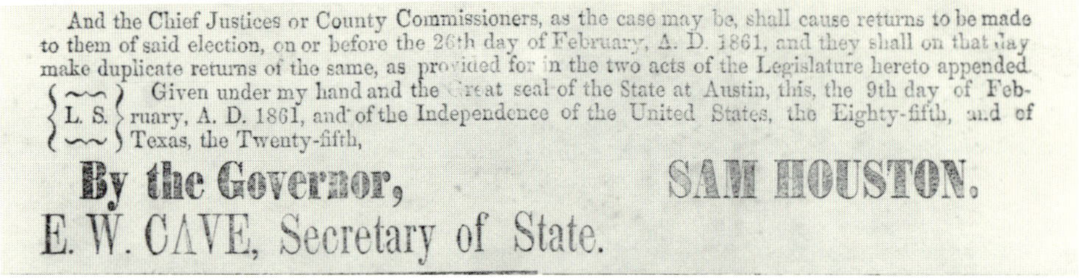

And the Chief Justices or County Commissioners, as the case may be, shall cause returns to be made to them of said election, on or before the 26th day of February, A. D. 1861, and they shall on that day make duplicate returns of the same, as provided for in the two acts of the Legislature hereto appended.

{L. S.} Given under my hand and the Great seal of the State at Austin, this, the 9th day of February, A. D. 1861, and of the Independence of the United States, the Eighty-fifth, and of Texas, the Twenty-fifth,

By the Governor, **SAM HOUSTON.**

E. W. CAVE, Secretary of State.

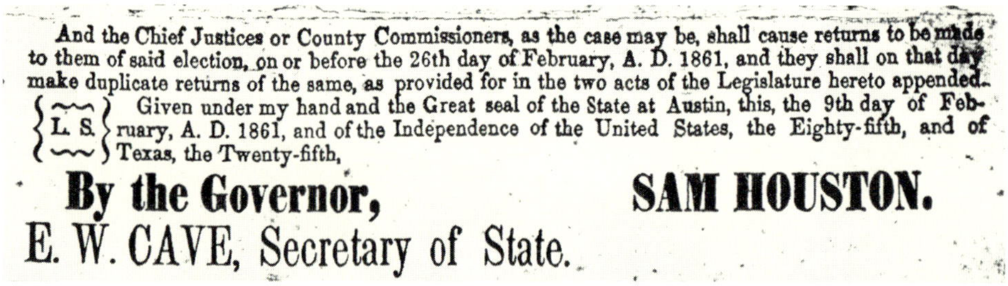

And the Chief Justices or County Commissioners, as the case may be, shall cause returns to be made to them of said election, on or before the 26th day of February, A. D. 1861, and they shall on that day make duplicate returns of the same, as provided for in the two acts of the Legislature hereto appended.

{L. S.} Given under my hand and the Great seal of the State at Austin, this, the 9th day of February, A. D. 1861, and of the Independence of the United States, the Eighty-fifth, and of Texas, the Twenty-fifth,

By the Governor, **SAM HOUSTON.**

E. W. CAVE, Secretary of State.

Plate 39. *Top:* Detail from the genuine copy of the Sam Houston Proclamation at the University of Houston, used to make the forgeries. Note that the capital *G* in *Great Seal* in line 4 is weakly printed. *Bottom:* Same lines from photocopy of a forgery (unfortunately, a photocopy was all that was available). Note that the *G* is a crude retouching of the letter, especially compared to the capital *G* at the beginning of the sentence.

Glorious News!

(Not in Streeter)

Thomas J. Rusk was Texas' Secretary of War and commander of the left wing of the army at San Jacinto. He had come to Nacogdoches pursuing swindlers who had "G.T.T." (Gone to Texas) with most of his money. He decided to stay, organized a company of volunteers in the fall of 1835, and later signed the Texas Declaration of Independence as a delegate from Nacogdoches. His wife and their three sons arrived from Georgia in December 1835.[1]

The victory at San Jacinto would have been glorious news indeed to the inhabitants of Nacogdoches, and D. E. Lawhon, the town's only printer, might well have been moved to use that happy salutation in a printing of Rusk's dispatch announcing the triumph, dated April 23. There was only one problem: Lawhon wasn't in Nacogdoches. Neither was anyone else, except for a small garrison of thirty men under General McLeod.[2] Lawhon's newspaper, the *Texean and Emigrant's Guide*, had suspended publication by March 24, 1836,[3] and the town had been abandoned in the Runaway Scrape prior to April 13.[4] In fact, there was not another newspaper in Nacogdoches until July of 1837, and the next separate Nacogdoches imprint recorded by Streeter was not printed until August 1838.[5]

Thus when I compared the types in this "Glorious News" broadside with every surviving Lawhon imprint (there are only seven, in addition to his newspapers), I was not surprised to discover that the types were not among those he used. Once again, the text was set from Linotype (12-point Century Bold), but for variety a handset foundry type was used for the display line: American Type Founders' Rockwell Antique.

In *Papers of the Texas Revolution* (6:32, no. 2843), John Jenkins credits the text of this broadside to the *Mississippi Free Trader & Natchez Gazette* for May 6, 1836. However, it had already appeared in the *Red River Herald* (Nachitoches) on April 30, and as an extra of the *Louisiana Journal* on May 2. Its first separate appearance, as a broadside extra to the *Lexington Intelligencer*, May 14, 1836, had a heading with a familiar ring: "The Glorious News Confirmed."[6]

Census

Fabrications:

1. American Antiquarian Society, Worcester, Massachusetts. Received as a gift from a Baltimore collector, who purchased it from Arkansas dealer Gary Hendershott (item 3 in an undated catalogue from late 1986), who acquired the document from John N. Rowe, who acquired it from John Jenkins.
2. Private Collection, Houston. Acquired from Dorman David in the early 1970s.
3. John Jenkins, Austin. Sold to a private collector, who returned it because of doubts as to its authenticity; subsequently listed as genuine in Jenkins Company fire claim in September 1987.
4. Private Collection, California. Purchased from Dallas dealer John N. Rowe, who acquired it from John Jenkins.
5. Star of the Republic Museum, Washington-on-the-Brazos. Source unknown; acquired before 1976.

Notes

1. Blount, "A Brief Study of Thomas J. Rusk," *Southwest Historical Quarterly*, 191.
2. Ibid.
3. Streeter, *Bibliography*, Part I, 2:539.
4. Webb, *Handbook*, 2:515.
5. Streeter 287 (*Bibliography*, Part I, 1:243).
6. The salutation "Glorious News!" was fairly commonly used in newspapers of the time to announce events of importance. By a nice irony the earliest appearance of "Glorious News!" in a Texas paper is in the *Texas Gazette* for October 13, 1829, heading an article describing Santa Anna's victory over the Spanish at Tampico. The news was celebrated in San Felipe "by the firing of cannon, and by other such demonstrations of joy, as the means of our infant town would permit."

Sam Houston Proclamation

(Winkler/Friend 202)

This broadside is the only one of those found to be forged that does not fall within the period covered by the Streeter *Bibliography* (1795–1845). It is connected to the earlier period by the powerful personality of Sam Houston, still a force to be reckoned with in Texas twenty-five years after the Battle of San Jacinto. He had been elected governor in 1859 in an astonishing comeback, after a defeat for the same office only two years earlier and removal from the United States Senate by the Texas legislature the same year because of his vote against the Kansas-Nebraska Act.[1] It was during the Senate debates over that legislation that he made his position on the Union clear, saying, "I know neither North nor South; I know only the Union."

Despite his victory in the 1859 election, his position was rendered hopeless by Lincoln's victory in the presidential election of November 1860, which assured secession by the southern states. South Carolina seceded on December 20, 1860, and on January 23, 1861, a convention was held in Austin to draft an Ordinance of Secession for Texas, with a provision for a popular vote on the matter added as a concession to Houston. Houston attended the convention, but the outcome was a foregone conclusion. By a vote of 167 to 7 the measure was passed and the Ordinance offered to the popular ballot on February 23. This broadside announces the forthcoming election, and it is worth noting that Houston offers it only "in obedience to law." He was still fiercely opposed to secession, and he set off on a tour of Texas, speaking defiantly against the measure.

In Galveston he declared prophetically, "Some of you laugh to scorn the idea of bloodshed as the result of secession. But let me tell you what is coming. . . . Your fathers and your husbands, your sons and brothers, will be herded at the point of the bayonet. . . . You may, after the sacrifice of countless millions of treasure and hundreds of thousands of lives, as a bare possibility, win Southern independence . . . but I doubt it."[2] When the election was held, the result was 39,415 for secession, 13,858 opposed. On March 4, Houston was called upon to take an oath of allegiance to the Confederacy. He refused, and the convention declared the office of governor vacant. On March 16, he addressed an eloquent explanation of his action "To the People of Texas," in which he lamented, "I am stricken down now, because I will not yield those principles, which I have fought for and struggled to maintain. The severest pang is that the blow comes in the name of the State of Texas."[3]

The forgery of his call for an election is something less dramatic. Made from a genuine original now at the University of Houston, it displays subtle (for this forger) touching up to the type, primarily in the lower portion of the document.

Census

Genuine copies:

1. University of Texas at Austin, Barker Texas History Center. Source unknown.
2. University of Houston. Source and date of acquisition unknown; this was the copy used to make the forgeries.

Forgeries:

1. John N. Rowe, Dallas. Acquired at Simpson Galleries auction, February 3, 1986, lot 505.

Untraced copy:

1. Sotheby's New York, sale no. 5315, May 1, 1985, lot 138. Sotheby's will not release the name of either the consignor or the purchaser.

Notes

1. United States Senators were elected by the state legislatures until the passage of the 17th Amendment to the Constitution in 1913.
2. James, *The Raven*, 410.
3. Williams and Barker, *Writings of Sam Houston*, 8:277.

Other Documents

In addition to the documents described on the preceding pages, there are two items that are highly suspect:

Arrival of Colonel García (Streeter 7)

This item is a small circular announcing the arrival of Lieutenant Colonel D. Luciano García in Bexar and his assumption of the office of governor. Four copies were located by Streeter in 1955—at Yale, the Texas General Land Office, the University of Texas (there are four copies in the Bexar Archive, but Streeter did not note multiple copies in his locations), and in Streeter's own collection. Another copy appears in Edward Eberstadt and Son's catalogue 162, probably the duplicate created when Yale acquired the Streeter Collection. There was one copy (perhaps the same one) in the Eberstadt's Texas Collection when it was acquired by the Jenkins Company in 1975.

Since 1975 at least four additional copies have surfaced, and they differ from those copies that are genuine in important respects: 1) The genuine copies, except the four copies that are in the Bexar Archive at the University of Texas, are signed by the appropriate officials in ink. None of the copies, with one exception, that have appeared in the last decade is signed. They are simply blank forms. 2) The blank copies that are in the Bexar Archive, as well as all of the copies that are filled out, are printed with deep impression from the type, and with even, black coverage of ink. The copies that have appeared recently are printed with very light impression, and with the muddy ink coverage typical of other forgeries.

However, there are no identifiable changes made to the small amount of type present on these broadsides; there is no record of Dorman David ever having possessed one or sold one; and cyclotron tests on the ink in a genuine copy from Yale and one of the later copies from Texas, do not allow conclusive interpretation. Thus, while I personally believe that the unsigned copies that have appeared in recent years are forgeries—and I believe this to the extent of having refunded the purchase price to someone who bought a copy from me—I do not feel that I have proved it beyond doubt. I would simply suggest that anyone being offered a copy of this broadside realize that there is reason to believe that forgeries of this document may exist.

Funeral of Sam Houston
(Winkler/Friend 935)

This is a small handbill announcing the funeral ceremonies of Sam Houston in Huntsville, Texas, on July 27, 1863. It was suggested to me that this was a good candidate for a forgery, because a number of copies have appeared in recent years. There are a good many copies of this handbill in circulation, and few of them are genuine. However, their source is not attributable to any of the principals in this book. The copies now in circulation were evidently produced as a facsimile of the original, probably for an event that took place in Huntsville in the 1940s. The Sam Houston Memorial Museum in Huntsville at one time had a package of about fifty of these pieces, and still has a number in its possession. I have not determined a reliable way to tell an original copy of this handbill from one of the modern reproductions. Until this can be done, it would be advisable to examine copies of this handbill with care.

BIBLIOGRAPHY

Books and Journals

Allen, O. F. *The City of Houston, From Wilderness to Wonder*. Temple, Texas, 1936.

American Book-Prices Current. Index 1965–1970. New York: Columbia University Press, 1974.

Barker, Eugene C., ed. *The Austin Papers*. 3 vols. Washington, D.C.: American Historical Association, 1924–28 (vols. 1 & 2). Austin: University of Texas Press, 1927 (vol. 3).

Barker, Eugene C. "The Texas Declaration of Causes for Taking up Arms Against Mexico." *Quarterly of the Texas State Historical Association*, vol. 15, no. 3, January 1912.

Binkley, William C., ed. *Official Correspondence of the Texan Revolution, 1835–1836*. 2 vols. New York: D. Appleton-Century, [1936].

Blount, Lois Foster. "A Brief Study of Thomas J. Rusk." *Southwest Historical Quarterly*, vol. 34, no. 3, January 1932.

Castañeda, Carlos E., ed. and trans. *The Mexican Side of the Texan Revolution*. Dallas: P. L. Turner Company, 1928.

Dixon, Sam Houston, and Kemp, Louis Wiltz. *The Heroes of San Jacinto*. Houston: Anson Jones Press, 1932.

Frantz, Joe B. *Gail Borden, Dairyman to a Nation*. Norman: University of Oklahoma Press, 1951.

Gravell, Thomas L., and George Miller. *A Catalogue of American Watermarks, 1690–1835*. New York: Garland Publishing, Inc., 1979.

Gray, A. C., ed. *From Virginia to Texas, 1835. Diary of Col. Wm. F. Gray. . . .* Houston: Gray, Dillaye & Co., Printers, 1909.

Green, Michael R. "To the People of Texas and All Americans in the World." *Southwestern Historical Quarterly*, vol. 91, no. 4, April 1988.

Green, Thomas J. *Journal of the Texian Expedition Against Mier*. New York: Harper and Brothers, 1845.

Greer, James K., ed. "The Journal of Ammon Underwood, 1834–1838." *Southwestern Historical Quarterly*, vol. 32, no. 2, October 1928.

Gulick, Charles A., Jr., et al., eds. *The Papers of Mirabeau Buonaparte Lamar*. 6 vols. Austin: 1921–1927.

Hayes, Charles W. *Galveston: History of the Island and the City*. Austin: Jenkins Garrett Press, 1974.

Hogan, William R. *The Texas Republic*. Norman: The University of Oklahoma Press, 1946.

James, Marquis. *The Raven*. Indianapolis: Bobbs-Merrill, 1929.

Jasbert, W. P.; Berry, W. T.; and Johnson, A. F. *The Encyclopedia of Type Faces.* 4th ed. London: Barnes and Noble, 1966.
Jenkins, John, ed. *The Papers of the Texas Revolution.* 9 vols. Austin: Pemberton Press, 1973.
Lubbock, Francis R. *Six Decades in Texas.* Ed. C. W. Raines. Austin: B. C. Jones, 1900.
Martínez Caro, Ramón. "A True Account of the First Texas Campaign." In *The Mexican Side of the Texan Revolution.* Ed. and trans. Carlos E. Castañeda. Dallas: P. L. Turner Company, 1928.
McMurtrie, Douglas C. "Pioneer Printing in Texas." *Southwestern Historical Quarterly*, vol. 35, no. 3, January 1932.
Quarterly of the Texas State Historical Association, vol. 1, no. 1, July 1897—vol. 15, no. 4, April 1912. Continued as *Southwestern Historical Quarterly.*
Santa Anna, Antonio López de. "Manifesto . . . Relative to his Operations during the Texas Campaign. . . ." In *The Mexican Side of the Texan Revolution.* Ed. and trans. Carlos E. Castañeda. Dallas: P. L. Turner Company, 1928.
Sibley, Marilyn McAdams. *Lone Stars and State Gazettes: Texas Newspapers Before the Civil War.* College Station: Texas A&M University Press, 1983.
Smithwick, Noah. *The Evolution of a State, or Recollections of Old Texas Days.* Austin: Gammel Book Company, 1900.
Southwestern Historical Quarterly, vol. 16, no. 1, July 1912—vol. 93, no. 3, January 1990. (See also *Quarterly of the Texas State Historical Association.*)
Streeter, Thomas W. *Bibliography of Texas, 1795–1845.* 5 vols. Cambridge: Harvard University Press, 1955.
Streeter, Thomas W. *Bibliography of Texas, 1795–1845.* 2nd ed., revised. Woodbridge, Conn.: Research Publications, Inc., 1983.
Tolbert, Frank X. *The Day of San Jacinto.* New York: McGraw-Hill, 1959.
Webb, Walter P., et al., eds. *Handbook of Texas.* 3 vols. Austin: Texas State Historical Association, 1952 & 1976.
Williams, Amelia W., and Barker, Eugene C., eds. *The Writings of Sam Houston, 1813–1863.* 8 vols. Austin: The University of Texas Press, 1938–1943.
Winkler, E. W., and Friend, L., eds. *Check List of Texas Imprints, 1861–1876.* Austin: Texas State Historical Association, 1963.
Wooten, Dudley G., ed. *A Comprehensive History of Texas, 1685–1897.* 2 vols. Dallas: W. G. Scarff, 1898.

Newspapers and Magazines

Belkin, Lisa. "Lone Star Fakes," *New York Times Magazine*, December 10, 1989.
"Couple Helps Crack 'Hot Document' Ring," *Fort Worth Star Telegram*, August 10, 1971.
Curtis, Gregory. "Forgery, Texas Style," *Texas Monthly*, March 1989.
"Documents Recovered in Waco," *Austin American-Statesman*, August 7, 1971.
Hewett, David. "Forgeries and Fraud in Texas," *Maine Antique Digest*, vol. 17, no. 1, January 1989.
Jones, Monty. "Fake! Bogus Papers Sold As Genuine Texana," *Austin American Statesman*, April 9, 1988.
Lewis, Glenn Nolan. "Inquiries Ongoing into Fires That Destroyed Rare Book Dealer's Wares," *Houston Post*, December 18, 1988.

Lewis, Glenn Nolan. "Rare Papers Discovered to Be Fakes," *Houston Post*, December 18, 1988.
"Rare Papers Target of Official Scrutiny," *Houston Chronicle*, June 15, 1972.
"State Begins Crackdown," *Houston Post*, September 17, 1972.
Telegraph and Texas Register, October 10, 1835–November 19, 1836.
"Texana Sale Nets $23,000," *Houston Post*, June 24, 1971.
Texean and Emigrant's Guide, November 28, 1835.
Texas Gazette, October 13, 1829, May 15, 1830.
Texas Republican, July 25, 1834.
Trillin, Calvin. "Knowing Johnny Jenkins," *The New Yorker*, October 30, 1989.
Tutt, Bob. "Dealer Repurchases Rare Texas Documents," *Houston Chronicle*, December 21, 1988.

Miscellaneous Papers

Jenkins, John. Letter to William Buck, Maxson Young Associates, March 7, 1988. 3 pages. Photocopy at DeGolyer Library, Southern Methodist University.
Jenkins, John. "Report to the Board of Governors of the Antiquarian Booksellers Association of America," November 2, 1988. 4 pages. Photocopy at DeGolyer Library, Southern Methodist University.
"Notes obtained in the arrest of Bill Gray, August 2, 1971." Typescript, 4 pages. Photocopy at DeGolyer Library, Southern Methodist University.
"Provisional Government of Texas to Baker and Bordens," July 6, 1836. Ms., Secretary of State Papers, 2–9/41 no. 5, Texas State Archive, Austin.

INDEX

This book has been designed and printed at the press of W. Thomas Taylor in Austin, Texas. The type is Linotype Janson, with Ludlow Bodoni Black for headings, composed at G&S Typesetters by Arno Frank. There are seventy copies specially bound and signed by the author.